P9-DDB-363

WON'T YOU BE MY NEIGHBOR?

WON'T YOU BE MY NEIGHBOR?

Race, Class, and Residence in Los Angeles

Camille Zubrinsky Charles

Russell Sage Foundation
New York

The Russell Sage Foundation

The Russell Sage Foundation, one of the oldest of America's general purpose foundations, was established in 1907 by Mrs. Margaret Olivia Sage for "the improvement of social and living conditions in the United States." The Foundation seeks to fulfill this mandate by fostering the development and dissemination of knowledge about the country's political, social, and economic problems. While the Foundation endeavors to assure the accuracy and objectivity of each book it publishes, the conclusions and interpretations in Russell Sage Foundation publications are those of the authors and not of the Foundation, its Trustees, or its staff. Publication by Russell Sage, therefore, does not imply Foundation endorsement.

Library of Congress Cataloging-in-Publication Data

Charles, Camille Zubrinsky, 1965–
Won't you be my neighbor? : race, class, and residence in Los Angeles/
Camille Zubrinsky Charles
p. cm.
Includes bibliographical references and index.
ISBN 10: 0-87154-162-9
ISBN 13: 978-0-87154-162-8
1. Discrimination in housing—United States. 2. Ethnic neighborhoods—United States. 3. Segregation—United States. I. Title.

HD7288.76.U5C43 2006
363.5′1—dc22

2006040880

The paper used in this publication meets the minimum requirements of American National Standard for Information Sciences—Permanence of Paper for Printed Library Materials. ANSI Z39.48-1992.

Text design by Genna Patacsil.

RUSSELL SAGE FOUNDATION
112 East 64th Street, New York, New York 10021
10 9 8 7 6 5 4 3 2 1

Contents

About the Author

Camille Zubrinsky Charles is associate professor of sociology and faculty associate director of the Center for Africana Studies at the University of Pennsylvania.

Acknowledgments

MANY PEOPLE ASSISTED me in a variety of ways during my journey to this book, and I would be remiss in not acknowledging the role that they have played in my life and career. This is not an exhaustive list, and I apologize to anyone I have inadvertently overlooked—it certainly is not because I am unappreciative, just that I am sleep-deprived!

First, I owe a great deal to Professors Lawrence D. Bobo, Melvin L. Oliver, and James H. Johnson, Jr., for seeing my potential and taking me under their wings at UCLA's Center for the Study of Urban Poverty. This experience was and continues to be invaluable; thanks to each of you for seeing in me what I have only recently begun to see in myself. Thank you Larry, for challenging me to work harder and think more deeply, for consistently providing thorough, honest assessments of my work, and for your continued mentoring and friendship. Melvin, thank you for looking out for me. Your timely "intervention" not only ensured my continuation in the Ph.D. program, but also led to my first academic job as a research assistant on the Multi-City project. And, not incidentally, thank you for arranging the visit to UCLA that clinched my decision to enroll in the first place. Jim, thank you for your enthusiasm and commitment, your creativity, and for teaching us the importance of grant money—it has served me well! Thanks to each of you for your dedication to the training and professional socialization of your students: for your encouragement and support, for lighting a fire under me when necessary, and for your persistence. The work was hard and the hours long, but I learned more about social science research than in any classroom.

There are several other MCSUI "teammates" I should formally acknowledge: Mary Jackman (MCSUI Advisory Board member) for the conversation that led to the creation of my "Multi-Ethnic Showcard," Alice O'Connor for keeping us on track if not always on time, and Reynolds Farley for leading the way in research on neighborhood racial composition preferences. Another perk was the terrific group of graduate students, post-docs, and early-career folks that I am privileged to call friends and colleagues. Big shout-outs to David "Bud" Grant, Julie Press, Devon Johnson, Beti Gonzales, Tarry Hum, Michael Lichter, Susan Suh, Michael Stoll, Abel Valenzuela, Jr., Maria Krysan, and Tara Jackson. Though we have spread far and wide, I think of you often and fondly as part of what made this such a great project.

Most recently, several of my colleagues at the University of Pennsylvania (both past and present) have been a wonderful source of support. In sociology, Douglas S. Massey and Janice Fanning Madden consistently read and commented on my work and helped me work through early drafts and analyses. I am also extremely grateful to my new "family" in the Center for Africana Studies. Tukufu Zuberi provided mentoring and encouragement, as well as a quiet place to write where no one could find me. The Center staff—Carol Davis, Gale Garrison, and Onyx Finney—were a constant calming and supportive presence, while at the same time making sure that I made time to take care of myself. Members of the Africana Studies Faculty Reading Group—Tukufu Zuberi, Barbara Savage, Ken Shropshire, Herman Beavers, and Guthrie Ramsey—went above and beyond the call of collegiality to read and comment on work that was outside the scope of their own research interests, and to finally convince me that I could do this. As the most junior member of this group, I also benefited from their wisdom and advice, and from their willingness to assist me in any way possible. Thank you for creating a space in which I could thrive!

I would also like to thank those institutions and foundations that provided financial support for my research. I am grateful to the Ford and Russell Sage Foundations for funding the original MCSUI project and to Russell Sage for awarding me a small grant to continue my research after graduate school. In addition, the United States Department of Housing and Urban Development's dissertation fellowship provided critical financial support, as did Grinnell College where I spent a year as a scholar-in-residence. The University of Pennsylvania provided internal grant money to support aspects of this research, and I am eternally grateful to D-L Wormley and Vicky Tam at the Cartographic Modeling Lab for the terrific maps.

I would be remiss if I did not acknowledge those who were involved in the actual nuts-and-bolts processes related to publishing this book. At Russell Sage Foundation, Eric Wanner has been terrific in his support of MCSUI and of my work in particular. To Suzanne Nichols, thank you for getting excited about my project and for helping to nurture it (and for remembering all of the times I got things in on time!). Two anonymous reviewers provided detailed and thoughtful comments that substantially improved the final product, and Cynthia Buck did a terrific job of copy-editing throughout.

In addition to all of the people in my professional life who have assisted me in myriad ways, there is a small group of family and friends that I would like to thank for their love, support, and patience. My parents were patient when I decided to "take a break" from college, and I am sure they were relieved when I said I wanted to pay for graduate school on my own. To my mother, Janell: your example spoke volumes about what it means to be a strong black woman. I did not always want to hear what you were saying, but I always watched what you did. Thank you for all you sacrificed and for instilling in me a belief that I can do anything I set my mind to, despite having "to work twice as hard to get half as far!" To my father, Gene: thank you for my early exposure to sociology and using it consistently as a way to understand my social world, and for all of the other ways that you have supported my decisions. Thank you both for all of your love and support—and for the meals, the plane tickets, etc.

My four best friends—Chrys, Julie, Lola, and Eleanor—put up with sometimes severe neglect on my part. Thank you for understanding my tendency to disappear for long periods of time, to forget birthdays, anniversaries, and other important dates, and my inability to return phone calls or emails in a timely manner. You have been excellent cheerleaders, and it means the world to me to know you are all on my side! A big shout-out to Emery and Emily (yes, Em and Em!) for hosting my working vacation when I was eight and a half months pregnant and trying (unsuccessfully) to finish this book. You took good care of me and I got some of my best work done in your home!

Finally, I cannot adequately express all that my husband, Scott, has done to encourage, support, and assist me. Not only has he loved me "in sickness and in health," but through insanity, sleepwalking and talking, insomnia, writer's block, tenure…the list is endless. Thank you for writing down the things I said in my sleep, "just in case they were important"; for pointing out that when I am in tears at 3 a.m. because I have run out of words it is time to go to sleep; for taking charge of family life when I needed to work late and/or on weekends; for "helping" me write the last paragraph of my dissertation; for loving me enough to leave California and follow me to Ohio, and for the life I always dreamed of but never believed I would have. And, thank you for our two greatest accomplishments: Zora and Sasha, who have shown me that there really is no "balance" between work and family (who knew?!), who love me no matter what, and whose smiles light up my life. Thank you for loving me unconditionally, and for the best job there is—Mom.

Introduction | Or, Why I Love Mister Rogers

My obsession with the racial composition of neighborhoods probably began when I was four years old. For much of my childhood (until I was fourteen), my mother and I were the only nonwhite people for miles around in the Ventura, California, neighborhood where I grew up. Local police once told my mother that the location of our house was identified with a red pushpin on the map that hung on the precinct wall—not because they thought we would cause trouble, but because they were concerned that others might cause trouble for us. From what I have been told—and from what I remember—I integrated the El Camino Elementary School when I entered kindergarten. Until about fourth grade, when students were bused in from a predominantly Latino neighborhood, I remember only one other black child, and even with busing there were few students of color. My fourth-grade teacher, Ms. Romero, was the only nonwhite teacher.

Nothing overtly bad ever happened to us in our neighborhood, but I never quite felt like I fit in either. There were other children around. We went to school together and were even friendly; still, something always felt a little amiss. I remember seeking out playmates and play dates with little reciprocity. For example, there were few sleepovers for many of those years. In hindsight, I see that my sense of not fitting in, of being excluded, had much more to do with the attitudes of the parents than with the children themselves. I also have vivid memories of nearly every argument I was a part of turning racial. For some of my closest friends—and for my staunchest adversaries—the first stone to be thrown was the "N-word."

I think it was this lack of predictability and subtle lack of a sense of belonging that made Mister Rogers so appealing to me. Throughout elementary school *Mister Rogers' Neighborhood* was one of my favorite television shows. In fact, to this day his theme song holds a special place in my heart:[1]

> It's a beautiful day in this neighborhood,
> A beautiful day for a neighbor.
> Would you be mine?
> Could you be mine?

This middle-aged white man was singing to *me*. The neighborhood he sang about was one where I and, I believed, others like me *belonged*.

> I have always wanted to have a neighbor just like you.
> I've always wanted to live in a neighborhood with you.

As a child, perhaps I wished that my own neighbors, teachers, and classmates (and their parents) could feel that way about me and my mom. Instead, I seemed always to be on edge, waiting for the next racial hand grenade to be thrown. This experience lasted for more than a decade of my formative years and fundamentally shaped the way I look at and think about cities and neighborhoods.

So began my obsession. Throughout my young adulthood, I naively believed that one day we would see Dr. King's dream realized, that, as Rodney King pleaded, one day we would all "just get along." It was impressed upon me that relations between the races were much better than they ever had been: opportunities and access were expanding, and attitudes among whites were becoming more favorable. At the same time, my mother taught me early that, because we were black, we would "have to work twice as hard to get half as far." Implicit in her lesson was an acknowledgment that prejudice and discrimination were alive and kicking, despite any assertions to the contrary. My father is a white man and a junior college sociology instructor; he explained American race relations to me using conflict theories. I came to understand that the racial prejudice of whites is motivated not just by ignorance but also by concerns about maintaining an advantaged position. My family's presence in a neighborhood of all-white, owner-occupied households challenged our neighbors' ideas about how things "ought" to be. And the fact that I excelled academically and earned my place at the head of the class—ahead of white students—challenged their beliefs about black intellectual inferiority.

In spite of the prejudice we encountered, I grew up believing that someday, somehow, I would see the day when Mister Rogers' Neighborhood (the one I imagined at least) was a reality, not just for me, but for our country as a whole.

Let's make the most of this beautiful day.
Since we're together we might as well say:
Would you be mine?
Could you be mine?
Won't you be my neighbor?
Won't you please,
Won't you please?
Please won't you be my neighbor?

Being a California girl, I looked at Los Angeles as a shining example of what was possible. We often visited the City of the Angels, only an hour away from home, to see extended family and friends. My paternal grandparents lived in the middle-class community of Burbank, and sometimes my mom and a friend of hers would pile us kids into the car on the spur of the moment to drive to South Central Los Angeles for a soul food dinner. Both of my parents took me to Los Angeles to experience its vast and diverse cultural opportunities—music, art, and theater. And of course, a little farther away was Disneyland. These experiences exposed me to people from all over the world, people of various hues, cultures, and religions, speaking many languages and eating all kinds of foods. Los Angeles was, quite simply, my promised land.

It wasn't until I moved to Los Angeles for graduate school that I began to realize just how segregated it is. Once again my dream was deferred, and once again I became obsessed with understanding why. It is a common misconception that a diverse city is logically an *integrated* city—particularly if "integrated" is taken to mean a high level of contact between and interaction with people from varying racial-ethnic, religious, and cultural backgrounds. School desegregation is subject to the same misconception: students of different racial-ethnic backgrounds may be in the same building, but they are not necessarily mingling, or mingling in friendly ways.

Another common misconception in some circles is that racial residential segregation is no longer a central concern. Advocates of this view argue that with the end of legalized segregation and the passage of the 1968 Fair Housing Act, any remaining segregation is the result of either group differences in objective social class characteristics or the race-neutral preferences of residents to be around people like themselves. Thus, according to this argument, racial residential segregation persists because that is the way everyone wants it: actual residential patterns reflect our unconstrained choices. Some might even say that each of these factors is influential. It is hard to convince those who hold this view that another influential factor is persisting racial prejudice and discrimination. Our national tendency to believe that negative racial attitudes are no longer problematic makes it painfully difficult to have any sort of national "conversation" about the salience of race in our country. Many Americans are willing to point to the end of legalized discrimination and the growing acceptance of "egalitarian principles" among whites as evidence that things are now okay; they argue that any remaining inequality is probably the result of "poor choices" or lack of impulse control among members of disadvantaged groups.

This volume represents my effort at understanding why and how race matters for the geographic distribution of racial-ethnic groups in cities. We now have ample evidence that where we live is consequential for our life chances: residential location influences experiences of long-term joblessness, out-of-wedlock births, school dropout, and exposure to crime and social disorder and is associated with lower average wages (Cutler and Glaeser 1997; Jargowsky 1996; Krivo and Peterson 1996; Massey and Denton 1993; Wilson 1987). Without sufficient resources, public services—particularly public schools—deteriorate in some residential areas as well. Racial residential segregation is deeply implicated in white-black differences in all these areas. This is so much the case that even after accounting for the social and economic disadvantages associated with residential segregation, David Cutler and Edward Glaeser (1997, 865) find that "a one-standard deviation reduction in segregation (13 percent) would eliminate one-third" of white-black differences in rates of school completion, single-parenthood, and employment, as well as earnings. It is also clear that economic inequality alone cannot account for the high degree of segregation in our cities—particularly that of blacks from whites.

Poor blacks are concentrated in neighborhoods characterized by extreme levels of disadvantage, and middle-class and affluent blacks are exposed to higher levels of neighborhood disadvantage than their status would seem to warrant (Alba, Logan, and Bellair 1994; Massey and Fischer 1999; Pattillo-McCoy 1999; Wilson 1987). Suburban blacks are as segregated as their central-city counterparts; indeed, their suburban enclaves are part of a contiguous set of black neighborhoods that collectively make up the ghetto and are differentiated only by their status as the "best, mixed, [or] worst [area]" (Patillo-McCoy 1999, 27; for similar assertions, see Galster 1991; Jargowsky and Bane 1991; Logan 2001a; Morenoff and Sampson 1997). The well-known perils associated with ghetto life and documented by quantitative researchers (Jargowsky 1996; Cutler and Glaeser 1997; Wilson 1987) and ethnographers (Anderson 1990, 1999; Edin and Kafalas 2004; Venkatesh 2000) are found, albeit to a lesser degree, in the neighborhoods of middle-class blacks (see, for example, Alba et al. 1994; Pattillo-McCoy 1999; Timberlake 2002).

Racial inequality and tense intergroup relations seem to become more likely and more pernicious as we become an increasingly diverse nation. Thus, it is vital that we confront not only the persisting segregation in our nation's neighborhoods but the primary importance of segregation for understanding patterns of economic inequality and the persistence of negative racial attitudes and relations. Moreover, it is long past time to expand all such analyses beyond black-white relations. We must look at the effect of the increase in racial-ethnic diversity not only on minority-group relations with whites but also on relations between minority groups. Does the introduction of new groups into the American "melting pot" change our racial hierarchy in any meaningful way? Specifically, do such changes in the racial hierarchy affect the position of blacks, or do they remain at the bottom? And what role does immigration play in understanding the increasing complexity of intergroup relations? Do immigrants' racial attitudes and perceptions of discrimination, for example, differ from those of their native-born counterparts? Does length of time in the United States or acculturation result in decreasing differences between the native- and foreign-born? How do beliefs about economic inequality or perceptions of racial group competition over scarce resources influence intergroup relations? How do all of these factors influence preferences for residential integration or segregation? And finally, to what extent do our preferences for neighborhood racial integration influence where we actually end up living?

Reducing racial residential segregation may be the most critical step toward eradicating economic inequality, a goal that would benefit all Americans, irrespective of race, class, or political stripe. Unfortunately, this is sometimes difficult for us to see. The findings reported in the following pages offer room for both optimism and concern. Mister Rogers didn't live long enough to see his neighborhood become a reality, and I may not either. Still, I hold out hope that my own daughters will grow to be as fond of Mister Rogers as I am—but for very different reasons.

Chapter One | Los Angeles: A Window on the Future of the Nation

Los Angeles is one of the most racially, ethnically, and culturally diverse cities in the world. The public schools offer instruction in 92 of the 224 identified languages spoken in the county. Restaurants span the cuisines of the world, including Thai, Vietnamese, Indian, Pakistani, Russian, Moroccan, Ethiopian, Caribbean, Argentinean, Cuban, and Guatemalan, not to mention the ubiquitous Mexican, Chinese, Italian, French, and Japanese venues, classic "American" soul food restaurants, and Jewish deli spots. The political landscape is equally diverse, with local officeholders and prominent public figures whose surnames run from Molina to Woo, Edelman, Ito, Yaroslavsky, Antonovich, Waters, Abramson, Burke, and Villaraigosa. Both residents and visitors to the city can partake in annual African marketplace festivals, Cinco de Mayo and Dia de los Muertos celebrations, Chinese New Year, the Israeli Festival, and Chosuk, a Korean Thanksgiving celebration. If there was ever a metropolis that holds forth the promise of a heady social melting pot, it would be La Ciudad de Los Angeles—the City of the Angels.

Behind this surface patina of rich diversity lies a vast array of racial and ethnic communities and social structures. To the rest of the world, the African American community in Los Angeles may be associated with the 1965 uprising in Watts, the more recent (and more destructive) uprisings of 1992, and South Central, made famous by rappers like Ice Cube, Dr. Dre, and TuPac. This well-established community also includes, however, strong and vibrant black institutions, such as Founders Bank and Trust and Broadway Federal Savings and Loan, both venerable, black-owned financial institutions. The Degnan Street area in Liemert Park features art galleries like Museum in Black—where the front is dedicated to the display and sale of African art and the back holds a permanent exhibit of art and memorabilia relevant to the African American experience—as well as black bookstores, import-export shops specializing in African art, textiles, and clothing, and the World Stage, a place where up-and-coming jazz musicians show their wares. Los Angeles supports two black newspapers, including *the Los Angeles Sentinel*, a weekly that has served the black community for more than sixty years. And not far from South Central is the "new West Side," where upwardly mobile blacks live in the hilltop communities of Ladera Heights and Baldwin Hills (fondly referred to by blacks as "Black Beverly Hills") and in the "tidy tractlands of suburban Inglewood and Carson" (Davis 1992, 304).

There is also a vast and growing Latino community in Los Angeles. In absolute terms, the city is home to the largest Latino population in the country. Spanish-speaking television and radio stations rival mainstream electronic media in viewers and listeners, and *La Opinión* is a thriving Spanish-speaking daily newspaper. Pico-Union and East L.A. have long histories as thriving Latino communities where businesses cater to the needs of Mexican and Central American residents: posters, billboards, and store signs are all in Spanish; Latin music blares from loudspeakers out into the streets; at parish fiestas, lottery jackpots are advertised in pesos; and in the bars and restaurants of Boyle Heights, children go from table to table selling novelties like those found in the stalls of Tijuana (Skerry 1993).

Los Angeles is also home to the largest Korean settlement in the United States and supports the most thriving and profitable Korean economy. Koreatown is a thriving business community for Korean merchants and small businesses. Korean commercial signs on this one-mile strip near downtown L.A. advertise "English spoken here" (Portes and Rumbaut 1996). In addition to the plethora of Korean restaurants and grocery stores, Koreatown includes Korean banks, import-export houses, garment factories, real estate offices, and a wide variety of retail stores, and *the Korea Times* is the newspaper of choice (Bobo et al. 1994; Portes and Rumbaut 1996). About eight miles east of downtown Los Angeles is Monterey Park, a middle-class, majority-Chinese suburb that is also home to a sizable number of Japanese residents.

Finally, there are the predominantly white areas that in many people's minds define Los Angeles: Brentwood, Bel Air, Beverly Hills, Hollywood, Malibu, and Burbank—the land of the rich and famous and beautiful, with sparkling beaches and big money. As the center of the entertainment industry, a Pacific Rim hub for business and finance, and the place that entertainers, industry executives and hangers-on, and corporate employees call home, this Los Angeles attracts tourists and the "up-and-coming" in droves. People come from around the world to see the L.A. that Huey Lewis sang about: the stars' homes, Universal Studios, the Hollywood

Walk of Fame, the Sunset Strip, Rodeo Drive, *The Tonight Show*, Venice Beach, and Disneyland.

As these "snapshots" attest, Los Angeles is the premier "prismatic metropolis": a city with many colors and cultures, "profoundly, irremediably ethnic. . . . In Los Angeles, late twentieth century America finds a mirror to itself" (Waldinger 1996, 447). By 1990 the population of Los Angeles was majority-minority: roughly 41 percent non-Hispanic white and nearly 40 percent Latino (blacks and Asians were each about 11 percent of the population; see table 1.1), making it one of thirty-seven "multiethnic metros" (Frey and Farley 1993).[1] This trend toward increasing racial-ethnic diversity is only expected to continue and to spread as the U.S. population becomes majority-minority by the year 2050 (Harrison and Bennett 1995).

Understanding the dynamic interplay of race, class, and residence in Los Angeles moves us toward a better understanding of the future of the country as a whole. Rapid changes in the population composition associated with massive immigration from Latin America and Asia; economic restructuring and persistent economic inequality along racial-ethnic lines; and patterns of intergroup tensions and often negative intergroup attitudes—all contribute to, and are consequences of, persisting residential segregation by race. There is much to be learned about racial inequality, broadly speaking, by understanding the dynamics of racial residential segregation in this truly multiethnic metropolis.

IMMIGRATION AND POPULATION COMPOSITION

The increasing racial-ethnic diversity of Los Angeles detailed in table 1.1 is indicative of the national trend toward a "browning" of the population as a consequence of high-volume, continuous immigration, primarily from Latin America and Asia, and the simultaneous decline in the share of the total white population. (Black population share has changed very little.) With no end to immigration in sight, non-Hispanic whites are projected to become a numerical minority in the United States sometime in the twenty-first century (Edmonston and Passel 1992; Massey 1995), and the trend is well under way: eight of the fifty largest metropolitan areas are already majority-minority (that is, whites are less than half the total population), and two others will be majority-minority by the next census.[2]

Los Angeles, one of the most popular destinations for immigrants, is now one of the nation's majority-minority metro areas. Table 1.2 illustrates the dramatic increase in the foreign-born population since 1980 at the city and county levels. In 1980, 22 percent of the population of Los Angeles County was foreign-born; the percentage was slightly higher for

Table 1.1 Racial-Ethnic Composition of Los Angeles County, 1990–2000

	White		Black		Latino		Asian	
Year	Population	Percentage	Population	Percentage	Population	Percentage	Population	Percentage
1990	3,634,722	40.70%	990,406	11.17%	3,306,116	37.96%	928,710	10.48%
2000	2,959,614	31.09	930,957	9.78	4,242,213	44.56	1,137,500	11.95
Change from 1990 to 2000		−18.57		−6.00		+28.31		+22.48

Source: U.S. Bureau of the Census.

Table 1.2 Native-Born and Foreign-Born Population in Los Angeles City and Los Angeles County, 1980 to 2000

	1980			
	Native-Born	Foreign-Born	Percentage Foreign-Born	Total
Los Angeles City	2,162,032	804,818	27%	2,966,850
Los Angeles County	5,812,710	1,664,793	22	7,477,503

the City of Los Angeles (27 percent). By the year 2000, the number of foreign-born residents in Los Angeles County had nearly doubled, totaling nearly 3.5 million—more than one-third of the total population. According to the U.S. Bureau of the Census, the majority of foreign-born residents are Latin American, followed by Asian immigrants; in 2000 Latin America and Asia accounted for 62.1 and 29.6 percent of foreign-born Angelenos, respectively. European immigrants were a distant third, accounting for roughly 5.6 percent of foreign-born residents in 2000, down from 15 percent in 1980 (see table 1.3).

The rapid change in L.A.'s population composition has had a major impact on the geographic distribution of racial-ethnic groups. Figures 1.1, 1.2, and 1.3 illustrate patterns of racial-ethnic concentration in 1980, 1990, and 2000, showing the predominant racial-ethnic group within census tracts over the two-decade period. (Tracts are identified as being over half non-Hispanic white, black, Latino, or Asian or as having no single majority.) Glancing at these figures, one can easily see the dramatic increase in the Latino population during this period, as well as the Latino movement into the historically African American South Central portion of the county. In addition to these areas, however, Latinos also remain concentrated in the historically Mexican American area of East Los Angeles and further east into El Monte and Downey. By the year 2000, Downey and the surrounding area had also become overwhelmingly Latino, as had a portion of south Los Angeles just west of Long Beach. The Latino population also increased in the San Fernando Valley area, where a substantial number of tracts became majority Latino.

Most of the change in the distribution of the black population in Los Angeles County from 1980 to 2000 is best described as a decrease in the number of predominantly black tracts, apparently the result of Latino settlement in the South Central portion of the area. Otherwise, the only noticeable change is a slight increase in the number of majority-black tracts just north of Pasadena, in the northern part of the county. Overall, the size

Table 1.2 *(Continued)*

1990				2000			
Native-Born	Foreign-Born	Percentage Foreign-Born	Total	Native-Born	Foreign-Born	Percentage Foreign Born	Total
2,148,733	1,336,665	38%	3,485,398	2,182,114	1,512,720	41%	3,694,834
5,968,098	2,895,066	33	8,863,164	6,069,894	3,449,444	36	9,519,338

Source: U.S. Bureau of the Census: 1980, tables 172, 116; 1990, tables 167, 138, and 27; 2000, table P21.

of the black population remained fairly constant as blacks continued to be concentrated in the South Central area but were a majority in an increasingly smaller number of tracts.

There was also a clear and significant increase in the number of majority-Asian areas between 1980 and 2000. Concentrations of Asians increased in the San Gabriel Valley area and emerged in several new areas in the southeastern and eastern portions of the county, closer to Orange and San Bernardino Counties. For the most part, however, pockets of Asian concentration are not adjacent to areas in which blacks predominate, and the newer, easternmost areas of Asian concentration are also distant from Latino areas. Thus, it appears that blacks and Latinos may be

Table 1.3 Foreign-Born Population by Place of Birth, Los Angeles City and Los Angeles County, 2000

	Los Angeles City		Los Angeles County	
Percentage	Population	Percentage	Population	Percentage
Latin America	996,996	65.9%	2,143,049	62.1%
Asia	376,767	24.9	1,022,289	29.6
Europe	100,252	6.6	194,503	5.6
Africa	20,730	1.4	43,024	1.2
North America (not Latin America)	13,859	0.9	34,003	1.0
Oceania	4,104	0.3	12,560	0.4
Born at Sea	12	0.0	16	0.0
Total	1,512,720		3,449,444	

Source: U.S. Bureau of the Census, 2000, table P21.

Figure 1.1 Los Angeles County: Racial-Ethnic Concentration, 1980

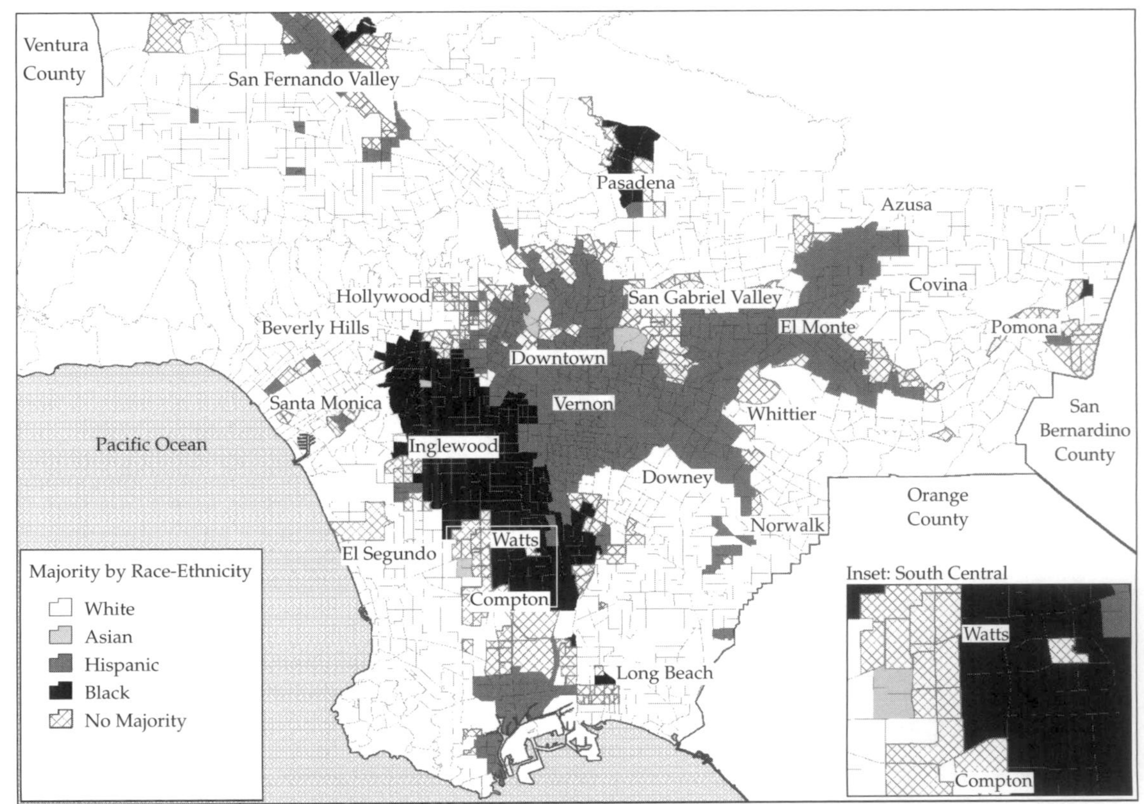

Source: GeoLytics (2003).

Figure 1.2 Los Angeles County: Racial-Ethnic Concentration, 1990

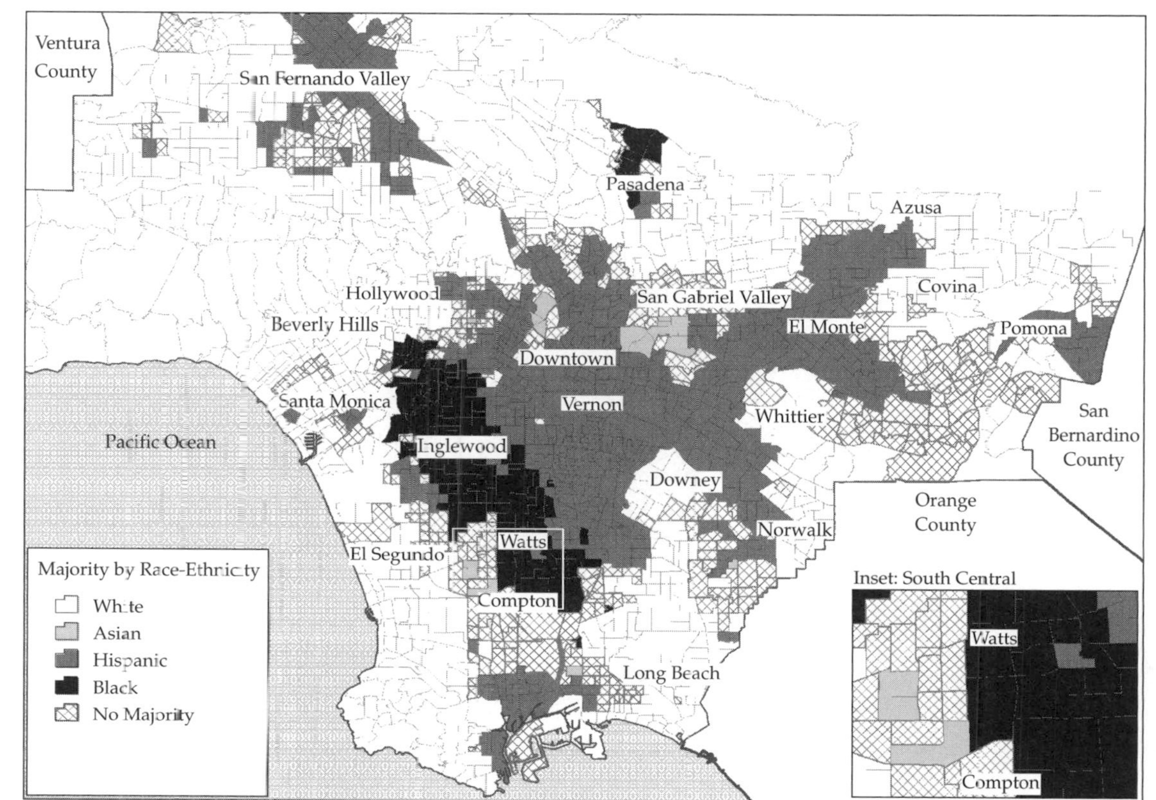

Source: GeoLytics (2003).

Figure 1.3 Los Angeles County: Racial-Ethnic Concentration, 2000

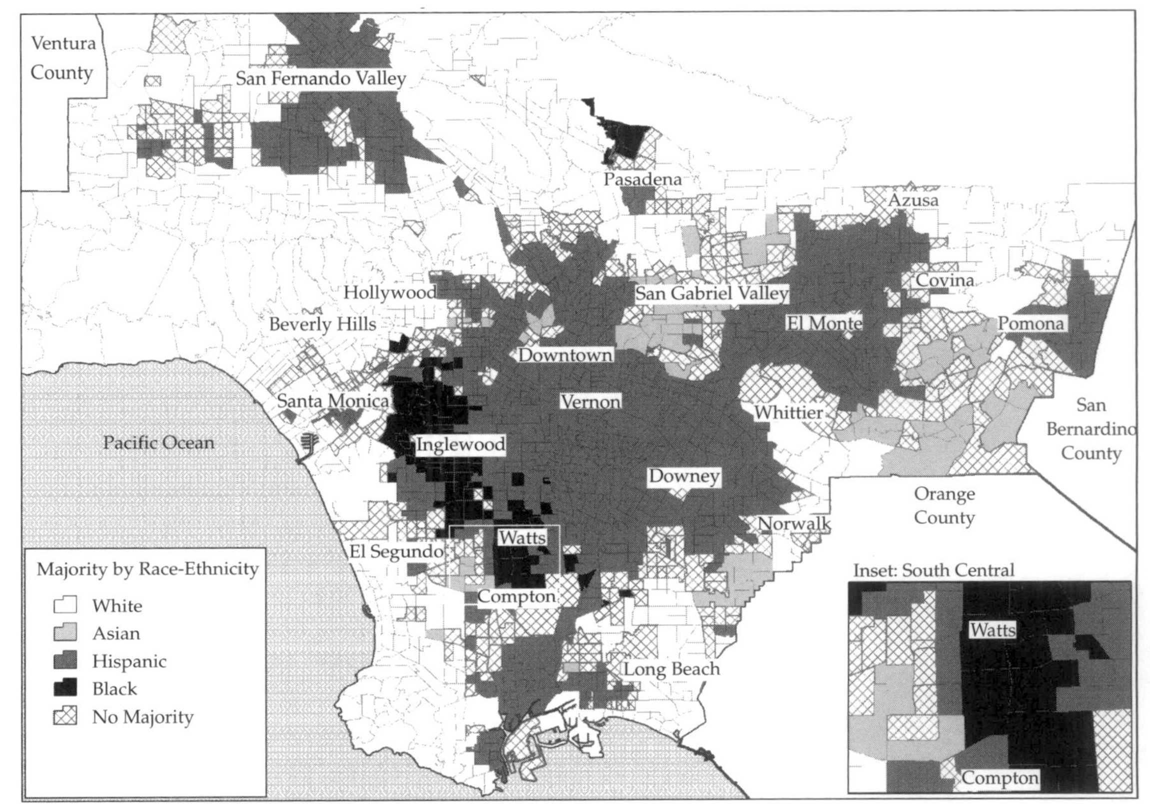

Source: GeoLytics (2003).

competing for residential space and local community resources, but that Asians are not nearly as likely to have similar issues of interminority-group conflict. And in keeping with the increasing diversity of the metro area as a whole between 1980 and 2000, there has also been a substantial increase in the number of tracts with no racial-ethnic majority.

Although the absolute numbers vary dramatically, municipalities across much of the nation are also experiencing drastic changes in the racial-ethnic composition of residents; immigration reform, bilingual education, and the provision of social services (particularly health care) for undocumented immigrants are all hotly contested political issues. Similarly, competition for already scarce resources—including residential location—may intensify as a consequence of rapid population change. And unlike the nineteenth- and early-twentieth-century immigration waves, the post-1965 wave is a migration "of color" to a nation that has historically been stratified along racial-ethnic lines. Thus, understanding the consequences of rapid population change is critical to any analysis of the impact of increasing diversity on other aspects of life in America.

PERSISTENT ECONOMIC INEQUALITY

Beginning in the mid- to late 1970s, fundamental changes in the structure of the national economy have had a profound effect on levels of economic inequality in the United States. The decline of central-city manufacturing jobs, the shift from a goods- to a services-producing economy, and the increasing bifurcation of the labor market into high- and low-wage sectors are factors that are all implicated in the widening of the distance between the haves and the have-nots (Kasarda 1993; Sassen 1990; Wilson 1987, 1996). Increasing joblessness in central-city communities is one severe consequence of the suburbanization of high-paying entry-level jobs—or a so-called spatial mismatch (Holzer 1987, 1988; Kain 1968, 1992)—and a mismatch of skills and available jobs in the central city (Kasarda 1989, 1993; Moore and Laramore 1990).

These more traditional mismatch hypotheses are less relevant in Los Angeles, as may also be true in other metro areas with a large and continuously replenishing pool of immigrant labor. Because immigrants with few or no skills easily find employment in such cities, they are considered prime settlement areas. Thus, high-volume immigration has an impact on economic restructuring when the expansion of the service economy generates demand for both high- and low-skilled labor but excludes the workers in between. Immigrants provide a cheap source of labor and are willing to work at low-status jobs with low wages and few if any benefits (Waldinger and Bozorgmehr 1996, 25–26). These are precisely the jobs that many African Americans feel they should no longer have to settle for (Bobo, Zubrinsky, Johnson, and Oliver 1995). Moreover, employers—both white and other-race minorities—are increasingly likely to prefer immigrant labor, because it is cheaper, easier to exploit, and because immigrants are stereotyped as hardworking while blacks are often labeled as lazy and/or unreliable (Bobo et al. 1994; Kirschenman and Neckerman 1991).

Economic restructuring has had a profound effect on patterns of economic inequality in the city of Los Angeles, where poverty rates have tended to exceed the national average. For example, in 1990 about 13 percent of the total population lived in poverty, compared to nearly 17 percent of the population in Los Angeles County; for 2000 the figures are 11.3 and 17.9 percent, respectively (U.S. Bureau of the Census 1990, 2000; United Way of Greater Los Angeles and Los Angeles Urban League 2005). Table 1.4 summarizes poverty rates in Los Angeles County by racial-ethnic group in 2000, highlighting the racial-ethnic patterning of economic inequality. Based on information from the most recent decennial census, nearly one-quarter of blacks and Latinos in Los Angeles County were living in poverty, compared to fewer than one-tenth of whites; 14 percent of Los Angeles County Asians lived in poverty.

In the recently published report *The State of Black Los Angeles 2005* (United Way of Greater Los Angeles and Los Angeles Urban League 2005), racial-ethnic inequality is measured with a series of indices that capture various dimensions of social life. These "equality index" measures point to persisting racial economic inequality. Initially developed to measure objectively the equality of conditions between blacks and whites nationally, these measures are useful in Los Angeles for measuring Latino and Asian inequality relative to whites. Thus, in all measures, whites are the baseline or comparison group and receive a constant score of 1. A minority-group index value less than 1 indicates relative disadvantage, while a value greater than 1 means that the minority group is better off than whites (United Way of Greater Los Angeles and Los Angeles Urban League 2005, 23–24).[3]

The results of this consideration of economic inequality provide additional insights into the nature of economic inequality in Los Angeles; table 1.5 summarizes the information used to calculate the economic index and provides a summary measure for each racial-ethnic group. Note that all racial-ethnic minority groups fare worse than whites; Asians are the group closest to parity, with a weighted index score of .79. Blacks and Latinos are about equally disadvantaged relative to whites, with weighted scores of .55 and .54, respectively. In addition to these poverty differentials, the individual dimensions of group-level economic status reveal severe differences in unemployment, labor force participation, and

Table 1.4 Race and Poverty in Los Angeles County, 2000

	Poverty Rate
Racial-ethnic group	
Non-Hispanic white	8.5%
African American	24.4
Latino	24.2
Asian	13.9
Total	17.9

Source: United Way of Greater Los Angeles and Los Angeles Urban League (2005).

income. Note too the greater proclivity toward small-business ownership found among Latinos and Asians compared to blacks. The so-called ethnic niches or enclaves that provide additional labor market opportunities for immigrants have historically been more illusive for blacks (Bobo, Oliver, Johnson, and Valenzuela 2000).

Racial-ethnic groups in Los Angeles, as in the nation as a whole, also

Table 1.5 Economic Indicators and Index of Economic Inequality in Los Angeles, 2005

	Whites	Blacks	Latinos	Asians
Key indicator				
Median household income in 2000	$53,798	$31,905	$33,820	$47,631
Median family income in 2000	69,396	37,190	33,363	54,108
Per capita income in 2000	35,785	17,341	11,100	20,595
Household income less than $35,000	32%	53%	52%	38%
Household income greater than $100,000	23	8	7	17
Unemployment rate	6	14	10	6
Adults in the labor force	64	59	59	59
Adults unemployed or not in labor force	40	49	47	44
Persons below poverty line	9	24	24	14
Own business	489,284	38,277	136,678	114,462
Own business with paid employees	127,345	3,359	16,757	37,596
Weighted economic index	1.00	.55	.54	.79

Source: United Way of Greater Los Angeles and Los Angeles Urban League (2005, 26).

differ significantly in their levels of accumulated wealth (Oliver and Shapiro 1995). Unlike income, one's assets—real estate, savings, stocks, and other property—may provide a cushion that enables one to afford the "extras" in life and to wade through difficult economic times. On average, whites in Los Angeles have $271,000 in assets; Asians are not far behind, with assets averaging just over $214,000. Blacks and Latinos have much smaller "nest eggs," averaging $50,000 and $65,000, respectively. Such differences in assets, combined with persisting economic inequality, have a profound impact on the ability to purchase housing in more desirable neighborhoods. Thus, persisting racial economic inequality—intensified by immigration and rapid changes in the racial-ethnic composition of the population—is implicated as both a cause and a consequence of racial residential segregation in Los Angeles and increasingly in the country as a whole. Racially patterned economic inequality is also both cause and consequence of the oppression, negativity, and conflict that mar intergroup relations in Los Angeles, where racial-ethnic groups are more often competitors than allies.

RACIAL-ETHNIC TENSIONS

For better or worse, increasing racial-ethnic diversity can add to intergroup tensions and intensify conflict, especially in a society marked by a history of racial-ethnic oppression, extreme racial residential segregation, and economic stratification along racial-ethnic lines. Without such a history—whether between the dominant group and minorities or between minority groups—the conflict engendered by increases in racial-ethnic diversity might not be especially severe (Bobo et al. 2000). In many ways, Los Angeles illustrates something close to a worst-case scenario: in this city, segregation, economic inequality, and major shifts in the racial-ethnic composition have combined with "well-defined racial and ethnic identities, and interethnic attitudes characterized by mutual suspicion and hostility" (Bobo et al. 2000, 23). Two events in L.A.'s fairly recent past—the 1965 Watts riot and the 1992 Los Angeles rebellion—offer some perspective on intergroup relations and tensions, and the differences between the two events show how the increasing Latino and Asian populations have changed these relations.

Both events erupted in response to what the black community saw as its continued mistreatment at the hands of the Los Angeles Police Department (LAPD). In 1965 the catalyst was the arrest and perceived mistreatment of a drunk black driver in South Central L.A. David Sears (1994, 239) cites three causal factors. First, the city was characterized by a high degree of racial spatial isolation and what he terms "symbolic racism"—a blend of traditional American values with "the mild, stereotyped white prejudice common to northern whites." Second, blacks held long-standing grievances related to police brutality, gouging by local merchants (most of whom at that time were Jewish), what they perceived as local discrimination in housing and public education, and the negative attitudes of white leaders, particularly the mayor and the police chief, toward the black community. The third factor was the presence of a new generation of urban blacks who were "northern socialized, better educated and more sophisticated" than the predominantly rural and southern blacks who had preceded them in migrating to the city; this new generation was also "more angry, disaffected, anti-white, and proud of being Black" (Sears 1994, 239–40). The riots served to further polarize blacks and whites in Los Angeles. Blacks viewed the unrest as a racial protest and a catalyst for social change. Whites were ambivalent: they viewed the "protest" as a wake-up call for themselves, but also supported the firm "law-and-order" stance taken by white public officials (Sears 1994, 241).

The City of the Angels erupted again in the spring of 1992 after an all-white jury in a white suburb just outside of Los Angeles County acquitted four white LAPD officers accused of beating the black motorist Rodney King. Twenty-seven years after the Watts riots, police brutality remained all too familiar to blacks—and to Latinos as well, for that matter. This time, however, there was a videotape of the beating; shown throughout the region and around the world during the twelve months preceding the verdict, the videotape gave both blacks and Latinos reason to believe that the right thing would finally be done. The acquittal came as a shock to many in the region, and within hours South Central was once again at the center of urban unrest in L.A. This time, however, Latinos and Asians played far more central roles in the conflict. Persisting grievances directed mainly at whites—and confirmed by the verdict—precipitated the unrest, but it became apparent almost at once that the pattern of violence and destruction that ensued expressed interminority-group tensions that had been simmering for quite some time.

Blacks were joined almost immediately by their new Latino neighbors (who were primarily new immigrants), and the violence quickly turned toward local merchants and landlords, most of whom were Korean (Waldinger and Bozorgmehr 1996). Tensions between blacks and Koreans were well known and long-standing. Blacks had long resented Koreans, whom they viewed as exploiting blacks for their own economic gain—charging high prices for low-quality merchandise, choosing not to invest in the inner city by employing local residents—and as generally treating black customers disrespectfully. Moreover, blacks often resented the relative economic success of Asian immigrants, which was attained, they believed, at the expense of blacks. Finally, blacks' resentment over being often compared to the "model minority" also contributed to black-Korean tensions (Freer 1994; Johnson and Oliver 1989).

What the 1992 unrest revealed to the rest of Los Angeles and the nation, however, was that Latinos had similar complaints about and conflicts with the Korean community. This previously "hidden conflict" was evident in the widespread participation of Latinos in vandalism directed at Korean-owned businesses and in the expressed attitudes of Latinos themselves in the weeks following the unrest. In a series of focus groups, Latinos expressed the same grievances against Korean merchants and business owners as blacks did, and they expressed equally problematic employer-employee relations: Latinos felt that they were exploited by Korean employers who took advantage of their economic distress and questionable legal status (Bobo et al. 1994, 121). Given the increasing tendency of blacks and Latinos to share residential space since 1970 and the concentration of Latino immigrants in low-skilled occupations, the commonality of their complaints is not necessarily surprising. Until the spring of 1992, however, it had gone largely unnoticed by the rest of Los Angeles and the nation.[4]

Although for this brief period blacks and Latinos were united against common foes—brutal treatment by the police and tense relationships with Koreans—black-Latino relations had also been characteristically tense for some time. Blacks viewed Latinos as having taken over their community—historically black South Central—and become direct competitors in the labor market. Latinos, on the other hand, believed that with their larger numbers relative to blacks, they were entitled to increased access to resources, including political influence (Johnson et al. 1992; Miles 1992; Oliver and Johnson 1984). Finally, data from the 1992 Los Angeles County Social Survey (LACSS) reveal substantial anti-black and anti-Latino sentiment among Asians; these attitudes were also expressed in focus groups with Asians. Moreover, the events of April 1992 would lead to an increase in Asians' anti-black hostility (Bobo et al. 1994).[5] Finally, in the wake of the verdict and the civil unrest that ensued, blacks in Los Angeles became "substantially more pessimistic about the problem of discrimination and whether, in a fundamental sense, they [would] ever be treated fairly in the United States of America"; as in 1965, economically successful blacks were the ones who expressed the most pessimism and frustration (Bobo et al. 1994, 126).

And so it seems that, in many ways, the more things change, the more they stay the same. The 1992 Los Angeles rebellion was sparked by issues that were strikingly similar to those that had set off the Watts riots nearly three decades earlier: ongoing tension between minority communities (blacks and Latinos) and the police and persisting economic exclusion (particularly of blacks, but also, in a slightly different way, of Latinos). In addition, changes in the population composition of the city had contributed to increased interminority-group tensions by 1992. Despite improvements, a majority of whites adhered to negative stereotypes of blacks and Latinos, and evidence indicates that blacks, Latinos, and Asians held negative views of one another as well (Bobo 2001; Bobo et al. 1994; Smith 1998). Whites and racial-ethnic minority groups had markedly different perspectives on the persistence of prejudice and discrimination—whites viewed it as largely a thing of the past, while minority-group members believed it to be systematic and pervasive. If these attitudes undoubtedly contributed to the feelings of alienation and frustration that erupted among blacks and Latinos in Los Angeles during the spring of 1992, they may also have factored heavily into the all-white suburban jury's decision to acquit the four white police officers accused of beating Rodney King in spite of videotape evidence and dispatch recordings that showed the officers' use of racial slurs in reference to King.

These attitudes, perceptions, and beliefs have combined with constrained economic and housing market opportunities patterned by race to set the stage for tense relations, which are exacerbated by rapid population change and patterns of racial residential segregation. Moreover, when life chances and status are perceived to be so closely tied to racial-ethnic identity, it is likely that competition will take on a racial character. Admittedly, instances of civil unrest represent the most obvious and extreme examples of racial tensions; however, as noted by Lawrence Bobo and his colleagues (2000, 25–26), the 1980s and 1990s saw more reports of racially motivated hate crimes and interminority-group conflict over residential, economic, and health care resources in Los Angeles. In short, interethnic conflict became both more frequent and more violent during the 1990s, and economic inequality worsened. Racial residential segregation is deeply implicated in these trends.

RACIAL RESIDENTIAL SEGREGATION

As detailed in the foregoing discussion of racial residential segregation in Los Angeles, it is abundantly clear that where we live has profound consequences for our economic well-being and overall quality of life, since it determines our proximity to good job opportunities, our safety from crime, and the quality of our social networks and educational opportunities (Jargowsky 1996; Massey and Denton 1993; Wilson 1987). Indeed, without racial residential segregation, the structural changes in the national economy "would not have produced the disastrous social and economic outcomes observed in inner cities. . . . Although rates of black poverty were driven up by the economic dislocations . . . it was segregation that confined the increased deprivation to a small number of densely settled, tightly packed, and geographically isolated areas" (Massey and Denton 1993, 8).

Across the nation there is tremendous variation in the quality of neighborhoods in terms of the availability and quality of services and amenities and exposure to social dislocations (such as poverty, crime, and poor-quality schools) (Bickford and Massey 1991; Massey, Condran, and Denton 1987; Massey and Fong 1990). Because racial residential segregation interacts with structural changes in the economy to concentrate poverty, disadvantaged groups are far more likely to live in undesirable neighborhoods. With their efforts to achieve homeownership confined to such neighborhoods, they are less able to reach favorable terms on mortgages and insurance. Moreover, when they do own homes, those homes are worth less. These barriers contribute to the lower levels of accumulated wealth among blacks and Latinos described by Melvin Oliver and Thomas Shapiro (1995). Finally, when members of disadvantaged groups live much of their day-to-day lives in racial isolation, they do not experience the kind of sustained and meaningful intergroup contact that would significantly improve their relations with other groups. For all of these reasons, understanding racial residential segregation is essential for understanding contemporary racial inequality in the United States (Massey and Denton 1993, 7).

In 1980 blacks in sixteen metropolitan areas were hypersegregated from whites—that is, they exhibited extreme isolation on at least four of five standard measures of residential distribution (Massey and Denton 1989).[6] By 1990 that number had nearly doubled: in twenty-nine U.S. metropolitan areas, containing 40 percent of the total black population, blacks experienced "extreme, multidimensional, and cumulative residential segregation" (Denton 1994, 49). The number of cities in which blacks were hypersegregated from whites remained unchanged by 2000, and Los Angeles was still on the list (Wilkes and Iceland 2004). Until recently, blacks were unique in this experience, which contrasts sharply with the typically limited and temporary segregation experienced by other groups (Denton 1994; Massey and Denton 1993); however, Rima Wilkes and John Iceland (2004) have recently identified two cities in which Latinos also experience hypersegregation—Los Angeles and New York. Though generally less segregated from whites than blacks are, both Latinos and Asians have seen their levels of segregation and isolation increase, owing at least in part to continuous high-volume immigration since 1970.[7]

Table 1.6 reports black, Latino, and Asian segregation from whites (D), isolation (P*xx), and exposure to whites (P*xy) for the fifty largest metropolitan regions in 2000 (and parenthetically the 1980-to-2000 change), including Los Angeles.[8] The percentage of blacks, Latinos, and Asians who would have to relocate in order to achieve a random spatial distribution in Los Angeles without regard to race is 68 percent for blacks, 63 percent for Latinos, and 48 percent for Asians. In Los Angeles and across the country, both Latinos and Asians have become increasingly segregated from whites and residentially isolated; they have also experienced declining exposure to whites. These trends are consistent with the rapid population growth in these groups, their settlement patterns, and the declining white population share.[9] Indeed, an important difference in the experience of residential segregation for groups with large immigrant populations is that residential segregation tends to be a temporary, transitional period in the larger process of immigrant adaptation and acculturation. For recent arrivals, residential segregation can be beneficial for "learning the ropes" and adapting to a new home surrounded by coethnics who can provide support and assistance (Lieberson 1963; Massey and Denton 1993; Park and Burgess 1969).

For blacks, on the other hand, segregation is a permanent aspect of life stretching across generations. Between 1980 and 2000, blacks continued to experience a high level of segregation on average, in spite of meaningful improvements in many metropolitan regions. They also experienced declines in racial isolation, but trends in exposure to whites were mixed, showing only a slight increase on average. In Los Angeles, blacks experienced no change in their exposure to whites between 1980 and 2000. Overall, these patterns are consistent with the shifts in population composition detailed previously and their anticipated effects on spatial distribution (see figures 1.1, 1.2, and 1.3). In many instances, the concentrations of Latino immigrants in areas of traditional black settlement contributed to the trend toward decreasing racial isolation for blacks by increasing black-Latino contact (Alba et al. 1995).[10]

Note that metro areas with the largest declines in black-white segregation (15 percent or more) tend to be multiethnic (an above-average presence of at least one other nonwhite group) and/or have a relatively small black population (between 5 and 10 percent); these areas tend to be located in the newer cities of the West and the Southwest (Farley and Frey 1994; Frey and Farley 1993; Logan 2001a). As a newer, western city that is multiethnic and has a relatively small black population, Los Angeles might be expected to be a less segregated metropolis, and relative to other large cities, particularly those in the Midwest and Northeast, this is certainly the case. On the other hand, Los Angeles County often scores

(Text continues on p. 28.)

Table 1.6 Black, Latino, and Asian Segregation from Whites in the Fifty Largest Metropolitan Regions, 1980 to 2000

	Blacks			Latinos			Asians		
Metropolitan Area	Dissimilarity	Isolation	Exposure	Dissimilarity	Isolation	Exposure	Dissimilarity	Isolation	Exposure
Western areas									
Los Angeles, Long Beach	68 (−14)	34 (−26)	16 (0)	63 (+6)	63 (+13)	17 (−17)	48 (+1)	29 (+14)	31 (−17)
Riverside, San Bernadino	46 (−9)	15 (−5)	38 (−17)	43 (+4)	50 (+17)	36 (−23)	38 (+7)	11 (+8)	46 (−27)
Orange County	37 (−9)	3 (−2)	48 (−17)	56 (+13)	54 (+21)	31 (−28)	40 (+12)	26 (+19)	46 (−29)
San Diego	54 (−10)	15 (−12)	38 (−6)	51 (+9)	44 (+16)	38 (−20)	47 (+1)	22 (+11)	45 (−17)
Seattle, Bellevue, Everett	50 (−18)	14 (−15)	59 (+4)	31 (+11)	8 (+6)	70 (−16)	35 (−5)	19 (+7)	65 (−8)
Oakland	63 (−11)	35 (−21)	26 (−2)	47 (+11)	30 (+12)	36 (−25)	42 (+4)	29 (+17)	41 (−22)
Portland, Vancouver	48 (−21)	16 (−16)	67 (+7)	35 (+14)	15 (+12)	74 (−17)	32 (+3)	9 (+6)	78 (−12)
San Francisco	61 (−7)	23 (−18)	31 (−3)	54 (+8)	34 (+12)	36 (−17)	49 (−2)	40 (+10)	38 (−12)
San Jose	41 (−8)	4 (−3)	38 (−18)	52 (+6)	41 (+9)	30 (−23)	42 (+9)	38 (+27)	37 (−28)
Sacramento	56 (−3)	18 (−4)	44 (−13)	40 (+5)	21 (+7)	52 (−17)	49 (+1)	20 (+7)	48 (−19)
Western area average	52 (−11)	18 (−12)	41 (−7)	47 (+9)	36 (+13)	42 (−20)	42 (+3)	24 (+13)	48 (−19)
Southwestern areas									
Houston	68 (−9)	47 (−19)	22 (−1)	56 (+5)	49 (+13)	31 (−19)	49 (+6)	15 (+9)	45 (−26)
Dallas	59 (−19)	42 (−26)	33 (+9)	54 (+5)	45 (+21)	37 (−23)	45 (+6)	11 (+9)	60 (−22)
Phoenix, Mesa	44 (−18)	9 (−14)	51 (+4)	53 (0)	46 (+12)	44 (−13)	28 (+1)	4 (+3)	70 (−13)
Denver	62 (−7)	24 (−19)	47 (+4)	50 (+1)	38 (+9)	50 (−13)	30 (+4)	5 (+3)	70 (−9)

Fort Worth, Arlington	60 (−18)	35 (−28)	40 (+10)	48 (0)	37 (+11)	46 (−17)	42 (+5)	8 (+6)	61 (−25)
San Antonio	50 (−12)	20 (−15)	34 (+1)	51 (−7)	66 (−1)	27 (−2)	32 (+2)	4 (+2)	49 (−13)
Las Vegas	43 (−20)	19 (−31)	48 (+7)	43 (+20)	34 (+23)	49 (−30)	30 (+9)	9 (+6)	62 (−20)
Salt Lake City, Ogden	37 (−20)	3 (−6)	74 (−1)	43 (+8)	22 (+12)	70 (−15)	30 (+5)	6 (+4)	76 (−13)
Austin, San Marcos	52 (−13)	21 (−22)	40 (+5)	47 (0)	40 (+4)	45 (−7)	41 (+6)	9 (+7)	63 (−13)
Southwestern area average	53 (−15)	24 (−20)	43 (+4)	49 (+4)	42 (+12)	44 (−15)	36 (+5)	8 (+5)	62 (−17)
Midwestern areas									
Chicago	81 (−8)	73 (−10)	16 (+5)	62 (−2)	48 (+10)	38 (−13)	44 (−3)	15 (+6)	63 (−12)
Detroit	85 (−3)	79 (0)	17 (−2)	46 (+4)	19 (+12)	62 (−13)	46 (+5)	8 (+6)	76 (−8)
Minneapolis, St. Paul	58 (−10)	23 (−6)	58 (−4)	47 (+10)	10 (+6)	67 (−20)	43 (+13)	12 (+10)	68 (−25)
St. Louis	74 (−9)	65 (−9)	32 (+8)	29 (0)	4 (+2)	77 (−4)	43 (+1)	5 (+3)	80 (−8)
Cleveland, Lorain, Elyria	77 (−8)	71 (−7)	25 (+5)	58 (0)	17 (+4)	65 (−9)	38 (+3)	5 (+3)	80 (−7)
Kansas City	69 (−9)	53 (−14)	38 (+9)	46 (+5)	17 (+7)	64 (−13)	35 (+1)	4 (+2)	77 (−7)
Cincinnati	75 (−4)	58 (−6)	39 (+4)	30 (−1)	2 (+1)	81 (+1)	42 (+2)	4 (+3)	82 (−5)
Indianapolis	71 (−9)	53 (−12)	41 (+7)	44 (+15)	7 (+6)	70 (−14)	39 (0)	3 (+2)	79 (−8)
Columbus	63 (−10)	48 (−9)	47 (+6)	38 (+9)	6 (+5)	71 (−12)	42 (−3)	7 (+5)	78 (−10)
Milwaukee, Waukesha	82 (−2)	67 (−2)	25 (−2)	60 (+4)	33 (+17)	51 (−20)	41 (+10)	5 (+4)	65 (−25)
Midwestern area average	74 (−7)	59 (−8)	34 (+4)	46 (+4)	16 (+7)	65 (−12)	41 (+3)	7 (+4)	75 (−12)
Southern areas									
Washington, D.C.	63 (−7)	59 (−8)	28 (−1)	48 (+16)	20 (+15)	45 (−25)	39 (+7)	14 (+9)	57 (−18)
Atlanta	66 (−11)	63 (−10)	28 (+2)	53 (+21)	20 (+18)	49 (−27)	45 (+9)	8 (+7)	59 (−27)

(*Table continues on p. 26.*)

Table 1.6 *(Continued)*

Metropolitan Area	Blacks			Latinos			Asians		
	Dissimilarity	Isolation	Exposure	Dissimilarity	Isolation	Exposure	Dissimilarity	Isolation	Exposure
Baltimore	68 (−7)	66 (−7)	29 (+4)	36 (+3)	4 (+2)	66 (−7)	39 (+1)	7 (+5)	71 (−10)
Tampa, St. Petersburg, Clearwater	65 (−14)	43 (−16)	42 (+7)	45 (−5)	23 (+4)	61 (−9)	34 (0)	4 (+3)	75 (−12)
Miami	74 (−7)	62 (−5)	11 (−7)	44 (−9)	71 (+13)	18 (−16)	31 (+3)	3 (+2)	29 (−29)
Orlando	57 (−17)	41 (−21)	41 (+5)	41 (+10)	27 (+21)	55 (−30)	36 (+4)	5 (+4)	62 (−26)
Fort Lauderdale	62 (−22)	53 (−18)	31 (+6)	32 (+4)	23 (+17)	55 (−29)	28 (+1)	4 (+3)	59 (−30)
Norfolk, Virginia Beach, Newport News	46 (−13)	52 (−9)	42 (+5)	32 (+1)	5 (+2)	60 (−11)	34 (−4)	6 (+2)	63 (−14)
Charlotte, Gastonia, Rock Hill	55 (−8)	45 (−10)	44 (+2)	50 (+18)	13 (+12)	55 (−18)	43 (−4)	4 (+3)	65 (−19)
New Orleans	69 (−2)	71 (0)	24 (−2)	36 (+9)	8 (+2)	61 (−10)	48 (−3)	11 (0)	51 (−7)
Greensboro, Winston-Salem, High Point	59 (−8)	49 (−11)	41 (+3)	51 (+19)	11 (+10)	58 (−16)	46 (+3)	4 (+3)	67 (−19)
Nashville	57 (−9)	46 (−10)	48 (+5)	46 (+23)	9 (+8)	68 (−12)	42 (−1)	4 (+3)	75 (−12)
Raleigh, Durham, Chapel Hill	46 (−6)	43 (−11)	46 (+1)	43 (+19)	12 (+11)	55 (−19)	41 (0)	7 (+5)	70 (−14)
Southern area average	61 (−10)	53 (−10)	35 (+2)	43 (+10)	19 (+10)	54 (−18)	39 (+1)	6 (+4)	62 (−18)

Eastern areas									
New York	82 (0)	60 (−3)	11 (−4)	67 (+2)	46 (+6)	21 (−10)	51 (+1)	27 (+11)	40 (−15)
Philadelphia	72 (−6)	62 (−7)	28 (+2)	60 (−3)	27 (+5)	43 (−7)	44 (+3)	10 (+7)	66 (−12)
Boston	66 (−11)	39 (−14)	40 (+4)	59 (+3)	21 (+9)	54 (−13)	45 (−3)	13 (+1)	71 (−7)
Nassau, Suffolk	74 (−3)	41 (−8)	34 (−8)	47 (+10)	23 (+13)	56 (−22)	36 (+5)	8 (+6)	75 (−14)
Pittsburgh	67 (−6)	47 (−7)	50 (+6)	30 (−1)	1 (0)	84 (−3)	49 (+3)	5 (+4)	85 (−7)
Newark	80 (−3)	67 (−3)	17 (−4)	65 (−2)	36 (+9)	36 (−11)	35 (+4)	9 (+7)	69 (−11)
Bergen, Passaic	73 (−7)	36 (−10)	27 (−6)	58 (−3)	39 (+11)	38 (−13)	36 (+2)	16 (+13)	65 (−20)
Providence, Fall River, Warwick	59 (−13)	13 (−10)	56 (−5)	68 (+18)	32 (+24)	48 (−31)	43 (+10)	6 (+5)	69 (−20)
Eastern area average	72 (−6)	46 (−8)	33 (−2)	57 (+3)	28 (+10)	48 (−14)	42 (+3)	12 (+7)	68 (−13)
Overall average	62 (−10)	41 (−12)	37 (+1)	48 (+6)	27 (+10)	51 (−16)	40 (+3)	11 (+6)	62 (−16)

Source: U.S. Bureau of the Census and Lewis Mumford Center for Comparative Urban and Regional Research.

Notes: Due to space limitations, indices and changes are rounded to the nearest whole number. Change from 1980 to 2000 is in parentheses.

worse than any other region in the West and Southwest on measures of segregation.

An alternative perspective on the shifting color line is to visualize changes in the diversity of neighborhoods over time, using a measure that suggests the magnitude of possible interracial contact. From this perspective, racial-ethnic diversity "is a function of racial *abundance* (the number of races in the population) and racial *evenness* (the evenness with which the individuals in the population are distributed among these racial categories)" (Zuberi 2001, 157, emphasis in original). The Index of Racial Diversity (IRD) offers an estimate of the probability that two randomly and independently selected individuals from a population will belong to the same group. Like other common measures of spatial distribution, values range from 0—complete homogeneity or the absence of diversity—to 1—even racial distribution or maximum heterogeneity (Zuberi 2001, 157). As an alternative to the illustrations of racial concentration highlighted in the discussion of immigration and population change (see figures 1.1, 1.2, and 1.3), figures 1.4, 1.5, and 1.6 illustrate changes in the IRD in 1980, 1990, and 2000, respectively.

What is interesting about these figures is that over the two-decade period there appears to have been declines in both the least (darkest) and most diverse (lightest) areas in Los Angeles County. By comparing the maps of racial concentration to those mapping racial diversity, we can also visualize the degree of diversity. Looking at the maps of racial diversity shows that, for example, the majority-white areas like Beverly Hills and areas west of Beverly Hills have experienced little change in diversity; however, the northeasternmost section of the county (north of Azusa) went from little or no diversity (0 to .25) to substantial diversity (.51 to .75). Indeed, the areas that saw the biggest increases in diversity seem to be those that were previously white; in the heavily black and Latino areas (such as South Central, Pico-Union, and East L.A.), changes were much more modest. In fact, the heavily Latino area just east of South Central (Vernon) has become less diverse over time, consistent with its rapid increase in population and its settlement patterns.

Thus, in terms of racial residential segregation, Los Angeles is arguably one of a very few large metropolitan areas that embody various national trends. A newer city located in the West—where segregation tends to be lower relative to the rest of the country—it is among the most racially and ethnically diverse cities in the world. It is a city that has experienced rapid population change as a result of high-volume immigration, primarily from Asian and Latin American countries, but from the rest of the world as well. Yet Los Angeles is also similar to the older cities of the Midwest and Northeast in the degree to which both blacks and Latinos

Figure 1.4 Los Angeles County: Index of Racial Diversity, 1980

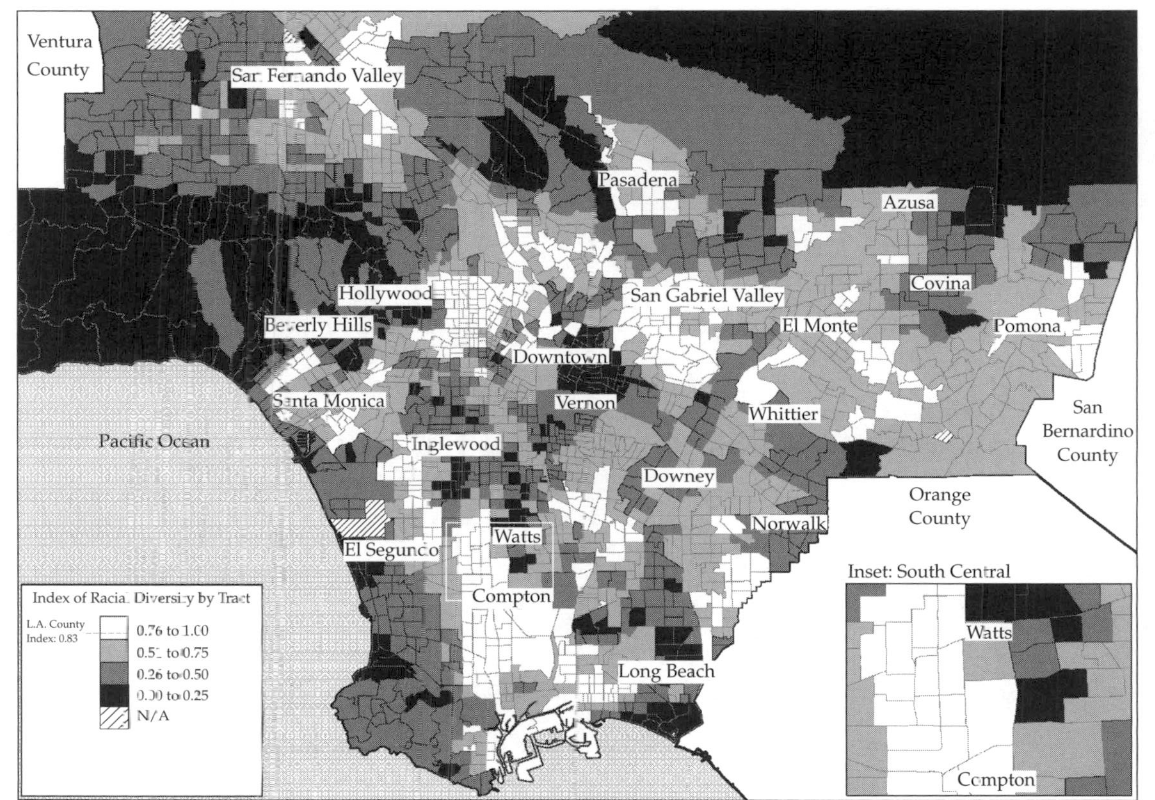

Source: GeoLytics (2003).

Figure 1.5 Los Angeles County: Index of Racial Diversity, 1990

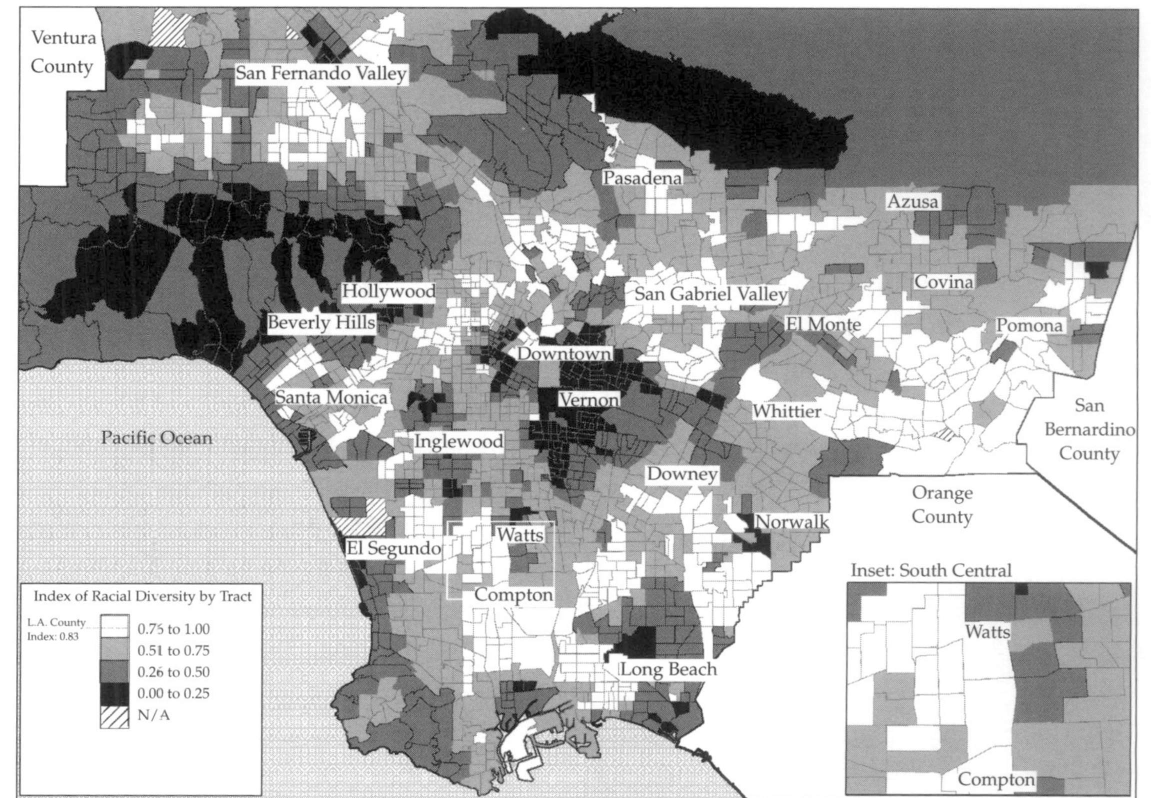

Source: GeoLytics (2003).

Figure 1.6 Los Angeles County: Index of Racial Diversity, 2000

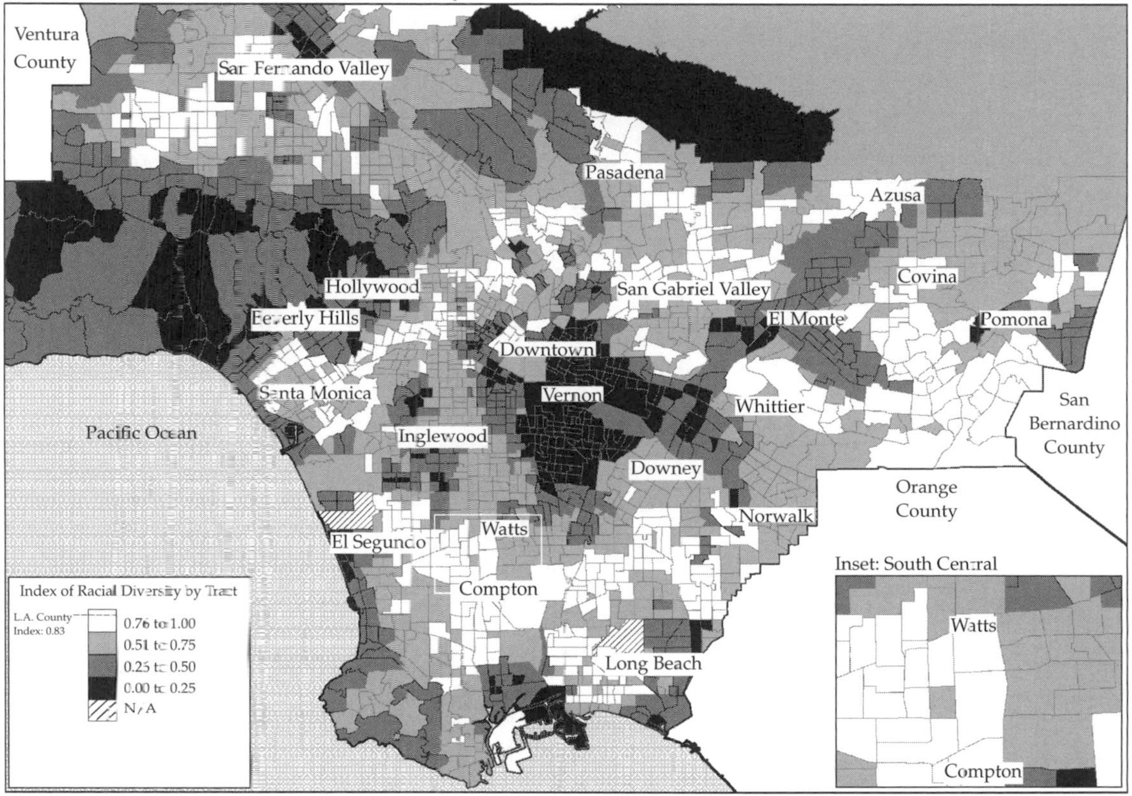

Source: GeoLytics (2003).

experience hypersegregation (particularly black-white segregation). Thus, to the extent that racial residential segregation is deeply implicated in persisting racial economic inequality and tenuous intergroup relations, and inasmuch as trends in Los Angeles point to our national urban future (Baldassare 1994; Waldinger and Bozorgmehr 1996), it is an optimal location for a case study of the dynamics of racial residential segregation.

THE 1992 TO 1994 LOS ANGELES SURVEY OF URBAN INEQUALITY

By and large, our knowledge of the factors that influence racial residential segregation has been limited in one or more of several ways: (1) studies have been limited to the attitudes and experiences of whites and blacks in an increasingly multiracial society (Farley et al. 1978; Farley et al. 1993; Farley et al. 1994; Ilandfeldt and Scafidi 2004; Krysan 2002; Krysan and Farley 2002; Timberlake 2000); (2) data sources have been used that allow for rigorous tests of *either* class- or race-based explanations (such as census data for class-based hypotheses and survey data or audit studies for race-based explanations), but that cannot accommodate a rigorous examination of the relative importance of competing explanations; and (3) attitudinal studies have relied on awkward measures of neighborhood racial composition preferences and/or a limited consideration of racial attitudes (Bobo and Zubrinsky 1996; Charles 2000a; Clark 1992; Farley et al. 1994; Zubrinsky and Bobo 1996).

The 1992 to 1994 Los Angeles Survey of Urban Inequality (LASUI) addresses each of these limitations. The LASUI is a large, multifaceted survey research project designed to examine crosscutting explanations for racial inequality broadly defined and to provide fresh data from one of the largest and most racially diverse metropolitan areas in the country.[11] More specifically, the goal of the interdisciplinary team of researchers behind the LASUI was to design and execute a study that would "broaden our knowledge and understanding of how three sets of forces—changing labor market dynamics, racial attitudes and relations, and residential segregation—interact to foster modern urban inequality" (Bobo et al. 2000, 6).

Devising the LASUI instrument was a long and arduous process. To assist us in the development of the questionnaire, we conducted a series of twelve focus groups: four Latino groups (two in English, two in Spanish), two Chinese American groups (both in Mandarin Chinese), two Korean American groups (both in Korean), two with blacks, and two with whites (for more details, see Bobo et al. 1994, 1995). Information from these focus groups, an extensive review of the literature, advice from a national advisory board, and careful instrument pretesting all went into a complicated but, in the end, thorough survey instrument.

The design of the LASUI instrument was intended to capitalize on the multiracial character of Los Angeles in three important ways: (1) large numbers of respondents from each of the four major racial-ethnic groupings were included;[12] (2) content moved beyond the traditional black-white dichotomy; and (3) survey-based experimental manipulations were used (Schuman and Bobo 1988) to avoid time-consuming redundancy and repetition. The survey-based experimental design allowed the examination of various types of integrated living arrangements and permitted a direct assessment of whether individuals "react in a uniform or racially discriminatory manner" (Bobo et al. 2000, 8).

The sample design includes non-Hispanic white, black, Hispanic, and Asians of Chinese, Korean, or Japanese descent. We had to restrict the Asian respondents included in the sample to these three Asian-ancestry groups owing to the great expense associated with multiple-language translation and interview staffing. Nevertheless, the LASUI covers three of the four largest such groups in Los Angeles. Equally important, these three groups represent analytically important cases. Respondents of Chinese and Korean origin were largely foreign-born, and a substantial proportion were recent immigrants to the United States (see tables 1.7 and 1.8). Both groups have diverse socioeconomic and cultural characteristics. On the other hand, Japanese-origin Asians were more likely to be native-born and affluent relative to other Asian subgroups—and to whites as well. Consistent with the actual population composition, the overwhelming majority of Latino respondents were of Mexican ancestry, with a varied set of social background characteristics. To ensure the inclusion of the experiences, attitudes, and opinions of these large immigrant populations, the English version of the LASUI instrument was also fielded in Spanish, Korean, Mandarin, and Cantonese.[13] The availability of non-English interview settings proved invaluable, since substantial majorities of Mexican, Central American, Chinese, and Korean respondents opted to complete their interviews in their native language.

The LASUI questionnaire covers a wide range of topics and goes into great detail about respondents' labor market experiences, residential segregation and attitudes about the housing market, and intergroup attitudes and relations. The research team also invested a considerable amount of time in gathering detailed social background and demographic information, including conventional measures like educational attainment, employment status, income, occupational status, and employment status. We also made a concerted effort to obtain the data necessary for more nuanced analyses of economic outcomes, including assets

Table 1.7 LASUI Sample Characteristics, by Race

	Whites	Blacks	Latinos	Asians
Sex				
Female	49.07%	54.21%	49.73%	51.04%
Male	50.93	45.79	50.27	48.96
Nativity status				
Native-born	100	100	26.27	11.96
Foreign-born	0	0	73.73	88.04
Mean age	44.96	42.08	36.78	44.43
Mean years of education	14.01	12.73	9.58	13.27
Mean family income	$53,714	$36,241	$27,284	$43,410
Mean net financial assets	10,561	2,753	1,304	6,383
Neighborhood poverty				
Less than 20 percent	96.43	60.44	52.78	79.44
20 to 40 percent	3.48	34.04	43.70	20.21
Over 40 percent	0.19	5.52	3.52	0.34
Neighborhood racial composition				
Mean percent white	63.42	23.57	23.27	41.29
Mean percent black	4.37	40.36	7.21	4.18
Mean percent Latino	21.54	28.25	59.27	28.05
Mean percent Asian	9.97	7.00	9.61	25.90
Mean percent same-race	63.42	40.36	59.27	25.90
Total number of cases	739	1,075	914	1,045

Source: 1993–94 Los Angeles Survey of Urban Inequality.

and debts; these data allow us to consider whether and how racial differences in accumulated wealth have an impact on housing outcomes. To address adequately the role of immigration in the social and economic well-being of Latinos and Asians, we also gathered information on nativity status, citizenship or residency status, length of time in the United States, and English-language proficiency.

The LASUI also gathered a considerable amount of information on people's beliefs about neighborhood and community issues. Some of it is especially pertinent to the purposes of this volume, such as amount spent each month on housing, whether respondents rent or own their current residence, and level of experience with public housing. In addition, respondents shared their beliefs about the prevalence of housing market discrimination against specific minority groups and their own neighbor-

Table 1.8 LASUI Sample Characteristics, by National Origin for Latino and Asian Respondents

	Mexican	Central American	Chinese	Korean	Japanese
Sex					
Female	48.51%	54.54%	46.80%	53.20%	55.68%
Male	51.49	45.46	53.20	46.80	44.32
Nativity status					
Foreign-born—five years or less in U.S.	10.97	28.77	26.08	24.94	4.89
Foreign-born—six to ten years in U.S.	14.54	17.81	14.32	36.18	1.74
Foreign-born—over ten years in U.S.	42.24	50.70	54.80	38.15	45.80
Native-born	32.25	2.72	4.80	0.73	47.58
Mean age	36.94	36.15	45.65	44.85	41.16
Mean years of education	9.57	9.65	12.87	12.84	14.93
Mean family income	$29,070	$20,244	$40,088	$35,698	$64,463
Mean net financial assets	1,680	−177	6,383	931	16,480
Language of interview					
English	39.72%	19.32%	33.83%	25.88%	99.80%
Other	60.28	80.68	66.17	74.12	0.20
Mean English proficiency (0 to 5 scale)	2.29	1.66	2.18	2.01	3.85
Neighborhood poverty					
Less than 20 percent	59.81%	25.06%	77.33%	71.77%	97.96%
20 to 40 percent	37.03	70.01	22.67	27.39	1.92
Over 40 percent	3.16	4.93	0	0.84	0.12
Neighborhood racial composition					
Mean percent white	25.25	15.49	33.04	42.53	55.78
Mean percent black	7.16	7.41	2.57	6.39	3.36
Mean percent Latino	57.73	65.32	30.58	28.77	21.56
Mean percent Asian	9.24	11.09	33.28	21.53	18.94
Mean percent same-race	57.73	65.32	33.28	21.53	19.94
Total number of cases	689	225	527	353	165

Source: 1993–94 Los Angeles Survey of Urban Inequality.

hood racial composition preferences. In fact, an entire section of the survey confronts racial attitudes on a variety of dimensions, including racial-group solidarity, a wide variety of racial stereotypes, and beliefs about racial-group competition for economic and political resources. All of these attitudes are critical to understanding attitudes about residential integration. Finally, the restricted-use data file includes tract-level characteristics taken from the 1990 census for each respondent's actual neighborhood, including poverty rate, racial composition, and median household income.

A core aim of the LASUI is determining the nature of racial attitudes and intergroup relations in a multiracial context. These are sensitive issues for many people; to minimize the likelihood of socially desirable responses, we made every effort to match the race of the interviewer to that of the respondent, and did so in 78 percent of the cases.[14] The end result is a face-to-face household survey of 4,025 adults twenty-one years of age or older, interviewed between September 9, 1993, and August 15, 1994.[15] The LASUI had an overall response rate of 68 percent, a nonresponse adjusted rate of 71 percent, and an overall cooperation rate (ratio of completed interviews to interviews plus refusals) of 73 percent. An incentive of $10 was offered to respondents for their cooperation, and the average interview lasted roughly ninety minutes.

The analyses in the following chapters are limited to samples of native-born whites (739), blacks (1,075), native- and foreign-born Latinos of Mexican or Central American ancestry (914), and native- and foreign-born Asians of Chinese, Korean, or Japanese ancestry (1,045), for a total sample size of 3,773.[16] Table 1.7 presents summary information by respondent's racial-ethnic group for distributions by sex, nativity status, age, education, household income, wealth, neighborhood poverty, and neighborhood racial composition. Wealth is measured as net financial assets—the remainder of assets (excluding home equity and car value) after accounting for household debt (excluding mortgage debt). Table 1.8 presents this information not only in relation to length of time in the United States, language of interview, and self-reported English-language proficiency but broken down by national-origin categories for Latino and Asian respondents.

AN OVERVIEW OF THE VOLUME

All told, the LASUI offers a unique opportunity for undertaking crosscutting analyses of racial inequality, intergroup relations, and residential processes in a multiracial context. Chapter 2 offers a review and critique of existing research that attempts to explain the persistence of racial residential segregation. This vast body of research emphasizes two competing explanations: the spatial assimilation model, which sees objective differences in socioeconomic status and immigration-related characteristics as primarily responsible for the racial distribution of groups across metropolitan areas, and the alternative explanation, the place stratification model, which focuses on persisting racial prejudice and discrimination, both among individuals and in the housing market (Alba and Logan 1993). Both bodies of research have made invaluable contributions to our understanding of residential processes, yet each also suffers from shortcomings that, I believe, can be addressed with the LASUI.

Chapter 3 thoroughly investigates the varying ways in which objective differences in the socioeconomic status of racial-ethnic groups facilitate or constrain their housing options, including the likelihood of homeownership, neighborhood proximity to whites, and neighborhood-level socioeconomic status.[17] This chapter attempts to bring together the best methods for testing the spatial assimilation hypothesis, using information that has been historically unavailable in these types of analysis.

In chapter 4, I provide an overview of trends in the racial attitudes of whites, blacks, Latinos, and Asians, paying particular attention to the attitudes most likely to be implicated in their preferences for neighborhood racial integration. I argue here that by situating preferences for racial integration within the larger context of racial identity, racial attitudes, perceptions of discrimination, and beliefs about inequality, patterns of preference for neighborhood contact with various racial-ethnic groups are better understood as a manifestation of more generalized intergroup attitudes. Chapter 5 tests this notion empirically by evaluating the role that various racial attitudes play in shaping the neighborhood racial composition preferences of whites, blacks, Latinos, and Asians in Los Angeles. Specifically, this analysis identifies the factors that shape preferences and assesses their relative importance. New to this analysis is the consideration of multiple dimensions of prejudice, as well as the consideration of minority-group perceptions of discrimination. In addition to these attitudes, I consider the roles of in-group attachment or ethnocentrism and perceptions of the social class status of racial-ethnic groups.

The final chapter presents a simultaneous equations model to test the impact of neighborhood racial preferences on actual housing outcomes. In a sense, chapter 6 revisits the class-based models presented in chapter 3 and expands them to include racial attitudes—something rarely done before, and never done across four racial-ethnic groups. Throughout the analysis, I give particular attention to how immigration-related characteristics shape residential processes and racial attitudes and preferences, using measures such as national origin, length of time in the United States, and English-language ability. Each of these characteristics is known to influence immigrants' residential patterns; here we also look at their influence on the various racial attitudes toward racial integration.

As a result of the interdisciplinary interests and concerns of the investigators, the racial and ethnic diversity of Los Angeles, and the position of the metropolis as a top destination for immigrants, the Los Angeles Survey of Urban Inequality offers a rare opportunity to examine the dynamic interplay between individual-level characteristics (such as social class status, race-ethnicity, nativity status, and racial attitudes) and neighborhood-level outcomes. All told, it is my hope that this volume makes an important contribution to the study of racial inequality and intergroup relations in the United States.

Chapter Two | Theoretical Perspectives on the Dynamics of Racial Residential Segregation

AT THE DAWN of the twentieth century, W. E. B. Du Bois (1903/1990, 120–21) recognized the importance of neighborhoods—the "physical proximity of home and dwelling-places, the way in which neighborhoods group themselves, and [their] contiguity"—as primary locations for social interaction, lamenting that the "color line" separating black and white neighborhoods caused each to see the worst in the other. Indeed, students of racial inequality from Gunnar Myrdal to Karl and Alma Taeuber have believed that segregation is a major barrier to equality. The Taeubers (1965, 1) asserted that segregation "inhibits the development of informal, neighborly relations" and "ensures the segregation of a variety of public and private facilities," and Myrdal (1944/1972, 618) believed that segregation permits prejudice "to be freely vented on Negroes without hurting whites." Moreover, as Douglas Massey and Nancy Denton (1993, 2–3) have observed, residential segregation "undermines the social and economic well-being" irrespective of personal characteristics.

By the late 1960s, unrest in urban ghettos across the country had brought residential segregation—and by implication racial inequality—to the public's attention, leading to the now-famous conclusion of the Kerner Commission (1968) that America was "moving toward two societies, one black, one white—separate and unequal," as well as to passage of the Fair Housing Act in 1968. In addition to ending legal housing market discrimination, the Fair Housing Act marked the end of public discussion of residential segregation, since many believed that antidiscrimination legislation would be the "beginning of the end of residential segregation." With legal barriers to educational, occupational, and residential opportunities removed, blacks could finally achieve full-fledged integration, and social scientists, politicians, and the general public would ignore the residential dimension of "the color line" for the next two decades (Massey and Denton 1993; Meyer 2000). By the late 1970s, with conditions in the nation's urban areas—where the majority of blacks were still concentrated—in precipitous decline, social scientists began scrambling to explain the emergence of a disproportionately black urban underclass, but they paid little or no attention to persisting residential segregation by race.

In *The Truly Disadvantaged* (1987), William Julius Wilson outlines the most widely accepted theory of urban poverty: geographically concentrated poverty and the subsequent development of a ghetto underclass resulted from structural changes in the economy combined with the exodus of middle- and working-class black families from many inner-city ghetto neighborhoods. The shift from a goods- to a services-producing economy caused huge declines in the availability of low-skilled manufacturing jobs that paid enough to support a family; owing to past discrimination, blacks were disproportionately concentrated in these jobs and therefore suffered massive unemployment. Wilson argues that middle- and working-class blacks, having benefited more substantially from affirmative action policies and antidiscrimination legislation, were able to take advantage of residential opportunities outside of the ghetto. These shifts led to an "exponential increase" in the now well-known social dislocations associated with sudden and/or long-term increases in joblessness—under- and unemployment, welfare dependence, out-of-wedlock births, and blatant disregard for the law. The out-migration of nonpoor blacks, Wilson (1987, 56–60) argues, removed an important "social buffer," leaving poor blacks in socially isolated communities that lacked material resources, access to jobs and job networks, and exposure to conventional role models, and therefore "generate[d] behavior not conducive to good work histories."[1]

Massey and Denton (1993) show, however, that, without residential segregation, structural changes in the economy would not have had monumentally disastrous social and economic effects on American inner cities. Retooling existing theories of urban poverty to include processes of racial residential segregation, they argue, resolves unanswered questions regarding the disproportionate representation of blacks and Puerto Ricans in the ranks of the underclass, as well as the concentration of underclass communities in the older, larger cities of the Northeast and Midwest. In the largest urban areas, blacks and Puerto Ricans have been the only groups to experience both extreme residential segregation and steep rises in poverty, owing to the fact that areas of black concentration were especially hard hit by the economic reversals of the 1970s (Massey and

Denton 1993, 146–47).[2] Emphasizing the interaction of segregation and rising poverty also furthers our understanding of the inability of nonpoor blacks to escape segregation and its consequences, despite increasing class segregation within black communities (Jargowsky 1996; Massey and Denton 1993, 146–47). Focusing on a black middle-class exodus, they argue, detracts attention from the devastating consequences of residential segregation for *all* blacks, irrespective of socioeconomic status.

Thus, the publication of *American Apartheid* (Massey and Denton 1993, 7) was singularly influential in shifting public discourse "back to issues of race and racial segregation" as "fundamental to . . . the status of black Americans and the origins of the urban underclass," because it argues persuasively that "the missing link" in all of the underclass theories prevalent at the time was "their systematic failure to consider the important role that segregation has played in mediating, exacerbating, and ultimately amplifying the harmful social and economic processes they treat."

Trends in the spatial distribution of groups in metropolitan areas (see chapter 1) suggest that residential segregation by race continues to be one of our nation's most pressing problems. Furthermore, as our population becomes increasingly diverse racially and ethnically, the factors that drive segregation become increasingly complex. Given how well we now know that segregation has negative consequences—including economic vulnerability, exposure to crime, compromised health, and racial misunderstanding—it behooves us to gain leverage on the factors that contribute to residential segregation by race in multiracial contexts. Historically, efforts at understanding this process have focused either on objective differences in the social class characteristics of various racial-ethnic groups or on various racial attitudes—particularly prejudice and discrimination or neutral expressions of in-group preference. A central purpose of this volume is to consider the importance of both, using a single data source in a truly multiracial-multiethnic metropolis. Before delving into that analysis, I assess the state of knowledge to this point.

A large body of sociological research attempts to explain the persistence of racial residential segregation—particularly among blacks—despite the passage of antidiscrimination legislation, more favorable racial attitudes among whites, and the dramatic expansion of the black middle class. The following sections summarize the three competing explanations for persisting racial residential segregation that garner the most research attention—objective differences in socioeconomic status, prejudice, and housing market discrimination—and review major research findings since about 1980. Explanations emphasizing group differences in social class status are consistent with the spatial assimilation model, while the place stratification model includes explanations that focus on persisting prejudice and discrimination. Where appropriate, I consider alternative explanations that do not fit neatly into either theoretical perspective.

THE SPATIAL ASSIMILATION MODEL

Racial-group differences in socioeconomic characteristics are well documented. On average, blacks and Latinos complete fewer years of school and are concentrated in lower-status occupations, earn less income, and accumulate less wealth compared to whites (Farley 1996a; Oliver and Shapiro 1995). The persistence and severity of these differences lead easily to the conclusion that residential segregation by race is simply the logical outcome of these differences in status and the associated differences in lifestyle (Clark 1986, 1988; Galster 1988; on class identities as involving lifestyle considerations, see Jackman and Jackman 1983). This assumption is the basis of the spatial assimilation model, which asserts that individuals convert socioeconomic gains into higher-quality housing, often by leaving ethnic neighborhoods for areas with more whites. For immigrants, the process also involves acculturation—the accumulation of time in the United States and acquisition of English-language fluency. It should also be noted that spatial assimilation is influenced by metropolitan-area characteristics such as group size, rates of group population change, and suburbanization (Alba and Logan 1993; Farley and Frey 1994; Kain 1968, 1992; Massey 1985).[3]

Tests of this hypothesis dominated segregation research over the past two decades, and findings consistently showed that Asians and Latinos are always substantially less segregated from whites than blacks are, and that as Asian and Latino socioeconomic status improves and generations shift from immigrant to native-born, segregation from whites declines substantially. Conversely, objective differences in socioeconomic status explain only part of blacks' residential outcomes (Alba and Logan 1993; Denton and Massey 1988; Kain 1968, 1986, 1992; Logan and Alba 1993, 1995; Logan et al. 1996; Massey and Denton 1987, 1993; Massey and Fischer 1999). Moreover, studies distinguishing between white, black, and mixed-race Latinos find that black and mixed-race Latinos' residential patterns mirror those of African Americans. The exceptional experience of groups with black skin leads Massey and Denton (1989; see also Denton and Massey 1988) to conclude that blacks pay a penalty for their race that is not explained by socioeconomic status disadvantage.

Until recently, the bases for these conclusions were aggregate-level analyses, primarily from the Massey-Denton segregation research project that culminated in the publication of *American Apartheid*.[4] Modeling aggregate-level studies suffers, however, from several potentially important limitations. In particular, modeling individual-level processes at the aggregate level (either the tract level or the metropolitan area level) risks problems of ecological inference and introduces multicollinearity that limits the number of explanatory measures (Alba and Logan 1993; Massey et al. 1987; see also Massey and Denton 1987). Particularly problematic is the fact that homeownership is never included in aggregate-level studies, despite its obvious implications for residential outcomes (Alba and Logan 1993; Charles 2001a; Oliver and Shapiro 1995; Yinger 1995).[5] Finally, these studies measure or predict segregation or, less frequently, central-city versus suburban location across metropolitan areas. It is just as important, however, to understand variations in the characteristics of the neighborhoods—both central city and suburban—where various racial-ethnic groups actually live. For example, suburban blacks tend to live in older, inner suburbs that are less affluent and less white, and they experience more crime and social disorganization compared to whites who live in comparable suburbs (Alba, Logan, and Bellair 1994; Logan and Schneider 1984; Pattillo-McCoy 1999); thus, not all suburbs are equal, and aggregate analyses cannot detail these important experiential differences.

Individual-level analyses address these limitations and substantially enhance our knowledge of residential outcomes by race; *locational attainment models* (Alba and Logan 1991, 1992a) have been particularly influential.[6] An innovative method introduced by Richard Alba and John Logan (1991, 1992a) transforms aggregate-level census data (mainly summary tape files 3 and 4) into the functional equivalent of individual-level PUMS (public use microdata sample) data with characteristics of each respondent's community of residence appended; this method eliminates issues of ecological inference and multicollinearity (Logan et al. 1996, 858; for a detailed explanation of the method, see Alba and Logan 1991, 1992a). Models employ a broad range of social class indicators, most notably homeownership and family status, to predict neighborhood-level outcomes (such as median income, exposure to crime, percentage non-Latino white, and suburban versus central-city residence). Rather than examine aggregate-level segregation, these analyses compare the characteristics of suburbs inhabited by whites, blacks, Latinos, and Asians.[7]

The improvements brought about by individual-level analysis have yielded interesting and important information. Most interesting perhaps is that at the individual level blacks exhibit a positive association between socioeconomic status and residential outcome, though returns to education and income for blacks are significantly lower than for other groups. Especially troubling is the negative effect of homeownership on blacks' residential outcomes. Black homeowners reside in neighborhoods that are more segregated and less affluent than those of their renting counterparts; far from reaping the benefits typically associated with owning rather than renting a home, they are *the only group consistently penalized for owning a home* (Alba, Logan, and Stults 2000b; Logan et al. 1996). Together, these differences keep blacks from reaching parity with whites at any level of affluence. Blacks live in neighborhoods that are, on average, 15 to 20 percent less affluent than those of other groups with comparable status. And contrary to the assertion that black residential segregation is unchanged by increasing socioeconomic status, Alba, Logan, and Stults (2000b) find that middle-class and affluent blacks in the most segregated U.S. cities live in areas with substantially more whites than their poor, inner-city counterparts do. This pattern is counterbalanced, however, by the generally lower status of their white neighbors. Thus, the suburban areas where middle-class and affluent blacks live are significantly less white *and* less affluent than those of comparable whites.

Patterns for Asians and Latinos, on the other hand, are more similar to those observed in the aggregate. Both groups show substantial residential gains with improved socioeconomic status, and the effects of homeownership are mixed (often nonsignificant and occasionally negative, though less so than for blacks); the effects of education and income are large enough, however, that "average" and "affluent" native-born Latinos and Asians live in communities that are roughly equivalent to those of comparable whites (Logan et al. 1996; Alba et al. 1999). A comparison of 1980 and 1990 data suggests a weakening of the traditional spatial assimilation model regarding the importance of acculturation. The characteristics of being native-born and speaking only English still improve Latinos' locational attainment, but speaking only English was less important in 1990 compared to 1980; by 1990, neither characteristic disadvantaged Asians. The emergence of ethnic suburban enclaves may account for this apparent weakening of the traditional spatial assimilation process by making residence in high-status, suburban communities an option for recently arrived, non-English-speakers with average or above-average social class characteristics (Alba et al. 1999; Alba, Logan, and Stults 2000a; Logan et al. 2002). And "perceptible African ancestry" costs black Latinos between $3,500 and $6,000 in locational returns, placing them in neighborhoods that are comparable to those of black Americans (Alba, Logan, and Stults 2000a, 613).

Much of the research discussed to this point focuses heavily on the use of statistically convenient but homogenizing racial categories. Considering characteristics specific to immigration may account for some intragroup diversity and is certainly a step in the right direction; however, an important body of research documents meaningful differences between national-origin groups within the same broad racial category, suggesting the importance of analyses that are sensitive to these differences (see, for example, Portes and Rumbaut 1996; Waldinger and Bozorgmehr 1996; Waters 1990, 1999). At the aggregate level, Massey and Bitterman's (1985) comparison of Mexicans in Los Angeles and Puerto Ricans in New York—demonstrating that differences in segregation are attributable to the latter group's generally lower socioeconomic status and "blackness"—represents both an important exception to this general tendency and evidence of potentially important intragroup variation.

A final advantage of the individual-level analyses detailed here is the serious attention paid by several studies to national-origin differences within each of the four major racial categories. Consistent with assimilation hypotheses, for example, Logan and Alba (1993) find that the more recently settled Irish-, Italian-, and Polish-origin whites tend to reside in lower-income neighborhoods than those whites who arrived earlier (for example, the British, French, and Germans) and other white ethnic groups, net of individual-level characteristics. For "blacks," results are consistent with those detailed here: Afro-Caribbean blacks experience more favorable outcomes and see better returns to their human capital than African Americans do (Alba et al. 1999; Crowder 1999; Logan and Alba 1993, 1995).[8]

National-origin differences are most pronounced among Asians and Latinos, the two most heterogeneous and rapidly growing groups. Logan and Alba (1993) find that Asian Indians, Filipinos, and Vietnamese tend to reside in less affluent neighborhoods than Chinese, Japanese, Korean, and other Asian groups do, and they suggest that this effect may be tied to the extreme poverty of their home countries compared to those of other Asian groups. Alternatively, Asian Indians and Filipinos are not at all disadvantaged by poor English skills—perhaps, the researchers suggest, because English is widely used in both India and the Philippines. Members of these groups arrive with more exposure to English, and therefore the "census self-assessment of English ability has a different meaning for them" (Alba et al. 1999, 457; see also Jasso and Rosenzweig 1990). The disadvantage associated with poor English skills, moreover, declined considerably between 1980 and 1990 for Chinese and Koreans but increased among the Vietnamese.[9] None of the Asian groups is meaningfully disadvantaged by recent arrival (Alba et al. 1999).

Both national origin and racial classification matter for Latinos. Puerto Ricans, Cubans, and all black Latinos reside, on average, in lower-SES neighborhoods relative to other Latinos, net of other individual characteristics (Logan and Alba 1993, 260–64). Poor English skills decrease the likelihood that Mexicans and Cubans will live in the suburbs rather than the central city but do not have this impact on Dominicans and Salvadorans; in sharp contrast to the Asian groups, however, recent immigration to the United States is detrimental to the likelihood of suburban residence for all Latino groups (Alba et al. 1999). Though limited in number, these analyses highlight important variations in residential outcomes and in the factors influencing those outcomes that are hidden by the use of broad, analytically convenient racial categories. Future research should continue to expose the complicated social realities hidden by this social science convention.

On the whole, then, the conclusions of aggregate-level studies remain intact. The experiences of Latinos and (for the most part) Asians are largely consistent with the spatial assimilation model; blacks (African Americans and black Latinos), on the other hand, do not see the same payoff for improved social class status. This is best illustrated by the negative effect of homeownership. Alba and his colleagues (1999) suggest that this negative effect is the outcome of the operation of a dual housing market that restricts black homeowners—but not black renters—to black neighborhoods: the difficulty they experience in entering some neighborhoods adds to the cost they pay for housing. The mixed effects of homeownership among Asians and Latinos suggest that such a dual housing market may operate to a lesser extent for them as well (Alba and Logan 1993; Alba et al. 1999; Logan et al. 1996; Massey and Denton 1993). Finally, non-Latino whites live in largely white and generally more affluent neighborhoods irrespective of their social class characteristics. Though distinctly different from one another, the experiences of blacks and whites contradict the tenets of spatial assimilation and suggest the persistence of an enduring system of racial stratification.

THE PLACE STRATIFICATION MODEL

Racially separate neighborhoods are the result of a combination of individual- and institutional-level actions. Scholars generally agree that all levels of government, as well as the real estate, lending, and construction industries, have played critical roles in creating and maintaining a dual housing market that constrains the mobility options of blacks (for detailed discussions, see Massey and Denton 1993; Meyer 2000; Yinger 1995). Many assumed that passage of the 1968 Fair Housing Act would mark the beginning of the end of segregation, but this has not been the case: residential segregation persists, and substantial evidence points to continued resistance among most white Americans to the presence of more than token numbers of blacks (and, to a lesser extent, Latinos) in white neighborhoods (Bobo and Zubrinsky 1996; Charles 2000a, 2001b;

Farley et al. 1993, 1994; Meyer 2000; Zubrinsky and Bobo 1996). Discriminatory practices in the real estate and lending markets persist as well (Massey and Lundy 2001; Galster 1990; Yinger 1995). The place stratification model highlights the centrality of these issues, arguing that "racial/ethnic minorities are sorted by place according to their group's relative standing in society, [limiting] the ability of even the socially mobile members to reside in the same communities as comparable whites" (Alba and Logan 1993, 1391). Because whites use segregation to maintain social distance, present-day residential segregation—particularly blacks' segregation from whites—is best understood as emanating from structural forces tied to *racial prejudice and discrimination* that preserve the relative status advantages of whites (Bobo and Zubrinsky 1996; Logan et al. 1996; Massey and Denton 1993; Meyer 2000).

Two variants of racial prejudice are relevant to attitudes toward residential integration. The first is closer to *traditional prejudice*, which stresses the primacy of simple hostility directed at one or more out-groups as predictive of individual attitudes about residential contact with out-groups (Allport 1954; Katz 1991; Pettigrew 1982). Typically, prejudice is defined as an irrational antipathy against minority groups and their members, heavily imbued with negative affect and negative stereotypes that make the prejudiced person's views unreceptive to reason and new information (Bobo and Zubrinsky 1996; Jackman 1994). This perspective would lead one to expect a strong association between negative stereotypes and neighborhood racial composition preferences.

The second prejudice-based explanation is rooted in Herbert Blumer's (1958) theory of *race prejudice as a sense of group position*. Instead of placing negative affect and stereotypes at the core, Blumer argued that prejudice involves a commitment to a specific group status or *relative* group position, since simple out-group hostility is insufficient for giving prejudice social force. What matters is the magnitude or degree of difference that in-group members have socially learned to expect and maintain relative to members of specific out groups. It is the degree of difference that in-group members perceive between themselves and out-groups that is most strongly associated with preferences for neighborhood racial integration, with differentiation understood as an indication of preferred or superior group position. The greater the perceived relative difference (that is, the more unfavorably out-groups are perceived), the less desirable out-group members will be as potential neighbors (Bobo 1988; Bobo and Zubrinsky 1996; Charles 2000a).

The perception of one or more out-groups as posing a competitive threat to scarce resources is another way in which the group-position variant of prejudice might be expressed (Bobo 1999; Bobo and Hutchings

1996). What matters most is "the concern with group entitlements, privileges, and threats to customary privileges" (Bobo and Johnson 2000, 86). Feelings of competitive threat may emerge or become intensified under conditions of immigration and rapid population change, increasing the likelihood of tension and conflict and reducing opportunities for mutual cooperation (Bobo and Johnson 2000). The group-position theory of prejudice as originally conceived refers to whites' attitudes about and behaviors toward blacks (Blumer 1958); however, research by Bobo and Hutchings (1996) shows that application of this perspective also adds to our understanding of interminority-group relations.

Despite general agreement regarding the role of prejudice and discrimination in the emergence of racially segregated neighborhoods, the extent to which these factors are implicated in the persistence of segregation remains contested. Alternative explanations downplay the continuing salience of prejudice and discrimination in favor of other race-related attitudes and perceptions. The in-group preference hypothesis argues that the "strong desires" of all groups for neighborhoods with substantial numbers of coethnics (Clark 1992, 451) reflect a simple, natural ethnocentrism rather than out-group hostility or an effort to preserve relative status advantages. A stronger version of this hypothesis contends that blacks' own preference for self-segregation explains current levels of black-white segregation (see, for example, Patterson 1997; Thernstrom and Thernstrom 1997). According to the racial proxy hypothesis (Clark 1986, 1988; Harris 1999, 2001) and the race-based neighborhood stereotyping hypothesis (Ellen 2000), it is the collection of undesirable social class characteristics associated with blacks or the neighborhoods where they are concentrated (joblessness, welfare dependence, proclivity to criminal behavior), not race per se, that motivates aversion to black neighbors, not only among out-groups but among blacks themselves.[10] Still, race is central to each of these alternative explanations. Since direct assessments of the role of prejudice often include one or more of these explanations, I address each of them within the context of stratification-based explanations.

Neighborhood Racial Composition Preferences A well-established literature details black-white differences in preferences for integration. In their classic article "Chocolate City, Vanilla Suburbs," Reynolds Farley and his colleagues (1978) introduced an innovative and highly regarded method for measuring views on residential segregation. In the experiment, white respondents were asked about their comfort with and willingness to enter neighborhoods that were integrated with blacks to varying degrees, as represented on "neighborhood cards," or showcards (see figure 2.1; for

Figure 2.1 Farley-Schuman Neighborhood Cards for White and Black Respondents: 1992 to 1994 Multi-City Study of Urban Inequality

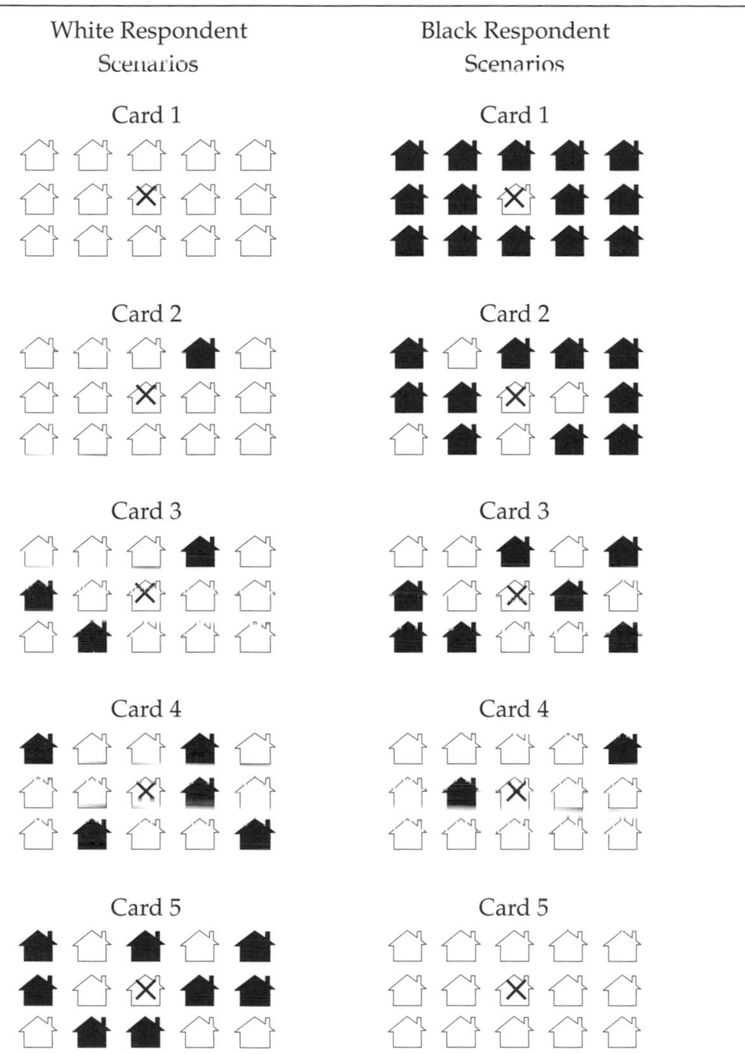

Notes: For multiethnic modification, shading is altered. Hispanic houses are always dark gray, and Asian houses are always light gray for both respondent and target-group representations.

details, see Farley et al. 1978, 1993); in a similar vein, black respondents also rated neighborhoods of various racial compositions from most to least attractive and indicated their willingness to enter each of the areas. The showcard experiment elicited realistic information about the residential experiences and options of both groups.[11]

The results revealed substantial resistance by Detroit-area whites to even minimal levels of integration: 25 percent said that the presence of a single black neighbor would make them uncomfortable; 40 percent said that they would try to leave an area that was one-third black; and nearly twice as many said that they would leave a majority-black neighborhood (Farley et al. 1978, 335). Blacks, on the other hand, showed a clear preference for integration. Eighty-five percent chose the fifty-fifty neighborhood as their first or second choice; when asked to explain their selection, two-thirds stressed the importance of racial harmony (Farley et al. 1978, 328). Virtually all blacks were willing to enter all three integrated neighborhoods, and 38 percent of Detroit-area blacks said that they would move into an otherwise all-white neighborhood.

As part of the 1992 to 1994 Multi-City Study of Urban Inequality (MCSUI), we replicated the Farley-Schuman showcard methodology in Atlanta, Boston, Detroit, and Los Angeles, and to enhance our understanding of preferences in multiethnic contexts we modified the experiment to include Latinos and Asians.[12] Analyses of neighborhood racial composition preferences based on the MCSUI data highlight the influence of both respondent and target-group race on attitudes toward residential integration (Charles 2001b; Clark 2002; Farley et al. 1993; Farley, Fielding, and Krysan 1997; Zubrinsky and Bobo 1996). Relative to the 1970s, whites expressed greater comfort with higher levels of integration, and fewer said that they would be unwilling to enter racially mixed areas. Although a sizable majority of whites expressed comfort with a one-third-out-group neighborhood, a rank-ordering of out-groups is evident: whites felt most comfortable with Asians and least so with blacks (Latinos fell in between), and their comfort level declined as the number of out-group members increased. The pattern of responses regarding whites' willingness to enter racially mixed neighborhoods is similar, except that the decline in willingness to enter begins earlier and is never as high as comfort with neighborhood transition; thus, 60 percent of whites were comfortable with a one-third-black neighborhood, but only 45 percent of whites were willing to move into that same neighborhood (Charles 2001b). Although MCSUI found meaningful improvements in the attitudes of Detroit-area whites, they nevertheless stood out as more resistant to integration compared to whites in the other cities (Farley et al. 1997).

Blacks, Latinos, and Asians all appear to want *both* meaningful integration and a substantial coethnic presence. The relative importance of these competing desires depends, however, on both respondent and target-group race. The overwhelming majority of blacks selected one of the two most integrated alternatives irrespective of out-group race, though the one with ten black and five out-group households was slightly more attractive to them than the one that best approximated a fifty-fifty neighborhood. For Latinos and Asians, on the other hand, target-group race was especially important: when potential neighbors were white, their most attractive neighborhoods were the same as those of blacks (cards 2 and 3), though the order was reversed. When potential neighbors were black, however, between 60 and 80 percent of both Latinos and Asians found one of the two least integrated alternatives most attractive (cards 1 and 2).

Across respondent racial categories, the all-same-race alternative was least attractive when potential neighbors were white; however, Latinos and Asians generally found this neighborhood more attractive than blacks did.[13] Both groups were also twice as likely as blacks to select the all-white neighborhood as their first or second choice (about 10 percent for Latinos and Asians, compared to 5 percent of blacks), though for all three groups the all-out-group alternative was the least attractive. Patterns of willingness to enter neighborhoods mirror those for attractiveness. For blacks, these patterns suggest a slight shift away from a preference for fifty-fifty neighborhoods since 1976 and a significant decline in willingness to be the only black family in an otherwise all-white area (Charles 2001b; Farley et al. 1993, 1997).

Other multiethnic studies of preferences yield similar results. In analyzing multiracial data, Lawrence Bobo and I measured attitudes toward one group at a time using a single forced-choice item (Bobo and Zubrinsky 1996). Consideration of a single target group is a limitation of the Farley-Schuman methodology in multiethnic contexts as well, as are differences between white and nonwhite experiments that make direct comparisons difficult. Elsewhere I have presented a major innovation on the Farley-Schuman experiment with the simultaneous consideration of whites, blacks, Latinos, and Asians as potential neighbors, using a single item in which all respondents were asked to draw their ideal multiethnic neighborhood (Charles 2000a).

Regardless of the measure of racial composition preferences, the pattern of results is the same. All groups exhibit preferences for both meaningful integration and a substantial presence of same-race neighbors, though preferences for same-race neighbors are not uniform across groups: whites exhibit the strongest preference for same-race neighbors, and blacks the weakest. Moreover, preferences vary by the race of the target group and demonstrate a racial rank-ordering of out-groups in which whites are always the most desirable out-group and blacks are always the least desirable. Finally, preferences for integration decline as the number of out-group members increases. These bivariate patterns make it clear that race is influential in the residential decisionmaking process. But *how* does race matter?

Prejudice Versus the Alternatives More than thirty years ago, the economist Thomas Schelling (1971) used a simple simulation exercise to demonstrate that minor differences in racial-ethnic-group preferences easily lead to severely segregated outcomes. In many ways, this simple demonstration has been the catalyst for subsequent efforts to understand what motivates our preferences for racial residential integration (or segregation). Though suggestive, the patterns detailed in this chapter are not conclusive evidence of the primacy of racial prejudice; however, several multivariate analyses detail whether and how race matters at the individual level. Using the MCSUI data for Detroit, Farley and his colleagues (1994) have shown that antiblack stereotypes are strongly associated with whites' discomfort with black neighbors, their likelihood of fleeing an integrating area, and their willingness to enter mixed neighborhoods. Similarly, Jeffrey Timberlake (2000) concludes that negative racial stereotypes and perceptions of group threat from blacks are the strongest predictors of whites' resistance to integration, based on his analysis of MCSUI data for Atlanta. For Atlanta blacks, negative racial stereotypes and (to a lesser extent) their perception of whites as tending to discriminate against other groups contribute to their integration attitudes. And in our analyses of multiracial data from Los Angeles, Lawrence Bobo and I (Bobo and Zubrinsky 1996; Charles 2000a) have concluded that negative out-group stereotypes reduce openness to integration across racial categories and influence preferences for both out-group and same-race neighbors.

Each of these analyses includes a measure of respondents' perceptions of the social class positions of out-groups relative to their own group as a test of the racial proxy argument; Bobo and Zubrinsky (1996), Charles (2000a), and Timberlake (2000) also include measures of in-group attachment to assess the relative importance of ethnocentrism. In all instances, racial stereotypes are the most powerful predictors of preferences. Effects for both perceived social class disadvantage and in-group attachment are always smaller and often nonsignificant; indeed, this pattern persists across respondent racial categories for both out-group and same-race neighbors (Charles 2000a). Nationally representative data from the 2000 General Social Survey (GSS) both confirm and strengthen the conclusions of these single-city analyses (Charles 2003).[14]

More recently, Maria Krysan and Reynolds Farley (2002) have supplemented quantitative analyses with an examination of black MCSUI respondents' open-ended explanations of their integration attitudes. Contrary to proponents of both the ethnocentrism and racial proxy hypotheses, they find that belief in the principle of integration and/or a desire to improve race relations drives blacks' preferences for integration: this was the most common explanation for the attractiveness of the two most popular (and most integrated) neighborhoods (see figure 2.1, cards 2 and 3). Moreover, strong desires for a substantial coethnic presence are "inextricably linked" to fears of discrimination and white hostility (Krysan and Farley 2002, 968–69); this conclusion is consistent with other descriptive analyses detailing an inverse association between perceived white hostility and overall neighborhood desirability (Charles 2001b; Farley et al. 1993; Zubrinsky and Bobo 1996). Krysan and Farley find virtually no support for either the ethnocentrism or the racial proxy hypothesis. Very few of their black respondents invoked ethnocentric attitudes, even when favoring the all-black over the fifty-fifty neighborhood, and contrary to the assertion that blacks (and whites) use race as a proxy for negative neighborhood characteristics, only 10 percent of their black respondents cited negative neighborhood characteristics as the primary reason to avoid all-black areas.

A similar analysis by Krysan (2002) examines open-ended elaborations from "whites who say they'd flee." Once again, there is little evidence of ethnocentrism among respondents asked to consider integration with blacks. Concerns about "cultural differences" were more salient for whites in Los Angeles contemplating integration with Asians and Latinos, and they were expressed mainly in terms of language differences. Consistent with the racial proxy and race-based neighborhood stereotyping hypotheses, whites were most likely to offer "race associated" reasons (such as concerns about crime and/or property values); however, meticulous analysis of the characteristics of whites who clearly offered "racial" versus "race-associated" responses finds that education made the difference. More educated whites were both less willing to stereotype out-groups negatively and more likely to offer race-associated explanations for their decision to flee an integrated area. Krysan (1998) has suggested that because better-educated respondents are both more susceptible to social desirability pressures and more adept at articulating their racial group's interest in more subtle ways (Jackman and Muha 1984), the difference between explicitly racial and so-called race-associated explanations is semantic: "In the end, each of the reasons is an articulation of a racial stereotype" (Krysan 2002, 693).

The analyses discussed to this point have made important methodological, empirical, and substantive contributions to our understanding of integration attitudes. Especially insightful are those analyses that elaborate preferences in multiethnic contexts and those that employ multiple methods to gain leverage on the complexities of racial attitudes. Nonetheless, critics correctly point to important limitations associated with studies that rely on measures of expressed preferences. In particular, because it is clear to respondents that their racial attitudes are at issue, their responses are susceptible to social desirability pressures and the difficulty of distinguishing between the direct effect of the racial composition of the neighborhood and the indirect effect of the neighborhood characteristics they may associate with the racial composition of the neighborhood. Although preference studies include a measure of perceived social class difference, other unmeasured aspects of the proxy argument (for example, crime or school quality) are left uncontrolled. Each of these limitations can bias results (Ellen 2000; Emerson, Chai, and Yancey 2001; Harris 1999). Alternatively, tests of the racial proxy hypothesis that use respondents' actual residential locations and the value of their homes as indicators of neighborhood desirability are confounded by the fact that "even if people prefer to live in racially mixed neighborhoods, they may not end up in such neighborhoods" because of discrimination or a shortage of housing (Emerson et al. 2001, 924).

A recent analysis by Michael Emerson, Karen Chai, and George Yancey (2001) stands out for creatively and effectively addressing these limitations, using a factorial experiment to assess whites' attitudes toward integration with blacks, Latinos, and Asians. Respondents were asked to imagine that they have two school-age children and are looking for a house; they have found a house they like better than any other that is both close to work and within their price range. Before whites are asked whether they would buy the home, they are offered a set of randomly generated neighborhood characteristics—public school quality, crime level, direction of property value change, home value compared to others in the neighborhood, and racial composition (between 5 and 100 percent Asian, black, or Latino). These authors find that the presence of Latinos and Asians does not matter to whites, but black neighborhood composition matters significantly even after controlling for proxy variables. Whites are neutral about buying a home in a neighborhood that is between 10 and 15 percent black but are unlikely to buy a home in a neighborhood over 15 percent black. This pattern is especially pronounced among families with children.[15]

The overall conclusion to be drawn is that active racial prejudice is a critical component of preferences for integration and therefore the persistence of racially segregated communities. Whites' racial prejudice is a "double whammy"—influential not only for its effect on whites' own integration attitudes but also for its implications for minority-group preferences and residential search behavior. Communities perceived as hostile toward particular minority groups are also perceived as less attractive, even when other aspects of the communities should be desirable (Charles 2001b). Indeed, blacks openly admit that fears of white hostility motivate their desire to have more than a handful of coethnic neighbors (Krysan and Farley 2002). Although the influence of racial stereotyping is the same for all groups, all three nonwhite groups wanted substantially more integration than whites did. Contrary to the popular adage that "birds of a feather flock together," ethnocentrism plays a minimal role at best. Moreover, the most thorough and detailed analyses to date suggest that whites move out *because* blacks move in; thus, black density matters because the presence of too many blacks (and to a lesser extent, Latinos and Asians) suggests a change in "traditional status relations of relative dominance and privilege" (Bobo and Zubrinsky 1996, 904; see also Charles 2000a and Krysan 2002).[16] In sum, the attitudes, preferences, and potential (and actual) behaviors of whites alone cannot fully account for residential patterns; all groups express some desire for coethnic neighbors, and these preferences may also play a role in shaping outcomes (Clark 2002). A much more sizable share of the available evidence points to the influential role of racial prejudice, both as a motivating factor in the avoidance of particular out-groups and as a motivator of minority-group preferences for same-race neighbors.

What About the Immigrants? The vast majority of the research on neighborhood racial composition preferences and most of what we have come to understand about the nature and manifestation of the various racial attitudes detailed here implicitly assume that all parties are native-born. It is quite likely, however, that there are important differences in both the nature of racial attitudes and the extent to which various racial attitudes impinge upon the preferences of immigrants relative to the native-born. In many ways, race-based explanations of preferences could benefit from the consideration given by the spatial assimilation model to the role played by immigrant adaptation and acculturation in residential mobility.

For instance, how immigrants think about the racial and ethnic composition of their neighborhood may be influenced directly by their relative ability to communicate in English or their length of time in the United States, the latter being suggestive of aspects of acculturation beyond language ability (for example, the need for parallel social institutions and social networks and the internalization of American culture, values, and norms). Immigrants enter the United States with vastly varying degrees of familiarity with American life: images of the stereotypic recent arrival beginning life in the United States with little or no English-language proficiency and few skills are countered by the actual immigrants who arrive with professional credentials and a strong command of English. Recent arrivals or those with little or no English proficiency may prefer more same-race and fewer other-race neighbors compared to the preferences of longer-term or native-born coethnics or those who speak fluent English. Alternatively, language ability and time in the United States may interact, and both characteristics may be more important for recent arrivals compared to their longer-term immigrant counterparts.

In addition, we know very little about the influence of immigration-related characteristics and acculturation on various other racial attitudes when immigrants are deciding with whom to share residential space.[17] The available evidence suggests that both the traditional and group-position variants of prejudice influence neighborhood racial composition preferences (Bobo and Zubrinsky 1996; Charles 2000a; Emerson et al. 2001; Farley et al. 1994; Krysan and Farley 2002; Krysan 2002). Yet if acculturating immigrants are encouraged not only to internalize patently American racial ideologies (such as negative stereotypes, perceptions of social distance, and a racial hierarchy) but to be aware of discrimination or racial-group competition, then both the strength of these attitudes and their effect on neighborhood racial preferences may intensify as immigrants accumulate time in the United States.

Increasing interminority-group conflict and competition between immigrant Asians and Latinos, on the one hand, and American-born blacks, on the other (Min 1996; Oliver and Johnson 1984; Yoon 1997), combined with residential preferences that clearly disfavor blacks, point to the potentially mediating role of immigration status. Under these circumstances, avoidance behavior may be tied to perceived racial-group threat, either instead of or in addition to negative stereotypes and in-group attachment (Mindiola, Niemann, and Rodriguez 2002). Aside from the tension and conflict that emerge after migrating, the spread of global media—such as television and music videos—has contributed to the global spread of negative images of African Americans (Forman and Kim 1999) and made it more likely that immigrants, especially Mexicans, will arrive with negative stereotypes of blacks (Henry 1980; Lambert and Taylor 1990; Niemann 1999). There is also evidence of strong antiblack attitudes among Asians in their native countries (Dikoetter 1994; Thornton 1985; Yuan 1989) and in the United States (Forman and Kim 2003). What we do not know is whether racial attitudes have the same effect on immigrants' preferences as they do among the native-born. It is possible that Latinos' similar socioeconomic status and similarly low status in society could lead to closer relations and coalition building with blacks (Henry and Munoz 1991), particularly with the accumulation of time in the United States as well as experiences of discrimination. In a similar vein, relations between Latinos and Asians could be facilitated by their recognition of sharing a similar status as immigrants as well as an ideology (Cheng and Espiritu 1989; Park 1991, 1995; Weitzer 1997; Yoon 1997). For the time being, however, there is considerable evidence that relations between Latinos and blacks and between Latinos and Asians are tense.

Concerns about the social class positions of out-groups may also be more salient for mobility-conscious immigrants, especially those who either entered American society in the middle of the stratification hierarchy or have accumulated some time in the United States and improved their socioeconomic status since they arrived. Many immigrants view the United States as "the land of opportunity" and are likely to believe that economically unsuccessful native-born Americans (such as blacks) lack intellectual character, are not oriented toward achievement, and tend toward moral deficiency (Cheng and Espiritu 1989; Forman, Martinez, and Bonilla-Silva 2003; Okazawa-Rey and Wong 1997). Newcomers learn early that whites maintain a privileged position in American society and that blacks are a stigmatized, low-status group.

Immigrants who are particularly concerned with improving their socioeconomic lot may seek to increase their residential contact with whites while avoiding contact with blacks at all costs (Loury 2002). Such an aversion to black neighbors accompanied by a strong preference for white neighbors may reflect beliefs about the relative economic standing of each group in American society; that is, preferences may be not necessarily about race per se but about the social class characteristics associated with various groups. (Aversion to Latino neighbors or preferences for Asian neighbors could also be understood in this way.) In short, immigrants may show above-average interest in avoiding residential contact with poor people and in seeking out coresidence with groups they perceive as well off.

And finally, the importance of in-group attachment for Asians and Latinos may vary substantially by their degree of acculturation. Three possible scenarios come to mind. First, in-group attachment may be more salient among recently arrived or less acculturated immigrants who still have strong ties to their homelands. For these individuals, the increase in both time in the United States and English proficiency may reduce feelings of in-group attachment. Second, recent arrivals or immigrants in general may embrace American individualism and opportunity to a greater extent than do longer-term immigrants or the native-born and may consequently be more inclined to believe that anyone willing to work hard can make it in America. After they have been in the United States for a longer period of time, however, these immigrants may also accumulate more experiences of racial discrimination, and these experiences—whether firsthand or vicarious through friends, family, or media reports—may strengthen their feelings of in-group solidarity and in-group attachment. In the third possible scenario, a continuous flow of new arrivals sustains feelings of group solidarity indefinitely (Massey 1995) and encourages a stronger sense of common fate among immigrants than is the case among their native-born counterparts.

Clearly, as our nation's population continues its rapid transformation it is important not only to understand the attitudes and preferences of immigrants compared to the native-born but also to examine the extent to which the internalization of American racial attitudes is simply one aspect of immigrant adaptation. It is equally important to gain insights into the effect of increasing racial-ethnic diversity on the relative status of groups in society. Lawrence Bobo and I have suggested that increasing diversity creates a "buffer" and increases blacks' opportunities for residential mobility and residential contact with whites, but our research revealed a clear rank-ordering of groups (Bobo and Zubrinsky 1996). Whites were at the top of the preference hierarchy, just as they have top billing in America's social and economic hierarchies. The least-preferred group was blacks, the group at the bottom of the social and economic hierarchies, and Asians and Latinos were in between (see also Zubrinsky and Bobo 1996). It appears, then, that interminority-group tensions, the generally more favorable societal stereotypes of Asians (the "model minority"), and the possible lack of phenotypic distinctions among some Latinos coalesce to keep blacks on the bottom rung of the racial status hierarchy (Forman and Kim 2003). A central goal of this volume is to address these issues in a more nuanced manner than has been done in the past.

Housing Market Discrimination The institutional practices that created and maintained residential segregation represent the translation of white prejudice into "systematic, institutionalized racial discrimination" in the housing market (Massey and Denton 1993, 51; see also Meyer 2000; Yinger 1995). A growing body of empirical evidence points to the persistence of discrimination in the housing market, though present-day discrimination takes a markedly different form than in previous eras (Bobo 1989; Cutler, Glaeser, and Vigdor 1999). Though formal barriers to integration have been eliminated, discriminatory white tastes and segregation persist, it is argued, through a kind of decentralized racism in which "whites pay more than blacks to live in predominantly white areas" (Cutler et al. 1999, 445). Thus, discriminatory behavior has become more subtle and more difficult for even its victims to detect (Galster 1990, 1992; Yinger 1995).

Since the mid-1950s, audit studies have proven useful in detecting these subtle forms of discrimination. In an audit study, pairs of trained testers with similar economic and family characteristics—one white and the other either black or Latino—successively inquire about housing. After a visit, each auditor completes a detailed report of his or her experiences with the real estate agent or landlord; discrimination is defined as systematically less favorable treatment of the black or Latino tester and is documented by direct observation during the interaction (Ondrich, Stricker, and Yinger 1998). Housing units are sampled randomly from metropolitan-area newspapers; examples of the experiences detailed by auditors range from aspects of seemingly race-neutral interactions—such as how promptly phone calls are returned or whether both members of an audit pair are shown additional units—to the obviously racially motivated act of steering minority auditors toward mixed or segregated areas.[18]

Studies on both the national and local levels find evidence of substantial discrimination that has not changed meaningfully over time (Yinger 1995, 1998). In a review of fifty local audit studies completed throughout the United States during the 1980s, George Galster (1990) concludes that racial discrimination is a dominant feature of the housing market. He conservatively estimates that (1) housing discrimination against black and Latino home- and apartment-seekers occurs in roughly half of their interactions with agents or landlords; (2) the discrimination is subtle and difficult for the individual to detect; and (3) the frequency of discrimination has not changed over time (Galster 1992, 647). These figures were confirmed by evidence from the 1989 Housing Discrimination Study (HDS). In *Closed Doors, Opportunities Lost*, Yinger (1995) presents a comprehensive and influential discussion of housing market discrimination, using HDS data to detail the incidence and severity of discrimination in housing transactions. At the beginning of a transaction, the client inquires about an advertised unit and then asks about the availability of other, similar units, at which time the agent may withhold information or limit the number of units shown to the client. In the second stage, agents are expected to take certain actions that facilitate the transaction, such as discussing terms and conditions, making a sales effort, and assisting the client in securing financing; at this point, the agent may offer less assistance to a minority client. Finally, the geographic location of units other than the initially advertised unit comes into play. Access to housing is constrained if a client is shown only housing in neighborhoods with particular racial-ethnic makeups (Yinger 1995, 31–33).

Yinger finds that blacks and Latinos were denied access to housing—that is, information was completely withheld—between 5 and 10 percent of the time. More often, he finds, minority access to housing was constrained: black and Latino testers learned about 25 percent fewer units than did comparable whites. Whites were also significantly more likely to receive other forms of favorable treatment, including follow-up calls, positive comments about an available unit, and special rental incentives (for example, one month's free rent or a reduced security deposit). Minority auditors suffered many minor inconveniences (such as waiting longer to be served), were more likely to have their housing needs ignored and their income overemphasized, and received less assistance with securing financing.

Steering was also quite common. Yinger estimates that for every four visits to a real estate agent, black and Latino home-seekers were steered away from predominantly white areas 40 percent and 28 percent of the time, respectively. Whites were more likely to hear negative comments about racially mixed areas. Both types of steering are prohibited by fair housing legislation, but steering through marketing practices is completely legal, and evidence suggests that real estate agencies do much of their steering through their marketing practices. Units in black neighborhoods are not advertised as often, have fewer open houses, and are more likely to be represented by firms that are not part of a multiple listing service (Fischer and Massey 2004; Yinger 1995). Such practices are also sometimes the norm for units in predominantly Latino areas and are the exact opposite of those used to advertise units in white neighborhoods (Yinger 1995, 55–59).[19]

More than a decade later, results from the 2000 Housing Discrimination Study offer a much-needed update, along with sorely needed research on housing market discrimination directed at Asians (Turner et al. 2002). Results offer mixed messages about changes in the incidence of housing market discrimination against blacks and Latinos since the 1989 study, revealing both improvement and persistent discrimination. The improvements in the sales market are encouraging: in 2000 both blacks and Latinos were significantly less likely than they were in 1989 to receive consistently unfavorable treatment relative to whites. For blacks, the overall incidence of white-favored treatment dropped to 17 percent in 2000, down twelve percentage points over the ten-year period. Despite this overall improvement, however, blacks were *more likely* in 2000 to be steered away from predominantly white neighborhoods than they were ten years earlier. The overall incidence of discrimination against Latinos declined by 7.1 percentage points over the decade (to 19.7), and the HDS study found no significant change in the likelihood of geographic steering (Turner et al. 2002).

On the other hand, the rental market experiences of blacks and Latinos offer little optimism. Blacks are significantly less likely to receive unfavorable treatment than in the previous decade, but the decline is much smaller (9 percent) compared to improvement in the sales market. More troubling, no significant change was found in the likelihood that Latino renters would receive unfavorable treatment relative to whites, and in 2000 their incidence of discrimination (26 percent) was greater than that of their black counterparts (Turner et al. 2002).

Phase 2 of HDS 2000 provides first-time information on the housing market experiences of Asians and Pacific Islanders (APIs) in eleven U.S. metropolitan areas. The findings reveal that both groups face meaningful discrimination in both the rental and owner markets, often at levels similar to those experienced by blacks and Latinos. In the rental market, API testers received consistently adverse treatment 21.5 percent of the time—about as often as for both blacks and Latinos. In the owner market, API testers received consistently adverse treatment about one-fifth of the time; this rate is roughly equal to that for blacks, but significantly higher than the level of owner-market discrimination against Latinos (Turner and Ross 2003). The API audit study also finds interesting differences based on the advertising sources. In particular, although discrimination against Asians and Pacific Islanders did not differ significantly by advertising source, API home-buyers faced a significantly higher incidence of discrimination when they inquired about units advertised in places other than major metropolitan newspapers (Turner and Ross 2003).

HDS 2000 also provides information on the incidence of housing market discrimination in Los Angeles.[20] In Los Angeles, the results suggest that Chinese and Korean renters "may face different patterns of adverse treatment" than their black and Latino counterparts (Turner et al. 2002, 4.18). Both groups were informed about and shown more units than their non-Asian-minority counterparts; on the other hand, black and Latino testers received better service from agents than both Asian groups. Discrimination against Chinese and Koreans in the sales market was similar to that of blacks and Latinos—indeed, among all of the minority groups studied in Los Angeles, Korean home-buyers experienced the highest overall net estimate of discrimination (22.2 percent) (Turner et al. 2002).

The important information provided by national audit studies comparable to both the 1989 and 2000 Housing Discrimination Studies is offset by the significant challenges involved in utilizing the method; in addition to training, recruiting, and maintaining minority testers, one major challenge is the substantial expense of such studies. Massey and his colleagues (Massey and Lundy 2001; Fischer and Massey 2004) designed a telephone-based audit study of housing market discrimination in the Philadelphia-area rental market as a lower-cost alternative to the in-person audit method used in the HDS. Citing evidence that individuals "are capable of making fairly accurate racial attributions on the basis of linguistic cues," the authors argue that a good deal of discrimination is likely to occur before a personal encounter can take place (Massey and Lundy 2001, 454). They find that this is in fact the case: compared to whites, blacks were significantly less likely to speak to the rental agent and, if they spoke to the landlord, significantly less likely to be told of a unit's availability. Alternatively, blacks were more likely than whites to have their creditworthiness mentioned as a potential obstacle in qualifying for a lease (Massey and Lundy 2001, 466).[21] A recent follow-up study by Fischer and Massey (2004, 237–38) finds that blacks' access to Philadelphia-area rental housing is "decisively lowered by certain ecological and realtor characteristics." Most notably, suburban location drastically reduces the odds that real estate agents will act favorably toward blacks.

Thus, in one way or another and to a greater or lesser degree, discrimination in the housing market constrains the ability of nonwhites to rent or purchase housing, and the likelihood of encountering discrimination seems to have changed relatively little since the passage of fair housing legislation and other antidiscrimination measures. Nonwhites' access to housing is constrained, the search process is more unpleasant for them (involving more visits and longer waits), they receive less assistance from lenders in the mortgage application process, they are more likely to have their applications denied, and their moving costs are higher. Yinger (1995, 95–103) estimates that every time black and Latino households search for housing—whether they encounter discrimination or not—they pay a "discrimination tax" of about $3,000. Cumulatively, he estimates that these groups pay $4.1 billion per year in higher search costs and lost housing opportunities. Included in this estimate is the decision by 10 percent of blacks and 15 percent of Latinos not to look for housing at all because they anticipate experiencing discrimination (for more on the impact of anticipated discrimination on search behavior, see Farley 1996b). By making it more difficult for minorities to purchase housing, discrimination contributes to racial disparities in homeownership and wealth accumulation, which in turn foster persisting residential segregation and economic inequality.

CONCLUSIONS

We have gained a great deal of insight from the research into the processes of racial residential segregation. Class-based explanations have been especially helpful, largely because both aggregate- and individual-level analyses based on census data provide the opportunity to test actual housing outcomes. That is, tests of the spatial assimilation model have actual neighborhood characteristics—the percentage white in a tract, for instance, or household median income—as their outcomes. Despite a strong circumstantial case, race-based analyses—particularly individual-level, attitudinal studies—fall short because they do not test whether attitudes do in fact influence housing-related behaviors (for notable exceptions, see Ilandfeldt and Scafidi 2002a, 2002b, 2004). These studies have also done an inadequate job of accounting for the degree to which characteristics specific to immigrants influence racial attitudes.

But the biggest shortcoming of the vast body of research in this area is its use of only one model—either spatial assimilation or place stratification—largely because of the nature of available data. The ideal empirical circumstance would be one in which the U.S. Bureau of the Census measures the American population's racial attitudes in addition to gathering detailed demographic information. This, obviously, is not likely to occur. An acceptable (and affordable) alternative is to include neighborhood-level characteristics from the census in large-scale, multiracial survey research projects like the 1992 to 1994 Los Angeles Survey of Urban Inequality.

We turn now to a consideration of the impact of the economics of housing on racial residential segregation.

Chapter Three | The Economics of Housing

The STRIKING DIFFERENCES in traditional measures of social class status presented in chapter 1 lead easily to the assumption that certain groups simply lack the financial resources of other groups and therefore cannot pay as much for housing. As such, racial residential segregation would be best explained as a consequence of economic disadvantage that leaves some groups with fewer (and arguably less desirable) housing options compared to economically advantaged groups. This assumption is consistent with the spatial assimilation model (Massey 1985), which posits that increasing socioeconomic status and (for immigrants) acculturation offer upward social mobility that includes movement into whiter or more affluent neighborhoods. Despite the commonsense appeal of this explanation, prior research makes it clear that this model is insufficient for understanding the aggregate-level housing patterns of whites and blacks (even as it provides a fairly accurate picture of housing outcomes for Latinos and Asians).

Nevertheless, well-known racial-group differences in objective social class status maintain the appeal of class-based explanations for residential segregation, and a preliminary examination of LASUI respondents' housing-related characteristics generally supports the tenets of the spatial assimilation model. First, blacks and native-born Latinos were significantly more likely than other groups to have had experience in public housing in the past, and just over 5 percent of blacks reported that they currently resided in public housing. Overall, however, the vast majority of respondents reported no experience with public housing and showed little difference in monthly housing expenditures across racial and nativity-status categories.[1] Like previous examinations of monthly housing expenditures (Zubrinsky and Bobo 1996; Charles 2000b; Charles 2001b; Farley et al. 1978, 1993), the findings reported in table 3.1 suggest substantial overlap across groups. In fact, only two groups—blacks and foreign-born Asians—differed significantly from whites: on average, blacks spent about $113 less per month on housing ($p < .05$), while foreign-born Asians spent $263 more per month on average ($p < .001$).

More telling are the group-level differences in homeownership detailed in the second row of table 3.1. In broad terms, patterns of homeownership by race are consistent with national trends: whites and native-born Asians had the highest rates of homeownership (roughly 52 percent and 77 percent, respectively), while blacks and Latinos reported significantly lower rates (36 percent of blacks, 45 percent of native-born Latinos, and 20 percent of foreign-born Latinos).[2] These figures are also consistent with group-level differences in socioeconomic status and accumulated wealth (see chapter 1), as well as with aggregate patterns of racial residential segregation, supporting class-based explanations for the latter. Differences in homeownership may contribute to racially separate neighborhoods to the degree that renters are more likely to be concentrated in apartment "communities" with fewer owner-occupied units. Similarly, the neighborhoods of homeowners may have less rental housing, particularly newer suburban communities that cater to families.[3]

Rather than look at monthly housing expenditures in absolute terms, we may find it worthwhile to consider housing costs as a percentage of household income, particularly for non-owners. According to Fannie Mae, lenders use a shared set of guidelines to determine prospective home-buyers' ability to comfortably pay their monthly mortgage. Although there is some flexibility, "guidelines generally state that a household should spend no more that 28 percent of its income on housing expenses and no more than 36 percent of its income on total debt obligations (including the monthly mortgage payment)" (Fannie Mae 2004). Thus, a housing payment that is comfortable for one household may give another household a problematic debt-to-income ratio, an important barrier to homeownership.[4] The third row of table 3.1 (housing as percentage of income) presents this alternative measure of housing costs, both overall and then separately by homeownership status. On average, non-Hispanic whites spent about one-quarter (26 percent) of their total family income on housing each month, and native-born Latinos (25 percent) and Asians (23 percent) spent roughly the same proportion. Blacks and foreign-born Latinos and Asians, on the other hand, spent between 48 and 58 percent of their family incomes on housing.

The percentage of household income spent on housing among non-owners is particularly telling. First, it should be noted that when we asked LASUI respondents about their monthly housing expenditures, non-owners were asked to include not only rent but utilities—an addi-

Table 3.1 LASUI Respondents' Housing-Related Characteristics, by Race and Nativity Status

	White	Black	Native-Born Latino	Foreign-Born Latino	Native-Born Asian	Foreign-Born Asian	Total
Housing characteristics							
Monthly housing costs[ab]	$705	$592	$608	$636	$896	$968	$679
	(35)	(34)†	(65)	(28)	(118)	(35)†††	(17)
Home ownership[b]							
Own or buying	51.84%	36.20%	45.08%	19.84%	76.96%	41.13%	39.90%
Renting or other	48.16	63.80	54.92	80.16	23.04	58.87	60.10
Housing as percentage of income[b]	26.03	47.72††	24.74	57.33†††	23.19	51.22†††	38.98
	(2.39)	(7.40)	(2.82)	(4.01)	(2.52)	(5.03)	(2.07)
Homeowners	16.22	19.57	19.95	40.93†††	23.26†	47.76†††	22.67
	(1.66)	(2.98)	(4.25)	(6.88)	(3.00)	(5.00)	(1.50)
Non-owners	36.14	63.73†	28.40	61.47†††	22.98†	53.54†	49.43
	(3.97)	(11.14)	(3.53)	(4.81)	(5.19)	(7.67)	(2.93)
Public housing experience[b]							
Never	95.67	80.87	87.88	94.75	96.33	97.04	92.82
In the past	3.88	13.94	11.66	4.52	3.67	0.70	5.93
Currently	0.45	5.19	0.46	0.73	0	2.26	1.25

Neighborhood characteristics							
Proximity to non-Hispanic whites[b]							
Less than 10 percent	1.38	48.02	25.67	41.78	4.73	15.27	21.80
10 to 25 percent	3.24	9.99	11.47	24.59	22.81	14.97	11.67
26 to 50 percent	12.55	21.29	32.30	24.35	29.76	24.15	19.71
51 to 70 percent	45.52	17.69	24.16	7.53	29.89	32.43	28.44
Over 70 percent	37.31	3.01	6.39	1.76	12.81	13.17	18.38
Mean proximity to non-Hispanic whites	63.42	23.57†††	34.88†††	19.13†††	45.67††	40.67†††	41.74
	(1.64)	(2.26)	(3.52)	(1.40)	(6.71)	(2.31)	(1.27)
Median household income	$44,695	$29,564†††	$33,892†††	$27,118†††	$47,705	$37,996†††	$36,456
	(1,865)	(982)	(903)	(772)	(6,396)	(1,032)	(966)
Median home value	264,022	181,793†††	182,872†††	173,057†††	271,240	275,579†††	221,112
	(11,282)	(9,641)	(7,518)	(4,758)	(33,477)	(9,726)	(5,968)
Poverty rate[b]							
Less than 20 percent	96.43%	60.44%	72.96%	45.58%	95.11%	77.30%	74.30%
20 to 40 percent	3.38	34.04	26.35	49.89	4.89	22.31	23.57
Over 40 percent	0.19	5.52	0.69	4.53	0	0.39	2.13
Mean poverty rate	8.28	19.26†††	13.49†††	22.20†††	8.30	13.43†††	14.36
	(0.45)	(0.90)	(1.07)	(0.87)	(1.05)	(0.83)	(0.45)

Source: Author's compilation.

a. The monthly housing expenditures of homeowners may or may not include taxes and insurance. Respondents were asked to respond with only principal and interest for all mortgages (including second mortgages and the like). A follow-up question confirms whether their response includes taxes, insurance, both, or neither.

b. Standard deviation values are listed in parentheses. $p < .001$. Where means differ significantly from whites, †††$p < .001$, ††$p < .01$, and †$p < .05$.

tional debt obligation of the sort that lenders account for in determining who can comfortably meet monthly mortgage payments. In reporting only rent and utilities, the average black respondent reported spending nearly two-thirds of household income on housing each month, and foreign-born Asian respondents reported spending over half; foreign-born Latinos are also strikingly overextended financially, spending roughly three-fifths of their household income on housing each month. Alternatively, native-born Latinos and Asians appear to be best situated financially to achieve their dream of homeownership, spending 28 and 23 percent of their family incomes, respectively, on housing and utilities each month. Whites, on average, border on being labeled bad credit risks; unlike minority-group members, however, whites tend to have enough net financial assets to offset the 36 percent of income they spend on housing.

This set of results, in particular, has clear and negative consequences for non-owner respondents' dreams of homeownership. In fact, when non-owners were asked what prevents them from purchasing a home in the Los Angeles area, 21 percent of whites and 34 percent of blacks and foreign-born Latinos said that they could not afford the monthly payments, and 11 percent of whites and 38 percent of blacks and foreign-born Latinos speculated that they would not qualify for a home loan. Considered in this light, then, the cost of housing—relative to family income—is critically important to understanding objective differences in neighborhood outcomes, given the connection between the proportion of income spent on housing and group-level differences in the rate of homeownership. Together, they support class-based explanations of racial residential segregation. This is particularly relevant to black-white segregation, since most research suggests that social class disadvantage plays only a minor role in the residential outcomes of whites and blacks.

The second panel of table 3.1 summarizes the objective neighborhood characteristics of LASUI respondents, which again mirror patterns of social class disadvantage across groups. On average, economically disadvantaged racial and nativity-status groups lived in neighborhoods that had fewer white residents and were less affluent relative to economically advantaged groups; this was especially true for African Americans, the group most residentially segregated from whites. Nearly half of blacks (48 percent) lived in neighborhoods that were less than 10 percent white, and at the same time blacks were the group most likely to live in high-poverty neighborhoods (5.52 percent, $p < .001$). Both native- and foreign-born Latinos lived in neighborhoods that were more similar to black neighborhoods than white neighborhoods, consistent with this group's increasing segregation from whites. In fact, foreign-born Latinos lived in neighborhoods with the lowest median incomes and home values and were exposed, on average, to more poverty than African Americans. The fact that foreign-born Latinos also had the least exposure to whites (19 percent, $p < .001$) may be a function of language barriers, which make coethnic neighbors both more desirable and necessary. Both native- and foreign-born Asians tended to live in neighborhoods with median incomes and home values more similar to those of whites; however, the foreign-born experienced significantly more neighborhood poverty and had less exposure to whites relative to the native-born.

This summary information on the housing characteristics of LASUI respondents suggests meaningful support for class-based explanations, particularly with regard to African Americans, since prior research has found that this connection for them is limited at best (Massey and Denton 1993; Massey and Fischer 2000; Alba and Logan 1993). Most interesting perhaps is the link between housing expenses—especially when considered as a percentage of family income—and homeownership. The remainder of this chapter delves into these issues in an effort to better understand these group-level differences in housing characteristics and the applicability of the spatial assimilation model. I begin by examining the degree to which economic inequality accounts for differences in monthly housing expenditures, then follow with similar tests of group differences in the likelihood of homeownership. Finally, I analyze residential-locational returns to human capital (Alba and Logan 1993)—that is, the degree to which individual characteristics like income, assets, and education yield similar residential returns across racial-group categories. The outcomes of interest here are neighborhood proximity to non-Hispanic whites and neighborhood socioeconomic status, measured as median income. This part of the analysis tests the utility of survey-based data (including tract-level census information) for replicating the prior work of Alba, Logan, and their colleagues based on data from decennial censuses, and it extends that research by including important measures not available from the census: experience in public housing and net financial assets as an indicator of accumulated wealth.

The chapter concludes with an assessment of whether and how both group and individual social class differences are useful in understanding aggregate-level neighborhood patterns in a diverse, multiracial city characterized by high-volume immigration.

MONTHLY HOUSING EXPENDITURES

Without question, the expenses associated with housing—rent or mortgage payments—are among the largest met by households each month, yet bivariate comparisons of monthly housing expenditures suggest few significant differences between households. It is nevertheless difficult to believe that significant differences in educational attainment, household income, net financial assets, homeownership, and residence in public housing do not play a role in how much individuals spend on housing each month.

To better understand how groups may differ in their housing expenses and what accounts for these differences, table 3.2 presents a series of OLS regression models estimating LASUI respondents' monthly housing expenditures.[5] Baseline model 1 illuminates basic racial-group and nativity-status differences.[6] The results reveal an interesting general pattern in housing costs: blacks and all categories of Latinos tended to spend less than whites, and Asians tended to spend more. These differences are often substantial. For instance, blacks and recent Latino immigrants spent about $170 per month less than whites, and more established Latino immigrants spent about $121 less (for all, $p < .001$). Native-born Latinos and Asians did not differ significantly from whites, nor did foreign-born Latinos with more than ten years in the United States. These results are consistent with the spatial assimilation model, which posits that immigrants are disadvantaged relative to the native-born but that the degree of disadvantage decreases with the accumulation of time in the United States. Most noteworthy in these results, however, is the finding that Asian immigrants spent between $160 and $365 more than whites each month and that accumulated time in the United States *increased* the difference between Asians and whites.

Model 2 rounds out the consideration of immigration-related characteristics with the addition of English-language ability (measured on a 0-to-5 scale where 0 indicates no English ability and 5 indicates high English proficiency or an English-only household), an aspect of acculturation that is also associated with educational attainment, social class status, and length of U.S. residence. As expected, English ability is positively associated with housing expenditures; for every one-unit increase in English ability, respondents spent nearly $47 more per month on housing, controlling for race and nativity status ($p < .01$). The inclusion of English-language ability does little to alter the black-white difference, while intensifying the difference between Asian immigrants and whites. Controlling for English ability differences, Asian immigrants spent between $290 and $472 per month more on housing than whites did (for all, $p < .001$). Among Latinos, on the other hand, accounting for English-language differences eliminates housing cost differences for immigrants with ten years or less in the United States, and the longest-term immigrants paid significantly more ($116.19) than whites ($p < .05$).

How much individuals spend on housing each month is also likely to vary by a number of housing-related characteristics. For instance, homeowners are likely to spend more each month on housing than nonowners; individuals who have lived in the same place for many years are likely to pay less for housing than those who have spent a comparatively short time at their current address; and current residents of public housing will report lower out-of-pocket housing expenses relative to those with no public housing experience. Model 3 considers the influence of each of these factors on racial and nativity-status differences in monthly housing expenditures. Homeownership status is measured as a dummy variable coded 1 if the respondent is a homeowner; length of time at the current residence is a scaled variable measured in five-year increments (coded 1 for less than five years through 5 for over twenty years); and public housing experience is coded as a set of dummy variables, with those having never lived in public housing as the referent.[7]

Each of these housing characteristics has the hypothesized effect on monthly housing expenditures. Homeowners spent significantly more—about $335—on housing each month than their non-owner counterparts ($p < .001$), and each five-year increase in years at current residence decreased housing costs by $155 ($p < .001$). Living in public housing—either in the past or in the present—was also negatively associated with monthly housing costs, reducing this expense by approximately $54 (in the past) and $262 (in the present) compared to those reporting no public housing experience, net of other factors ($p < .05$ and .001, respectively). Equally striking, however, is the powerful influence that controlling for these differences has on the race and nativity-status differences detailed in models 1 and 2: the black-white difference is cut almost in half, to roughly $97, and the remaining immigrant Latino differences from whites are either eliminated (for intermediate-term immigrants) or substantially reduced (for recent Latino immigrants). Immigrant Asian expenses still significantly outpaced those of whites (by between $127 and $324 per month), yet even these differences are significantly smaller compared to the previous model, as is the effect of English-language ability. Further evidence of the importance of housing-specific characteristics is the more than twofold increase in the overall explanatory power of model 3 ($r^2 = .26$) compared to model 2.

Model 4 introduces the financial characteristics that are often at the center of class-based discussions of racial differences in housing outcomes—household income and net financial assets, a measure of accumulated wealth. The anticipated relationship between each of these variables and monthly housing expenses is fairly straightforward: according to the spatial assimilation model, increasing income allows individuals to spend more for what they hope is better housing. On the other hand, we might

Table 3.2 Factors Influencing Respondents' Monthly Housing Expenditure: OLS Regression Coefficients (with Robust Standard Errors)

	Model 1		Model 2	
	B	SE	B	SE
Constant	662.82***	23.77	450.97***	66.46
Race or nativity status				
White (ref)	—	—	—	—
Black	−169.14***	29.36	−164.31***	29.52
Native-born Latino	−76.05	44.04	−44.52	44.94
Foreign-born Latino: ten years or more in the U.S.	−9.30	43.42	116.19*	52.25
Foreign-born Latino: six to ten years in the U.S.	−121.39***	26.80	30.35	51.36
Foreign-born Latino: five years or less in the U.S.	−170.18***	32.54	−4.92	58.27
Native-born Asian	3.09	58.05	7.34	58.96
Foreign-born Asian: ten years or more in the U.S.	364.29***	55.75	471.98***	66.47
Foreign-born Asian: six to ten years in the U.S.	203.83***	55.73	335.88***	64.94
Foreign-born Asian: five years or less in the U.S.	159.87**	45.84	291.69***	59.07
English Ability (0 to 5 scale)			46.90**	13.16
Housing characteristics				
Homeowner (1 = yes)				
Years at residence (/5)				
No public housing experience (ref)				
Past public housing experience				
Currently in public housing				
Financial characteristics				
Income (dollars/5000)				
Missing income (1 = yes)				
Net financial assets (dollars/5000)				
Missing net financial assets (1 = yes)				
Sociodemographic characteristics				
Age in years				
Age squared				
Degree attainment (0 to 4 scale)				
Married with children (1 = yes)				
Household size				
Interactions				
Homeowner × assets				
R-Squared	.10		.11	

Source: Author's compilation.

Notes: N = 3,579. Monthly housing expenditure is measured as rent plus utilities for renters; for owners, respondents were asked for the amount of the principal and interest for all mortgages. In a follow-up item, homeowner respondents were asked to confirm whether

Table 3.2 *(Continued)*

Model 3		Model 4		Model 5		Model 6	
B	SE	B	SE	B	SE	B	SE
741.9115***	65.53	656.35***	59.60	198.48*	75.56	204.71**	76.28
—	—	—	—	—	—	—	—
–97.24***	25.55	–36.39	21.15	–40.79	21.32	–41.57	21.43
–74.64	41.80	–66.98	37.87	–67.96	40.29	–69.24	40.75
23.13	44.97	44.97	42.62	–26.39	39.56	–28.59	39.85
–64.81	48.33	–44.54	43.13	–109.64*	42.98	–111.46*	43.06
–120.74*	55.34	–103.23*	49.30	–137.06**	46.15	–137.94**	46.06
3.02	50.16	16.94	48.44	1.15	45.64	2.96	44.97
323.79***	57.66	261.40***	50.38	218.00***	47.61	214.38***	48.06
189.51**	59.20	170.44**	56.70	108.60*	53.81	105.51	53.63
127.35*	51.67	127.15*	49.39	76.71	46.60	70.45	46.46
25.99*	11.85	0.09	11.58	–8.04	9.80	–8.58	9.84
335.44***	35.79	218.78***	37.21	191.36***	36.19	209.48***	38.83
154.90***	11.25	–138.97***	11.14	–120.12***	11.91	–119.80***	11.96
—	—	—	—	—	—	—	—
–53.73*	22.87	–36.14	19.77	–37.25	20.08	–36.58	20.06
–261.87***	33.53	–192.11***	31.99	–140.61***	21.74	–139.23***	21.60
		26.86***	2.58	21.12***	2.65	21.30***	2.61
		–51.49	29.64	–32.89	28.15	–33.43	28.29
		13.19**	4.00	–10.41**	3.95	–0.68	3.98
		26.35	31.98	13.76	30.74	15.14	30.97
				18.38***	2.50	18.12***	2.47
				–0.20***	0.03	–0.20***	0.03
				34.81***	9.09	34.84***	9.01
				73.99***	20.67	73.22***	20.65
				24.69***	5.14	24.71***	5.17
						–15.29*	7.02
.26		.32		.35		.35	

the monthly housing expenditure included taxes and/or insurance. Models 3 through 6 control for whether homeowners included taxes, insurance, or both in their monthly housing expenditure (the reference category is principal and interest only).

*** p < .001; ** p < .01; * p < .05

expect that access to wealth reduces the amount of money spent each month while still ensuring higher-quality housing compared to those with fewer or no assets, particularly for homeowners. Income is measured as the respondent's self-reported total family income in the year prior to the survey, divided by $5,000; net financial assets—also measured in increments of $5,000—are the total value of assets (not including homes or cars) minus debts (also not including homes or cars). Again, results are generally consistent with expectations: each $5,000 increment in family income increased housing expenditures by $26.86, and each $5,000 increase in net financial assets decreased expenses by about $13, net of other factors (for both, $p < .001$). Accounting for differences in respondents' financial characteristics produces only modest declines in the effects of each of the housing-related characteristics but eliminates the remaining race and nativity-status differences for blacks and all but the most recent Latino immigrants, who spent just over $100 per month less than whites on average ($p < .05$). The differences associated with English-language ability are also eliminated, probably because English-language proficiency is highly correlated with income. Variations in respondents' financial characteristics apparently account for little of the difference between Asian immigrants and whites and, more generally, result in a 23 percent increase in the explanatory power of the model.

To round out the analysis, model 5 adds a set of sociodemographic characteristics to account for group-level differences in age, educational attainment, family structure, and household size that may also influence housing-related outcomes. For instance, we might expect the youngest and the oldest respondents to spend less than the middle-aged on housing. The youngest group members may still live at home (paying little or no rent to their parents), while older group members are more likely than others either to own their homes free and clear or to live with their grown children—again, paying little or no rent. The effect of education should be similar to that of income—monthly housing expenditures should be higher among the better educated. And to the extent that more expensive housing is associated with better neighborhood amenities, we might expect married families with children to spend more than others for housing, both because they have additional financial resources (assuming a dual-income situation) and because they want to provide their children with the safest and best schools and recreational facilities. Age is measured in years and includes a squared term to check for the nonlinear relationship previously described. Degree attainment is measured on a 0-to-4 scale coded for highest degree obtained (0 for less than high school through 4 for a graduate or professional degree); household structure is measured with a dummy variable coded 1 if the respondent is married or cohabitating and has minor children in the household; and household size is measured as a continuous variable.

Each of these factors, as expected, is positively associated with monthly housing costs. Age is positively associated with housing costs but also exhibits the anticipated nonlinear relationship: the youngest and oldest respondents spent less on housing each month than their middle-aged counterparts.[8] Increasing educational attainment also corresponds to an increase in monthly housing expenses (about $35 for each additional degree); coupled respondents with children spent roughly $74 more each month on housing compared to other household structures, net of other factors. Increasing household size is also associated with higher monthly housing expenditures, with each additional householder bringing an average increase in housing costs of nearly $25. Taking account of relevant social background characteristics improves the overall explanatory power of the model by only 3 percent (only a .03 increase in r^2, to .35) and produces only modest changes in effects for financial and housing-related characteristics relative to the previous model.

In practical terms, the addition of social background characteristics does not substantially attenuate race and nativity-status differences: differences between whites and immigrant Asians (especially recent immigrants, who are no longer significantly different from whites) are slightly reduced, and the gap between whites and the two shortest-term Latino immigrants is slightly increased ($137, $p < .01$, and $110, $p < .05$, for less than six years and six to ten years in the United States, respectively). The addition of an interaction term for homeownership and net financial assets (model 6) confirms that accumulated wealth is important for reducing housing costs for homeowners only; otherwise, this model differs little in practical terms from model 5.

Prior research on group-level differences in monthly housing expenditures reveals both meaningful differences in average monthly housing costs and substantial overlap in these payments more generally (Charles 2000b; Farley et al. 1978, 1993; Zubrinsky and Bobo 1996). The overlap in expenditures is substantial enough to conclude that such disparities cannot account for residential segregation by race. This analysis takes a closer look at monthly housing expenditures in an effort to better understand both the source and the severity of previously documented racial-group disparities.

Overall, the results suggest that racial and nativity-status group differences in social class do influence what each group spends on housing each month. First, although average differences in monthly housing costs tend to be small or nonsignificant, there are critical differences in the percentage of total household income spent on housing (particularly and most importantly among non-owners). Most disconcerting for the prospects of increasing minority homeownership is that blacks in particular and immigrants (both Latino and Asian) spend far too much of their income on housing, disqualifying themselves for conventional home mortgage financing despite their strong desire for homeownership. Moreover, all racial and nativity-status differences in absolute monthly housing costs are completely eliminated by accounting for income and net financial assets, the two direct measures of economic status. Housing-related characteristics such as homeownership status and residence in public housing—indirect measures of economic status—are also important factors. Thus, even if group differences in monthly housing expenditures are probably not a direct cause of residential segregation by race, they do have a meaningful influence on housing options.

HOMEOWNERSHIP

LASUI respondents' rates of homeownership (see table 3.1) are generally consistent with national rates for the time period in question (Yinger 1995; U.S. Bureau of the Census 1990). Low rates of homeownership among racial minority groups reflect differential access to the wealth necessary to inherit property, afford a down payment, and/or obtain credit for a mortgage (Oliver and Shapiro 1995; Yinger 1995). For immigrants, citizenship status may also contribute to lowered rates of homeownership. The purchase of a home is a huge financial investment that may not be in the best interests of immigrants who are not yet citizens or who are planning to stay in the United States for only a limited amount of time. If differences in socioeconomic status result in differential rates of homeownership, then these differences may have consequences for aggregate-level residential patterns.

Differences in rates of homeownership across racial categories are important in and of themselves, given what homeownership means for the accumulation and intergenerational transmission of wealth. These group-level differences, however, are accompanied by other, associated inequities. For example, not only are blacks and Latinos less likely to own homes, but those who do own homes have lower property values compared to whites, after controlling for socioeconomic status differences (Yinger 1995). This is relevant to our understanding of racial residential segregation. White homeowners are overwhelmingly concentrated in newer, suburban developments equipped with high-quality services and amenities, and some have argued that whites avoid residential contact with minorities because they associate such contact with neighborhood decline (Clark 1986; Harris 1997).

Alternatively, minority homeowners are likely to move into the neighborhoods that whites have left behind. These communities, made up of older housing stock, tend to be located within the city limits and to offer lower-quality services and amenities (Massey and Denton 1993; Yinger 1995). Moreover, because these areas tend to have lower property values, they are more accessible to individuals who have insufficient assets for a large down payment but income sufficient to cover a larger monthly mortgage payment. (With a smaller down payment, the monthly payment must include the cost of private mortgage insurance.) The combination of minority concentration and lower property values makes these neighborhoods less attractive to whites, who continue to leave them or avoid them when searching for housing. Equally important, however, is the negative impact of stagnant or declining property values on the accumulation of equity: with less equity in their property, it is more difficult for minority homeowners to invest in better housing even as their income and occupational status improve.

For these reasons, understanding racial-group differences in the likelihood of homeownership is relevant to a discussion of the role that social class disparities play in perpetuating racially separate neighborhoods. Table 3.3 summarizes a series of logistic regression models predicting the likelihood of homeownership for LASUI respondents, excluding those respondents currently residing in public housing and beginning with a baseline model that details racial-group and nativity-status differences. Blacks, all categories of Latinos, and Asian immigrants with ten years or less in the United States are all significantly less likely than whites to own their homes. Only two categories of nonwhite respondents compare favorably to whites: the longest-term Asian immigrants do not differ significantly from whites in their likelihood of homeownership, and native-born Asians are nearly two and a half times *more* likely than whites to own their homes ($p < .001$).

It appears, however, that many of the racial and nativity-status differences are a consequence of related differences in English-language proficiency. That is, controlling for race and nativity status, the more proficient an individual is in English, the more likely he or she is to be a homeowner (model 2). Each one-unit increase in English ability corresponds to a 1.45 increase in the odds of homeownership: an individual with excellent English-language skills (scoring a 5) is 7.25 times more likely to own his or her home than someone who speaks no English at all (a score of 0). Controlling for English-language ability, moreover, produces important changes in patterns of homeownership among immigrants. Among Latinos, neither the native-born nor the longest-term immigrants differed significantly from whites; however, foreign-born Latinos with ten years or

Table 3.3 Factors Influencing Homeownership: Logistic Regression Coefficients (with Robust Standard Errors)

	Model 1		
	B	SE	Odds Ratio
Constant	–0.12	0.12	—
Race and nativity status			
White (ref)	—	—	—
Black	–0.59***	0.16	0.55
Native-born Latino	–0.39*	0.19	0.67
Foreign-born Latino: ten years or more in the U.S.	–0.94***	0.20	0.39
Foreign-born Latino: six to ten years in the U.S.	–2.57***	0.37	0.08
Foreign-born Latino: five years or less in the U.S.	–3.82***	0.55	0.02
Native-born Asian	0.90***	0.23	2.46
Foreign-born Asian: ten years or more in the U.S.	0.27	0.18	1.30
Foreign-born Asian: six to ten years in the U.S.	–0.81**	0.28	0.44
Foreign-born Asian: five years or less in the U.S.	–1.06***	0.23	0.35
English ability (0 to 5 scale)			
Public housing experience			
Never lived in public housing (ref)			
Lived in public housing in the past			
Financial characteristics			
Income			
Less than $20,000 (ref)			
$20,000 to $39,999			
$40,000 to $59,999			
$60,000 to $89,999			
$90,000 or more			
Missing income (1 = yes)			
Net financial assets			
Negative or none (ref)			
Up to $5,000			
$5,001 to $10,000			
Over $10,000			
Missing net financial assets (1 = yes)			
Sociodemographic characteristics			
Age			
21 to 29 (ref)			
30 to 39			
40 to 49			
50 to 59			
60 to 69			
70 and older			
Degree attainment (0 to 4 scale)			
Married with children (1 = yes)			
Household size			
Log pseudo-likelihood		–2,143.76	
Pseudo R-Squared		.08	

Table 3.3 *(Continued)*

Model 2			Model 3			Model 4		
B	SE	Odds Ratio	B	SE	Odds Ratio	B	SE	Odds Ratio
−1.80***	0.23	—	−2.73***	0.25	—	−5.50***	0.32	—
—	—	—	—	—	—	—	—	—
−0.56***	0.16	0.57	0.37†	0.19	1.44	0.36*	0.18	1.44
−0.15	0.20	0.86	0.38	0.24	1.46	0.53†	0.28	1.70
0.01	0.21	1.01	0.69**	0.23	2.00	0.94***	0.24	2.55
−1.42***	0.39	0.24	−0.88†	0.46	0.41	−0.10	0.49	0.91
−2.57***	0.59	0.08	−1.84**	0.56	0.16	−0.79	0.59	0.45
0.96***	0.24	2.60	0.44*	0.22	1.56	0.72**	0.26	2.05
1.11***	0.22	3.03	0.71**	0.25	2.03	0.90**	0.26	2.45
0.17	0.32	1.18	0.06	0.33	1.07	0.45	0.35	1.57
−0.05	0.28	0.95	−0.55†	0.30	0.58	0.16	0.33	1.17
0.37***	0.04	1.45	0.11*	0.05	1.12	0.33***	0.06	1.39
			—	—	—	—	—	—
			0.22	0.18	1.25	0.10	0.19	1.10
			—	—	—	—	—	—
			0.81***	0.10	2.24	1.01***	0.12	2.75
			1.40***	0.16	4.07	1.78***	0.17	5.94
			2.57***	0.17	13.01	2.90***	0.20	18.23
			1.98***	0.25	7.25	2.25***	0.24	9.45
			−0.12	0.12	0.88	−0.19	0.14	0.83
			—	—	—	—	—	—
			.38**	0.13	1.46	0.32*	0.15	1.38
			1.47***	0.16	4.37	1.39***	0.17	4.02
			2.01***	0.12	7.43	1.59***	0.14	4.92
			−0.12	0.13	0.89	−0.19	0.15	0.83
						0.66***	0.17	1.93
						1.20***	0.18	3.31
						2.01***	0.18	7.46
						2.29***	0.20	9.87
						2.86***	0.21	17.43
						−0.07	0.06	0.93
						0.53***	0.13	1.71
						0.18***	0.03	1.19
	−2,100.15			−1,689.21			−1,520.70	
	.10			.28			.35	

Source: Author's compilation.

Notes: N = 3,587. Respondents currently living in public housing are excluded from this analysis.

*** $p < .001$; ** $p < .01$; * $p < .05$; † $p < .10$

less in the United States remained significantly less likely than whites to be homeowners. Among Asians the reverse is true: immigrants with ten or fewer years in the United States were as likely as whites to own their homes, while the native-born and the longest-term immigrants in this group were between two and a half and three times more likely than whites to own their homes, controlling for English-language ability.

Model 3 introduces relevant housing and financial characteristics. (Keep in mind that respondents currently residing in public housing are excluded from this portion of the analysis.) For ease of interpretation, each of these items—public housing experience, income, and net financial assets—is measured as a series of dummy variables. Income and wealth have the anticipated effect on the odds of homeownership, net of other factors. The importance of wealth accumulation is particularly evident. Recall from chapter 1 that roughly 42 percent of whites and 56 percent of native-born Asians reported over $10,000 in net financial assets. LASUI respondents with access to this level of assets were nearly seven and a half times more likely to own a home than those reporting zero or negative assets—and more than half of blacks and native-born Latinos and nearly 70 percent of foreign-born Latinos fell into this extremely disadvantaged category. Note too, however, that as little as $5,000 or less in assets significantly increased the odds of owning a home. Equally important is the impact of controlling for social class and housing characteristics on racial and nativity-status differences in homeownership. Few statistically significant differences remain: given equal financial resources, most categories of nonwhites were at least as likely as whites to own homes. Some minority group members, both native- and foreign-born, were more likely than whites to do so—especially Asians, among whom only the most recently arrived immigrants remained disadvantaged. Prior residence in public housing does not have a significant impact on the likelihood of homeownership.

This tendency persists (and for some groups becomes stronger) with the introduction of controls for basic social background characteristics (model 4). Blacks and native-born Latinos were 1.44 and 1.70 times more likely than whites, respectively, to be homeowners; similarly, the longest-term Latino immigrants were more than two and a half times more likely than whites to own their home. Controlling for social background factors also increases the homeownership advantage that native-born and long-term-immigrant Asians exhibit over whites (with odds ratios of 2.05 and 2.45, respectively). In each of these cases, differences from whites are statistically significant. No significant differences remain between whites and the remaining racial and nativity-status groups.[9] Thus, the overall pattern is one in which, *given equal financial resources, nativity status, and other social background characteristics, the proclivity to own a home is stronger among disadvantaged minority groups than it is among whites.*

These results are largely consistent with prior studies on racial-group differences in rates of homeownership. This research shows that Latino disadvantages in homeownership are entirely the result of differences in their economic resources and immigrant status (Coulson 1999; Krivo 1995; Painter, Gabriel, and Myers 2001) and that, other things being equal, most Asian subgroups' rates of homeownership do not differ significantly from rates for whites. Moreover, prior research on Asian homeownership has consistently found that Chinese-origin Asians have homeownership rates of up to 20 percent higher than those of comparable whites (Painter, Yang, and Yu 2003; Skaburskis 1996). To investigate this possibility, I reestimated the final model, using national-origin categories for Latinos and Asians and separate dummy variables for length of time in the United States. The results support the "Chinese effect" detailed in previous research: net of nativity status and other characteristics, Chinese-origin Asians are nearly three and a half times more likely than whites to own their homes ($p < .001$), but Japanese- and Korean-origin Asians do not differ significantly from whites. Moreover, the "Latino advantage" (see table 3.5) is specific to those of Mexican ancestry. Controlling for time in the United States and other characteristics, Mexicans are roughly twice as likely as whites to own their homes ($p < .01$).[10]

These results differ from prior studies only insofar as they relate to black-white differences in homeownership. In this case, controlling for economic and social background characteristics substantially attenuates the gap (see, for example, Alba and Logan 1992a; Gabriel and Painter 2003a, 2003b; Painter et al. 2001); however, the results reported here represent the first instance of reversal. These results may differ because prior studies do not have measures of wealth (Alba and Logan 1992a), or perhaps because they measure wealth as simply dividend and interest income (Gabriel and Painter 2003a, 2003b; Painter et al. 2001). This analysis measures net financial assets—the assets that remain after accounting for debts. Given the greater percentage of income that blacks (and other racial and nativity groups) spend on housing, accounting for differences in debt—and assets relative to debt—is crucial to understanding patterns of homeownership.

The independent effect of age is positive, as expected; similarly, married couples with children were 1.7 times more likely than other family types to own their homes, net of other factors ($p < .001$). And other things being equal, increasing household size significantly improves the likelihood of homeownership. Effects for income and wealth persist, and the full model still suggests that individuals with prior public housing experience did not differ significantly from those without such experience in their likelihood of homeownership; however, results from a series of additional analyses run separately by race (but not shown here) indicate that prior residence in public housing was an advantage for Latinos: controlling for other factors, members of this group with prior public housing experience were nearly 2.6 times more likely to own homes compared to those without public housing experience.[11]

Thus, economic inequality is directly implicated in racial and nativity-status differences in homeownership. In fact, the most striking finding may be that, other things being equal—especially income and net financial assets—blacks, Latinos, and Asians are generally *more* likely than whites to own their homes. It is certainly plausible that homeownership signifies middle-class status and the attainment of the American Dream for socially and economically disadvantaged groups as well as for immigrants, often characterized as having come to America to improve their lot. Evidence of this difference in orientation regarding homeownership can be seen in the pattern of responses to a question about preferences for homeownership. When LASUI non-homeowners were asked whether they wanted to own a home, nearly 60 percent said yes. The desire for homeownership differs significantly, however, according to racial-group membership: nearly two-thirds of blacks and Latinos expressed a preference for owning a home, compared to about half of whites and 41 percent of Asians.[12]

For blacks, the importance of homeownership as a symbol of "making it" is evident in cultural representations as varied as Lorraine Hansberry's play *A Raisin in the Sun*, the 1970s sitcom *Good Times*, and, most recently, MTV's *Cribs*.[13] A desire for homeownership is also consistent with a tendency among blacks to embrace mainstream American values and to aspire to the American Dream. For example, attitudinal studies consistently show that the value and importance that blacks place on education exceeds that expressed by whites; after accounting for differences in household and economic endowments, research also indicates that blacks are substantially more likely than whites to be enrolled in college (Alexander, Holupka, and Pallas 1987; Bauman 1998; Bennett and Xie 2003; Charles, Roscigno, and Torres, forthcoming; Hauser 1993; Kane and Spizman 1994; McDonald and LaVeist 2001; Monk-Turner 1995; Rivkin 1995). With respect to the apparent Asian homeownership advantage, evidence points to a cultural explanation: homeownership is a deeply rooted aspect of Chinese culture (Chen 1992), and there is substantial within-group peer pressure to own a home (Zhou 1992). Immigrant Chinese also indicate feeling less secure when they do not own their home

(Zhou 1992). For this group, then, homeownership is important over and above the value placed on it in American society.

At the very least, differences in rates of homeownership are a cause of concern because, to the extent that owner-occupied housing and rental housing are located in separate, distinct areas, class-based disadvantage is again at least indirectly implicated in continuing racial residential segregation, particularly for black and Latino segregation from whites.[14] What matters ultimately, however, is the impact of racial and nativity-status group differences in socioeconomic status and related monthly housing expenditures and/or homeownership on actual neighborhood outcomes.

THE PRICE OF ADMISSION: RESIDENTIAL RETURNS TO HUMAN CAPITAL

To this point, there is credible evidence that objective differences in socioeconomic status can be linked to racial and nativity-status differences in both monthly housing expenditures and the likelihood of homeownership. The final step in making the case for class-based explanations for residential segregation by race is to determine the extent to which disparities in these individual-level characteristics account for differences in the objective neighborhood characteristics of whites, blacks, Latinos, and Asians in Los Angeles. The approach taken here is a replication and extension of the locational attainment models developed by Richard Alba and John Logan (for an overview, see chapter 2; for details, see Alba and Logan 1991, 1992b).

Owing to the size and scope of the LASUI, the analysis employs survey data rather than aggregate-level census data to provide information on respondents' individual-level characteristics; data on objective neighborhood characteristics were obtained from the 1990 census (STF3A) and appended to each respondent's record. An additional difference—and an important improvement—is the inclusion of three individual-level characteristics that are not available from the census: net financial assets (a measure of accumulated wealth), monthly housing expenditures, and residence in public housing. Measures of net financial assets are thought to be particularly relevant to understanding racial-group differences in residential outcomes (Conley 1999; Oliver and Shapiro 1995) and are often not available in the large datasets used to study these issues. Measures of monthly housing costs and experience with public housing are also not generally available from the census but may be useful in describing how people find housing.

The central tenet of the spatial assimilation model is that increasing socioeconomic status—in education, income, occupational status, and so forth—should correspond with improvements in neighborhood-level outcomes; for immigrants, acculturation also plays an important role (Massey 1985). An implicit assumption in this model is that similar levels of socioeconomic status yield similar "residential returns" irrespective of racial classification or nativity status. That is, an advanced degree and a household income of over $90,000 per year should "purchase" the same proximity to whites and neighborhood affluence for anyone in possession of such human capital. Prior research based on decennial census data suggests, however, that some groups get more for their human capital than others.

Proximity to non-Hispanic whites is a neighborhood-level characteristic considered here because it is indicative of the potential for interracial contact and thus speaks to issues surrounding intergroup relations.[15] Contact with whites is also among the most popular ways in which scholars have studied racial residential segregation, the idea being that increasing contact with whites, the dominant group both socially and economically, signals upward social mobility (Massey 1985). The other neighborhood-level characteristic under investigation here, a neighborhood's median household income, speaks more directly to tangible group differences tied to the economic characteristics of neighborhoods.

Neighborhood Proximity to Non-Hispanic Whites

How do members of racial and nativity-status groups end up in neighborhoods that differ in their proximity to whites as a consequence of their personal or household characteristics? To address this issue, table 3.4 summarizes a series of OLS regression equations for LASUI respondents. The individual and household characteristics taken into account are consistent with those used throughout this chapter and can be summarized as housing-related characteristics (homeownership and experience with public housing), financial characteristics (family income and net financial assets), and sociodemographic characteristics (age, education, household structure, nativity status, English-language ability, and national origin). The greater the extent to which improvements to social class are associated with increasing contact with whites and returns to human capital characteristics are similar across groups, the stronger the case for class-based explanations for racial residential segregation.

At first glance, the results support class-based explanations, to the extent that better-educated individuals and those with higher incomes tend to reside in neighborhoods with greater proximity to whites. A closer look, however, exposes substantial racial-group differences in "exchange

Table 3.4 OLS Regression Coefficients Predicting LASUI Respondents' Neighborhood Proximity To Non-Hispanic Whites, by Race

	Whites		Blacks		Latinos		Asians	
	B	SE	B	SE	B	SE	B	SE
Constant	28.09***	4.93	10.85***	2.71	15.68***	3.12	11.79*	5.03
Homeowner (1 = yes)	3.21	2.36	–5.32*	2.19	–2.61	2.28	4.44†	2.25
Public housing experience								
Never (ref)	—	—	—	—	—	—	—	—
In the past	–4.95	3.96	–0.80	1.59	6.31*	2.69	4.05	4.52
Currently	–9.52†	4.88	0.79	2.54	–3.45	3.59	3.96	4.50
Income								
Less than $20,000 (ref)	—	—	—	—	—	—	—	—
$20,000 to $39,999	11.05***	2.64	2.19	1.27	5.56***	1.36	4.62*	2.10
$40,000 to $59,999	16.20***	3.39	6.81**	2.20	14.59***	2.95	13.23***	2.82
$60,000 to $89,999	16.15***	3.50	9.69**	2.93	22.13***	5.70	18.94***	3.63
$90,000 or more	15.91**	4.74	13.47**	4.33	13.98*	6.70	18.95***	3.50
Missing income (1 = yes)	–0.26	2.68	0.56	1.49	0.76	1.75	2.36	1.44
Net financial assets								
Negative or none (ref)	—	—	—	—	—	—	—	—
$1 to $5,000	–0.41	2.77	1.18	1.01	0.71	1.56	1.22	2.00
$5,001 to $10,000	2.96	2.97	–0.04	1.75	0.30	3.26	1.19	2.73
Over $10,000	5.82**	2.17	2.05	1.89	0.20	4.46	2.76	2.46
Missing net financial assets (1 = yes)	–8.03**	2.74	–0.88	1.52	–1.94	1.78	–4.75*	2.20
Age								
21 to 29 (ref)	—	—	—	—	—	—	—	—
30 to 39	–3.83	2.41	–1.01	1.49	2.13	1.28	–0.19	2.16
40 to 49	–4.84*	1.94	–2.45	1.53	5.45**	1.91	0.72	2.33
50 to 59	–4.38	3.17	–2.54	1.67	7.26**	2.20	0.27	2.63
60 to 69	0.07	3.16	–1.01	2.27	6.30*	2.72	–3.93	3.30
70 or older	–1.56	3.30	–1.54	2.13	7.15	4.75	1.67	3.38

(*Table continues on p. 86.*)

Table 3.4 (*Continued*)

Education								
Less than high school (ref)	—	—	—	—	—	—	—	—
High school graduate or GED	12.22***	3.33	1.40	1.11	0.31	1.10	5.83**	1.89
Some college	10.88**	3.59	0.48	1.17	4.51	3.57	8.79**	3.00
Bachelor's degree	9.48*	4.17	2.75	2.06	6.90	3.57	11.72***	2.54
Advanced degree	13.39**	3.88	16.03**	4.76	19.66*	7.35	8.65*	3.64
Household structure								
Married with children (1 = yes)	1.48	2.33	1.92	1.47	2.11	1.28	0.13	1.92
Household size	1.49*	0.74	−1.24**	0.35	−0.90**	0.30	0.94	0.57
Nativity status								
U.S.-born (ref)					—	—	—	—
Foreign-born: over ten years in the U.S.					−8.14**	2.82	4.05	3.44
Foreign-born: six to ten years in the U.S.					−7.30*	3.21	5.50	3.84
Foreign-born: five years or less in the U.S.					−6.27†	3.35	4.65	4.00
English language ability								
None (ref)					—	—	—	—
Low					3.56**	1.28	0.21	1.78
Medium					4.84*	1.86	0.87	2.17
High (English only household)					8.90†	4.86	−1.92	3.60
National origin								
Mexican (ref)							—	—
Central American					−2.55†	1.36		
Japanese (ref)							—	—
Chinese							−4.22†	2.43
Korean							−3.64	3.41
R-Squared	0.22		0.10		0.28		0.28	
Nunber of cases	739		1,075		914		1,045	

Source: Author's compilation.
Notes: *** $p < .001$; ** $p < .01$; * $p < .05$; † $p < .10$

rates." Beginning with family income as an example, note that whites, Latinos, and Asians generally exhibit a fairly powerful, monotonic, and statistically significant relationship between income and neighborhood proximity to whites—that is, increasing income is associated with increased proximity to whites, net of other factors—and that these increases are nearly always in the double digits. Conversely, the association between income and neighborhood proximity to whites is much weaker for blacks. Only three of the four categories of income are associated with significant gains, and only the highest-income blacks see a double-digit return on their investment. Similarly, both whites and Asians exhibit sizable increases in contact with whites at each level of education. Among blacks and Latinos, however, only an advanced degree significantly increases neighborhood contact with whites (by 16 and 20 percent, respectively). Note also that the return on an advanced degree experienced by both blacks and Latinos is greater than it is for comparably educated whites and Asians. We should bear in mind, however, that these groups are also the least likely to hold advanced degrees.

Net financial assets, homeownership, and public housing experience are generally less consistent predictors of neighborhood proximity to whites. Among white respondents, the accumulation of more than $10,000 in assets yields a modest increase in neighborhood contact with whites; however, none of the other groups experiences significant gains. Homeownership generally is expected to improve neighborhood outcomes but only modestly increases Asians' proximity to whites, and it has no significant effect for white and Latino respondents' neighborhood exposure to whites. Most troublesome, however, is the statistically significant *negative* effect of homeownership experienced by blacks: on average, black homeowners live in neighborhoods with about 5 percent fewer whites than their non-owner counterparts ($p < .05$).

Experience with public housing has a significant impact on neighborhood proximity to whites only twice. First, net of other factors, the neighborhoods of whites currently living in public housing are roughly 10 percent less white than those of their counterparts with no public housing experience; given the overrepresentation of minorities in public housing, this is not especially surprising (Bickford and Massey 1991).

More surprising, however, is that prior residence in public housing has the opposite effect on Latinos, propelling this group into areas with significantly more white neighbors compared to coethnics with no public housing experience (6.31 percent, $p < .05$). Recall that prior residence in public housing doubled the odds of homeownership for this group. Without additional, qualitative information, we can only speculate about the sources of this association. Certain characteristics of public housing, such as concentrated poverty and close proximity to blacks, make it extremely difficult to separate race and poverty. Moreover, it is quite plausible that high-volume immigration has a self-selection effect in that Latinos may experience the same heightened concern with upward mobility that no doubt motivated them to migrate in the first place. To the extent that residence in public housing that is disproportionately occupied by African Americans represents the absolute bottom of the U.S. social hierarchy, homeownership in a predominantly white neighborhood may symbolize important social distance from stigmatized statuses (black and poor) and, equally important, the attainment of elevated status.

To assess the impact of high-volume immigration on the residential outcomes of Latinos and Asians, I included in models for these groups measures of nativity status, English-language ability, and national origin. The results highlight important differences in the importance of acculturation for these groups. Neither Latinos nor Asians exhibit any meaningful national-origin differences, but this is all they have in common in this examination of the role played by immigration-related characteristics in neighborhood proximity to whites. As anticipated, increasing acculturation improves residential outcomes for Latinos: the foreign-born have significantly less contact with whites than their native-born counterparts do (for recent immigrants, $p = .059$), and greater English-language proficiency tends to increase residential proximity with whites significantly; however, neither measure of acculturation has a significant impact on Asians' residential contact with whites. The contradictory pattern of immigration-related effects among Latinos and Asians is consistent with the census-based work of Alba, Logan, and their colleagues. In the past, researchers found this pattern difficult to explain, but more recent work (Logan, Alba, and Zhang 2002) finds the key to the puzzle in the emergence of *ethnic communities*: neighborhoods that are residential rather than economic in nature (that is, ethnic enclaves) and that offer both natives and immigrants access to affluent but predominantly coethnic neighborhoods.

In addition to interpreting and comparing individual coefficients across groups, it is also useful to evaluate the overall ability of these models to predict neighborhood proximity to whites. Immediately apparent is the lackluster performance of this set of variables in explaining black respondents' neighborhood contact with whites. The 10 percent of total variation explained is low, both in absolute terms and relative to the other groups. Alternatively, the explanatory power of both the Latino and Asian models (28 percent each) is respectable and the highest of the four groups, suggesting that the spatial assimilation model is more applicable to the residential experiences of these groups than it is for either whites

(22 percent of total variation explained) or African Americans. It could be argued, however, that in a city as diverse as Los Angeles, the percentage of non-Hispanic whites in one's neighborhood is not the best indicator of one's ability to achieve upward mobility. Although it is true that we have traditionally associated assimilation and improved status with proximity to whites, we have also associated predominantly white neighborhoods with greater affluence. The final step in making the case for social class as an explanation for persistent racial residential segregation is to assess the similarities and differences in the ability of LASUI respondents to exchange their human capital characteristics for residence in more affluent neighborhoods—ignoring racial composition.

Neighborhood Socioeconomic Status

Table 3.5 summarizes results from models predicting neighborhood median income. Immediately evident is that LASUI respondents' human capital characteristics predict neighborhood affluence far better than proximity to non-Hispanic whites. Not only do these characteristics explain between 27 and 35 percent of the total variation in neighborhood median income, but in several instances patterns of effects for individual variables are stronger and more likely to be statistically significant. Especially striking is the improved explanatory power for blacks and whites compared to the previous model: for blacks, the same set of individual and household characteristics explains 2.7 times more of the total variation in neighborhood median income compared to proximity to whites.

Income and homeownership also appear to be more strongly associated with neighborhood affluence across groups. Notably, the effect of homeownership is positive for all four groups, but statistically significant only for whites and Asians. Note too the more substantial role of household income in predicting neighborhood affluence, particularly for African Americans. Here again, however, the returns to income experienced by blacks are consistently lower than those of whites and Asians; Latinos also experience lower returns to income relative to these groups.

Beyond this cursory initial evaluation, however, lie important racial-group differences worth highlighting. As we might expect, all groups are disadvantaged by current residence in public housing; this is particularly true for whites and Asians, who, on average, reported declines in neighborhood affluence of $7,361 and $9,754, respectively. Blacks, on the other hand, are least disadvantaged by residence in public housing, net of other factors. (Latinos may represent an exception, although for this group the effect of current residence in public housing only narrowly misses conventional levels of statistical significance, with $p = .062$.) Recall, however,

Table 3.5 OLS Regression Coefficients Predicting LASUI Respondents' Neighborhood Socioeconomic Status, by Race

	Whites		Blacks		Latinos		Asians	
	B	SE	B	SE	B	SE	B	SE
Constant	18,534***	2,940	19,011***	1,396	22,992***	1,834	23,537***	4,192
Homeowner (1 = yes)	6,351***	1,465	1,515	1,271	1,807	1,227	5,890**	1,903
Public housing experience								
Never (ref)	—	—	—	—	—	—	—	—
In the past	–3,596	1,948	521	689	3,982*	1,662	4,560	4,186
Currently	–7,361*	3,712	–5,043**	1,454	–5,465†	2,929	–9,754**	3,400
Income								
Less than $20,000 (ref)	—	—	—	—	—	—	—	—
$20,000 to $39,999	5,550***	1,452	4,120***	897	3,606***	652	2,792†	1,417
$40,000 to $59,999	8,604***	1,774	7,985***	1,776	7,603***	1,489	7,460**	2,367
$60,000 to $89,999	11,647***	2,500	9,258***	2,127	10,164***	2,178	12,496***	2,680
$90,000 or more	16,633***	3,469	16,011***	3,315	11,219**	3,510	19,369***	3,641
Missing income (1 = yes)	4,371	2,935	–307	1,069	261	945	1,921	1,360
Net financial assets								
Negative or none (ref)	—	—	—	—	—	—	—	—
$1 to $5,000	550	1,391	365	794	566	573	–541	1,463
$5,001 to $10,000	4,614	2,703	1,090	1,300	–2,422	1,968	2,928	2,134
Over $10,000	5,689**	2,049	1,320	1,473	–450	1,748	7,078**	2,544
Missing net financial assets (1 = yes)	–2,269	2,333	371	1,060	320	891	–3,490*	1,712
Age								
21 to 29 (ref)	—	—	—	—	—	—	—	—
30 to 39	–2,910	1,692	–367	1,016	–216	729	–3,654*	1,830
40 to 49	–5,040*	1,970	–1,074	1,062	1,385	952	104	1,871
50 to 59	–4,362	2,388	–1,615	1,195	3,376**	1,133	–3,305	2,166
60 to 69	3,597	3,477	–900	1,621	2,285	1,566	–3,844	2,497
70 and older	–2,516	2,614	–2,212	1,352	3,690	3,151	–964	2,713

Education								
Less than high school (ref)	—	—	—	—	—	—	—	—
High school graduate or GED	6,040***	1,617	1,638**	505	114	340	2,349	1,629
Some college	7,834***	1,879	1,083	788	−98	1,530	5,894*	2,274
Bachelor's degree	7,208**	2,457	3,071*	1,334	2,938	1,747	8,405***	1,896
Advanced degree	12,967***	3,237	8,515*	3,181	11,752**	4,202	8,998**	3,207
Household structure								
Married with children (1 = yes)	−2,938	1,672	−712*	882	513	610	−232	1,448
Household size	2,083**	590	−234	222	−46	200	1,602**	576
Nativity status								
U.S.-born (ref)					—	—	—	—
Foreign-born: over ten years in the U.S.					−3,442**	1,236	−1,522	3,090
Foreign-born: six to ten years in the U.S.					−3,967**	1,410	−797	3,353
Foreign-born: five years or less in the U.S.					−3,896*	1,465	−1,232	3,142
English language ability								
None (ref)					—	—	—	—
Low					1,295†	737	190	1,581
Medium					2,053*	945	−2,745	1,693
High (English only household)					5,473**	1,775	−6,686†	3,412
National origin								
Mexican (ref)					—	—		
Central American					−3,234***	792		
Japanese (ref)							—	—
Chinese							852	1,700
Korean							1,164	2,371
R-Squared	0.34		0.27		0.35		0.35	
Number of cases	739		1,075		914		1,045	

Source: Author's compilation.

Notes: Coefficients and standard errors are rounded to the nearest whole dollar.

*** $p < .001$; ** $p < .01$; * $p < .05$; † $p < .10$

that blacks are roughly five times more likely than most other groups to reside in public housing (see table 3.1) and are therefore more often disadvantaged in this way. That blacks are least impacted by residence in public housing is consistent with race-based explanations for residential segregation; the implication is that escaping what is known to be a segregated circumstance does little to change the overall racial character of their neighborhoods. Lending credence to the possibility that, for Latinos, residence in public housing is a stigma to be eradicated is the fact that Latinos again appear to benefit from past residence in public housing: these respondents lived in neighborhoods that were about $4,000 more affluent than those of their counterparts with no public housing experience.

Only whites and Asians appear to benefit from accumulated wealth or from increasing educational attainment; for these groups, having more than $10,000 in net financial assets significantly increases neighborhood affluence ($5,689 and $7,078, respectively; $p < .05$). A high school diploma increases whites' neighborhood SES by more than $6,000, while an advanced degree increases their neighborhood affluence by nearly $13,000, compared to their counterparts with no such degree. For Asians, the comparable improvements are $2,349 (p = not significant) and $8,998, respectively. For these two groups, moreover, nearly every incremental increase in education significantly enhances neighborhood median income. This is not true for blacks or Latinos. Indeed, for both blacks and Latinos, only an advanced degree yields significantly improved neighborhood affluence ($11,752 for Latinos, $8,515 for blacks). Bear in mind, however, that blacks and Latinos are among the least likely to attain this level of education—roughly 6 percent of blacks and slightly under 1 percent of Latinos hold an advanced degree, compared to 10 percent of whites and 11 percent of Asians.

Characteristics associated with immigration have a significant impact on the neighborhood affluence experienced by Latinos. In general, immigrants live in neighborhoods that are between $3,400 and $4,000 less affluent than those of the native-born; this disparity declines only slightly with increasing time in the United States. Increasing English-language proficiency is associated with more substantial improvements in neighborhood median income: medium ability is associated with an increase of about $2,100, while high proficiency increases neighborhood affluence by more than $5,400. Even those with low English-language ability are slightly better off, showing an increase in neighborhood affluence of $1,295 ($p < .10$). National-origin differences benefit Latinos with Mexican ancestry by a little more than $3,200. Once again, however, almost none of the immigration-related characteristics significantly influence the neighborhood affluence experienced by Asians; the lone exception is for Asians with high English proficiency. Paradoxically, these individuals see a marginally significant decrease in neighborhood socioeconomic status of nearly $6,700 ($p < .10$).

CONCLUSIONS

What does all of this mean for the actual residential outcomes of whites, blacks, Latinos, and Asians in Los Angeles? To continue assessing the applicability of the spatial assimilation model to processes of residential attainment in Los Angeles, this chapter ends by looking at how things shake out in the "real world" and considering how these results play out for individuals with comparable individual and household characteristics from each racial and nativity-status group. Table 3.6 presents predicted values for each neighborhood outcome for four types of individuals—poor immigrants, poor natives, affluent immigrants, and affluent natives—to provide a clear, easy-to-interpret picture of the real-world consequences of the results detailed here.[16] A "poor native" is an individual who is U.S.-born, has high English proficiency (in the case of Latinos and Asians), does not own his or her home, and is in the lowest income, assets, and education categories (earns less than $20,000 annually, has zero or negative net financial assets, and has less than a high school diploma). A "poor immigrant" is similar to a poor native except that he or she has recently immigrated to the United States (within the last five years) and speaks little English ("low" English ability). An "affluent native" is a U.S.-born homeowner with "high" English proficiency (again, for Asians and Latinos) and income, assets, and education in the highest categories ($90,000 or more in income, over $10,000 in net financial assets, and an advanced degree). Finally, an "affluent immigrant" has been in the United States for over ten years, has "medium" English ability, owns his or her home, and is otherwise comparable to the affluent native. In all cases, the values for remaining characteristics are standardized to the overall sample mean.

The results offer interesting insights. After controlling for background characteristics, differences among native whites and Latinos—both poor and affluent—are relatively small. The two categories of native Latinos are nearly equivalent to whites in residential contact with whites: poor native members of both groups can expect to live in neighborhoods that are just over one-quarter white, with proximity to whites increasing to 67 and 58 percent, respectively, for affluent native whites and Latinos. In terms of neighborhood median income, poor native Latinos actually exceed the residential attainment of comparable whites by more than $9,000; affluent native Latinos experience a disadvantage relative to

Table 3.6 Predicted Values of Neighborhood Proximity to Non-Hispanic Whites and Neighborhood Median Household Income, by Race

Neighborhood Outcome	Whites	Blacks	Latinos	Asians
Proximity to non-Hispanic whites				
Poor native	27.63%	4.65%	26.88%	10.32%
Poor immigrant	—	—	15.27	17.10
Affluent native	65.96	30.88	58.11	45.12
Affluent immigrant	—	—	45.91	51.96
Median household income				
Poor native	\$20,013	\$16,894	\$29,304	\$22,979
Poor immigrant	—	—	21,230	28,623
Affluent native	61,652	44,255	53,632	64,315
Affluent immigrant	—	—	46,770	66,733

Source: Author's compilation.
Notes: Poor immigrants have five years or less in the United States, speak little English, do not own their homes, and are in the lowest categories for income, assets, and education (less than \$20,000 in income, zero or negative assets, and less than high school). Poor natives are comparable to poor immigrants, except that they are U.S.-born and have high English ability. Affluent natives are U.S.-born, have high English ability, are homeowners, and place in the highest categories for income, assets, and education (\$90,000 and over in income, over \$10,000 in assets, and an advanced degree). Affluent immigrants are comparable to affluent natives, except that they have been in the United States more than ten years and report having "medium" English ability. All other characteristics are standardized to the overall sample mean.

whites of roughly \$8,000. Also noteworthy are the predicted outcomes for poor immigrant Latinos: compared to poor native whites (the closest comparison group), poor, foreign-born Latinos reside in neighborhoods that are about 10 percent less white but about equally affluent.

The general story is slightly different for Asians, who experience less proximity to whites but greater neighborhood affluence. Poor natives have a predicted level of neighborhood affluence that slightly exceeds that of comparable whites; however, their neighborhood contact with whites lags substantially behind that of similar whites and Latinos, at 10 percent. Likewise, affluent native Asians are also predicted to reside in neighborhoods with fewer whites relative to the contact with whites experienced by white and Latino respondents, while at the same time they have the highest predicted level of neighborhood affluence, with a median neighborhood household income of over \$64,000. Poor immigrant Asians' predicted proximity to whites is similar to that of similarly situated Latinos; however, at $28,623, this group's predicted neighborhood affluence exceeds that of nearly all other comparable groups—that is, poor native whites, blacks, and Asians and poor immigrant Latinos. (Poor immigrant Asians' neighborhood affluence is roughly comparable to that of poor native Latinos.) Compared to all other categories of Asians, the affluent immigrants fare best of all, living in neighborhoods just over half-white (bested only by affluent native whites and Latinos) and earning a median household income of nearly $67,000—the highest income of all.

Consistent with all of the results presented thus far, blacks fare the worst of all groups. Poor native blacks can anticipate residence in neighborhoods that are less than 5 percent white. Although this figure improves considerably to 31 percent for affluent native blacks, it lags behind comparable groups by a low of 14 percent (Asians) to a high of about 35 percent (whites). In fact, affluent blacks' exposure to whites is not much different from that of poor native Latinos. Blacks' predicted levels of neighborhood affluence are equally troubling. Poor native blacks have the absolute lowest predicted neighborhood median income: at just under $17,000, this median income is lower than that of both poor immigrant and poor native Latinos and Asians. Once again, the within-racial-group comparison suggests vast improvement—affluent blacks reside in communities with median incomes of more than $44,000. Nevertheless, affluent blacks live in neighborhoods that are $9,300 to $20,000 less affluent than those of comparable out-groups, and the gap between affluent native blacks and affluent immigrant Asians is even larger, at nearly $22,500.

The patterns of association between blacks' individual characteristics and neighborhood outcomes are consistent with those documented with decennial census data (Alba and Logan 1993; Logan and Alba 1995; Massey and Mullan 1984) and again provide powerful evidence that objective differences in social class status cannot account for all of the racial residential segregation evident in Los Angeles—particularly that experienced by blacks. To put it plainly, blacks do not experience the same neighborhood outcomes as others with comparable human capital characteristics; in fact, poor immigrants get more than blacks do with less human capital. Therefore, even when differences in the distributions of those characteristics are held constant, blacks' neighborhood outcomes never reach parity with those of comparable whites. Particularly damning is the negative effect of homeownership on proximity to whites, which supports the idea that a dual housing market exists that confines black homeowners to black neighborhoods, makes it difficult for them to enter some communities, and adds to the housing costs they bear. As a consequence, efforts aimed at decreasing black-white economic inequality—increasing access to higher education, eliminating income inequality, increasing access to homeownership—may improve the residential outcomes of some blacks (clearly affluent blacks have better neighborhood characteristics than poor blacks do), but these efforts will not be sufficient to eradicate the extreme level of residential segregation in Los Angeles.

Prior research suggests that class-based explanations of racial residential segregation best describe housing outcomes for Latinos and Asians. Results from these analyses, however, offer mixed results. In support of class-based explanations, the native-born report higher rates of homeownership and spend more each month on housing, net of other factors. Consistent with the assumptions of acculturation, as immigrants' time in the United States and English-language proficiency increase, they become more likely to own their homes or to spend more each month on housing. In fact, Asian immigrants with more than ten years in the United States spend more on housing than any other group, including whites, once social class and other nativity-status characteristics are accounted for. Asian immigrants with fewer than ten years in the United States do not differ significantly from whites; nor do the native-born. The story is a little different for Latinos: the native-born and immigrants with more than ten years in the United States do not differ significantly from whites in their monthly housing expenditures, but shorter-term immigrants are disadvantaged relative to whites.

Similarly, the residential attainment models predicting neighborhood proximity to whites and neighborhood median income exhibit the best explanatory power for Latinos and Asians. At the same time, however, comparisons of the "purchasing power" of their individual and household characteristics with that of whites raise questions about spatial assimilation for these groups. Latinos, for example, do not appear to benefit from homeownership or accumulated wealth, and they reap residential rewards from only the highest levels of education. Nonetheless, Latinos are often well situated to reach neighborhood parity with whites (see table 3.6). Moreover, prior experience in public housing appears to have a uniquely positive effect on several of this group's housing-related outcomes: it increases the likelihood of homeownership and proximity to whites, as well as neighborhood median income. For Asians, on the other hand, the reverse seems to be true: immigration-related characteristics—length of time in the United States, English-language proficiency, and national origin—have virtually no effect on residential outcomes; however, homeownership, income, net financial assets, and educational attainment are strong, consistent predictors of residential outcomes for Asians. Finally, Asians' lower-than-expected levels of neighborhood exposure to whites, given their higher-than-expected neighborhood median incomes, further complicate their story.

There are two plausible explanations for these mixed results. First, with the emergence of suburban ethnic communities in Los Angeles, these groups have coethnic, affluent residential alternatives that are not available to African Americans (Logan et al. 2002). This would explain the nonsignificant effects for Asians' acculturation-related characteristics, as well as the contradictory predicted values of relatively low exposure to whites but better-than-comparable neighborhood affluence (see table 3.6). The emergence of ethnic communities would also make sense of the relatively high neighborhood affluence predicted for Latinos (both poor immigrants and poor natives). Another possibility is that a dual housing market operates in Los Angeles that puts Latinos and Asians—particularly those of Chinese and Korean descent—at a disadvantage similar to what blacks experience (Alba et al. 1999; Logan et al. 1996; Massey and Denton 1993). That this may be the case was suggested by the results of the 2000 Housing Discrimination Study, which revealed not only persisting discrimination against blacks and Latinos in both the sales and rental markets but meaningful discrimination against Chinese and Koreans as well, particularly in the sales market, where discrimination against Chinese and Korean home-seekers is comparable in both kind and frequency to the discrimination experienced by blacks and Latinos (Turner et al. 2002).[17]

The first of these alternatives—residence in suburban ethnic communities—suggests that Asians and Latinos may *choose* to have less residential contact with whites, possibly because they are seeking support from coethnics while adjusting to life in the United States. The other explanation—a dual housing market—points to racially discriminatory practices that constrain residential options not only for African Americans, as a voluminous body of research has already shown, but also for Latinos and Asians, groups whose experiences are often characterized as "textbook" spatial assimilation. Each of these explanations points to the importance of race in mapping processes of residential attainment. If this examination of the relationship between social class status and residential outcomes confirms that class does indeed matter, it also lends support to race-based explanations, to which we now turn.

Chapter Four | A Racialized Housing Market?

RACE AND RACE-RELATED issues are a concern for most Americans, whether or not we are willing to say so openly and whether or not we are even consciously aware of these issues. Our concern is tied to both our own racial-group membership and our attitudes about and perceptions of those we label racial "others." Although many public discussions of racial attitudes center on what white people think, the housing choices made by members of all groups are a function, in part at least, of racial attitudes and preferences. For example, many nonwhites believe that the presence of a "critical mass" of coethnics offers both the comfort of familiarity and a buffer against potential hostility. Racial integration in a neighborhood—especially a strong same-race showing—signals to outsiders that "people like us" are valued and welcomed there. Similarly, areas that are overwhelmingly white, or at least largely devoid of coethnics, are often perceived by nonwhites as hostile and unwelcoming. And although we tend to place racial prejudice squarely in the purview of white America, it also plays a role in nonwhites' preferences, even as they express concerns about racial hostility directed at themselves. Whites also prefer a meaningful coethnic presence. In fact, this preference is often stronger among whites than it is with any of the nonwhite groups. The preferences of whites appear to be more directly shaped by active racial prejudice, however, than by fears of out-group hostility or neutral ethnocentrism.

Thus, in important ways, racial attitudes and intergroup relations are critical aspects of neighborhood outcomes that are often downplayed or neglected in efforts to improve housing options, increase neighborhood residential integration, or reduce inequality more generally. As the United States is demographically transformed, and as our sprawling metropolitan communities continue to change shape, understanding these attitudes and preferences becomes ever more crucial. Again, Los Angeles, as a metropolis on the cutting edge of that transformation, offers a unique opportunity to visualize our national future.

This chapter provides an overview of recent trends in racial attitudes. Paying particularly close attention to aspects that are relevant to understanding neighborhood-level outcomes, I briefly discuss broad national trends but turn quickly to the attitudes of Los Angeles–area whites, blacks, Latinos, and Asians. I follow with an examination of neighborhood racial composition preferences—a set of race-related attitudes heavily implicated in aggregate-level residential patterns (Charles 2000a; Farley et al. 1978, 1993; Krysan 2002; Krysan and Farley 2002; Massey and Denton 1993; Zubrinsky and Bobo 1996); this discussion sets the stage for a detailed consideration of how racial identity and other racial attitudes are implicated in patterns of neighborhood preference. Once again, a central feature of this analysis is consideration of nativity-status differences among Latino and Asian Angelenos.

Before moving headlong into a survey of intergroup attitudes, it is helpful to consider variations across groups in attachment to a racial-ethnic identity, since such attachment may well be relevant to understanding group differences in the patterns of other racial attitudes. It is generally accepted among social scientists that one's racial-ethnic background, as a core element of individual social identity, serves as an important basis for individual behavior and social action (Bobo et al. 1998). Even without face-to-face interaction or any other meaningful social ties, group membership can lead to behaviors that favor one's own group (Tajfel 1982; Turner, Brown, and Tajfel 1979).

A commonly used indicator of racial-ethnic group attachment is an individual's sense of common fate identity—the belief that "what happens to my group happens to me." Research suggests that feelings of common fate are important aspects of both African American (Dawson 1994; Gurin, Hatchett, and Jackson 1989; Tate 1993) and Asian American group identities (Espiritu 1992; Tuan 1999) and that important national ancestry attachments among Latinos are critical to their self-concept (De la Garza, Falcon, and Garcia 1996). The LASUI measured common-fate racial identity in two steps. First, respondents were asked: "Do you think what happens generally to [own racial group] people in this country will have something to do with what happens in your life?" Those who answered yes were then asked whether their particular racial-group membership would affect them "a lot," "some," or "not very much"; the responses provided a measure of both the presence and strength of respondents' common fate identity.

The results, summarized in table 4.1, show that clear majorities of all groups—between 54 and 72 percent—expressed at least "some" degree of

Table 4.1 Common Fate Identity, by Respondent Race and Nativity Status: Summary Statistics

	Whites	Blacks	Native-Born Latinos	Foreign-Born Latinos	Native-Born Asians	Foreign-Born Asians
Sense of common fate***						
None	27.12%	21.60%	38.20%	27.97%	17.16%	22.69%
Not very much	9.26	6.19	7.51	5.31	24.05	9.51
Some	43.38	35.24	36.59	35.69	52.92	47.19
A lot	20.23	36.97	17.70	31.03	5.87	20.61
Mean**	1.57	1.88††	1.34	1.70	1.48	1.66

Source: Author's compilation.
*** $p < .001$; ** $p < .01$; †† Mean value is significantly different from whites, $p < .01$

common-fate racial identity, yet there are also substantial racial and nativity-status group differences. For instance, nearly two out of five blacks expressed "a lot" of common-fate racial identity (37 percent) compared to fewer than one in four native-born Latinos (18 percent). Native-born Asians were the least likely to express a strong sense of common fate identity (6 percent). Whites and foreign-born Latinos and Asians fall between these extremes, though foreign-born Latinos were more likely than either of the other two in this category to express "a lot" of common-fate racial identity. At the same time, between 17 and 38 percent of each group professed that their racial-group membership had nothing to do with their own life chances.

It should not go unnoticed here that among both Latinos and Asians the foreign-born expressed a stronger sense of common fate identity than did their native-born counterparts. A comparison of means by national origin within the foreign-born groups and separately by race found no significant differences among Asians. Among Latinos, however, Central Americans expressed a significantly higher sense of common fate than did Mexican-origin Latinos ($p < .05$). These patterns of difference, by both nativity status and to a lesser extent by national origin, suggest that immigrants used the common-fate racial identity query as an opportunity to express what may more likely be a national ancestry or ethnic identity (see Bobo and Johnson 2000).[1] Mean values for this item (bottom row of table 4.1), which range from 0 (none) to 3 (a lot), nicely summarize these overall trends.

In short, while the majority of Los Angeles–area adults expressed some level of common-fate racial identity, there were meaningful differences in the strength of common-fate identity as expressed by the different racial and nativity-status groups. As a core aspect of individual identity, such feelings of in-group attachment are likely to have an impact on both our perceptions of our own group and our sense of out-group differentiation. If, as Bobo and Johnson (2000, 92) assert, these attitudes occur, "at least logically, prior to perceptions of racial group competition or particular social policy views," then clearly they have a profound impact on how we see ourselves and others, whether we are negotiating the housing market or other aspects of modern life. Have our fundamentally held racial attitudes changed in recent U.S. history?

TRENDS IN RACIAL ATTITUDES

In a recent overview of trends in American racial attitudes and relations, Lawrence Bobo (2001, 294) concludes that "the glass is half-full or the glass is half-empty, depending on what one chooses to emphasize." The good news is that the second half of the twentieth century was a period of "steady and sweeping movement toward general endorsement of the principles of racial equality and integration" (269). Although blacks have a long history of endorsing racial equality and integration, this has not been the case for a substantial portion of the white population.[2] But by the early 1970s the vast majority of whites endorsed equal employment access and the integration of public transportation. The shift in white attitudes toward school integration was slower; nonetheless, by the mid-1990s whites almost universally endorsed this principle as well (Bobo 2001; Schuman et al. 1997). Whites still show less support for equality of access to housing, however, despite substantial improvements, and they show less support still for interracial marriage; indeed, recent analyses of trends in racial attitudes caution that the greatest evidence of growing endorsement of principles of racial equality and integration is in the most public and impersonal societal arenas (Bobo 2001; Schuman et al. 1997).[3]

Still, these trends are characterized as "sweeping and robust" and illustrative of a positive shift "in fundamental norms" regarding race (Bobo 2001, 273). Combined with other noteworthy improvements—the increasing size and relative security of the black middle class, the increasing presence of blacks and other minorities in seats of political and corporate power, and small but meaningful declines in residential segregation—these trends suggest that we have never been closer to resolving the "American Dilemma" (Myrdal 1944/1972).

Unfortunately, another set of trends supports the more pessimistic "glass-half-empty" interpretation. Socioeconomic inequities by race stubbornly persist. Although the root causes of these inequities continue to be debated, their patterns are well known: relative to whites, blacks and Latinos complete fewer years of school and are concentrated in lower-status jobs; they earn less income and accumulate less wealth (Farley 1996a; Oliver and Shapiro 1995). There is substantial evidence of systematic racial discrimination against blacks—in the labor and housing markets and in interpersonal relations—irrespective of their social class status (Bertrand and Mullainathan 2004; Bobo and Suh 2000; Feagin and Sikes 1994; Feagin and Vera 1995; Kirschenman and Neckerman 1991; Turner et al. 2002; Waldinger and Bailey 1991; Yinger 1995). More recent evidence suggests that both Latinos and Asians also face substantial racial discrimination in the housing market (Turner et al. 2002).

RACIAL STEREOTYPES

The proportion of whites who hold uniformly negative stereotypes of minorities has declined substantially; however, antiminority stereotypes remain common among whites (Bobo 2001; Charles 2000a). A majority of whites—between 54 and 78 percent, depending on the trait—still express some negative stereotypes of blacks and Latinos, and for nearly one-quarter of them, these are firmly negative views. A much lower percentage of whites (between 10 and 40 percent, again, depending on the trait) stereotype Asians negatively (Bobo 2001; Charles 2000a, 2001b; Smith 1990; Sniderman and Carmines 1997). How whites express negative racial stereotypes has also changed, becoming more qualified and less categorical than in previous eras, more likely to be rooted in cultural and volitional explanations than in beliefs of biological inferiority. Moreover, whites are not alone in the tendency to stereotype: although the story is more complicated, minority groups also hold negative stereotypes of both whites and each other (Bobo 2001; Bobo and Massagli 2001; Charles 2000a, 2001b).

Our attitudes, beliefs, and perceptions of other racial-ethnic groups as well as our own group are essential features of intergroup relations (Allport 1954; Ashmore and Del Boca 1981; Bobo 2001; Jackman 1994; Stephan 1985) and are relevant to understanding a wide range of outcomes related to inequality (Bobo et al. 1998). The LASUI included a substantial number of bipolar trait ratings to gauge respondents' racial stereotypes and related attitudes. These traits were chosen on substantive grounds and reflect a mix of considerations relevant to the groups under consideration. For instance, the "rich/poor" trait taps beliefs about the absolute and relative economic positions of groups and is directly tied to concerns associated with our achievement-oriented society. Four items—"intelligent/unintelligent," "prefers self-sufficiency/prefers welfare," "speaks English poorly/well," and "involvement in drugs and gangs (or not)"—tap aspects of traditional prejudice and are central components of American racial ideology. Prejudice is heavily imbued with negative stereotypes and negative affect that make the prejudiced person unreceptive to reason and new information. The "easy/difficult to get along with socially" trait is useful not only because it taps into perceptions about particular groups (for example, some Asian groups—including but not limited to Koreans—have cultural styles of interaction that many Americans view as brusque), but also because it provides a measure of perceived social distance—an affective component of racial prejudice. Those groups (including one's own group) that one perceives as "easy to get along with" should make more desirable neighbors, coworkers, and so on, than those one perceives as "difficult to get along with." Finally, the "tends to discriminate" stereotype seems to tap racial minority groups' perceptions of whites, though it may be applied to other groups as well (Bobo and Johnson 2000; Charles 2000a).[4]

There are two ways to interpret the responses to these items: in absolute terms, looking at scores on individual traits and an index measure that is the average score across traits; and in comparative terms, using a difference score to measure the relative difference that respondents perceive between their own group and a particular out-group. Absolute measures—the individual trait-rating items and the overall ratings—range in value from 1 to 7, with high scores reflecting negative ratings. Difference scores range from –6 to +6, with low scores reflecting a more favorable rating of an out-group relative to one's own group and high scores reflecting a more unfavorable rating of an out-group relative to one's own group; a score of 0 indicates a perception of no difference between the respondent group and the target group. Thus, for both the trait ratings and the difference scores, the higher the value, the more negative or unfavorable the perception of the target group (see also Bobo and Johnson 2000; Charles 2000a, 2000b; Krysan 2002).

So what are the most commonly held racial stereotypes? Can overall patterns of racial stereotypes across groups be characterized as consensual, or are there substantial differences? How much social distance do groups perceive between themselves and various out-groups? To what extent do minority groups perceive whites as discriminatory, and again, is this perception consensual? Equally important, to what extent do LASUI respondents' racial attitudes deviate from the broad trends discussed in the previous section? Table 4.2 reports mean responses for each of the individual traits, an overall absolute rating for the measures of tra-

Table 4.2 Perceived Social Class Disadvantage, Racial Stereotyping, Social Distance, and White Discrimination, by Respondent Race and Nativity Status and Target-Group Race: Summary Statistics

Target Group and Traits	Whites	Blacks	Native-Born Latinos	Foreign-Born Latinos	Native-Born Asians	Foreign-Born Asians
Whites						
Social class disadvantage						
Poverty	3.63	2.87	3.10	2.35	3.28	3.00
Difference score	—	–2.21	–1.64	–3.12	0.11	–0.61
Racial stereotyping						
Unintelligent	3.05	3.45	3.59	2.88	3.31	3.09
Prefers welfare	2.47	2.88	2.81	2.93	2.38	2.74
Poor English	1.95	1.95	1.76	1.42	1.76	1.37
Drugs and gangs	3.01	4.01	3.55	3.56	2.92	3.46
Absolute rating	2.62	3.08	2.93	2.70	2.59	2.67
Difference score	—	–0.63	–1.35	–1.58	–0.04	–0.21
Social distance						
Hard to get along with	3.21	3.98	3.66	3.67	3.08	3.82
Difference score	—	0.87	0.83	0.95	0.23	0.90
Discrimination						
Discriminates	4.05	5.31	4.71	4.97	4.62	4.60
Blacks						
Social class disadvantage						
Poverty	5.21	5.09	5.03	4.92	5.29	5.36
Difference score	1.57	—	0.29	–0.55	2.13	1.74
Racial stereotyping						
Unintelligent	3.82	3.39	4.05	3.90	4.03	4.44
Prefers welfare	4.16	4.04	5.04	5.63	4.27	5.25
Poor English	3.42	2.71	3.36	2.51	2.94	2.06
Drugs and gangs	4.60	4.68	5.21	5.36	4.90	5.01
Absolute rating	4.00	3.71	4.41	4.35	4.04	4.19
Difference score	1.38	—	0.14	0.07	1.41	1.32
Social distance						
Hard to get along with	3.83	3.11	3.69	4.54	3.45	4.35
Difference score	0.62	—	0.87	1.83	0.61	1.42
Discrimination						
Discriminates	4.70	3.96	4.92	4.94	4.81	4.13

Table 4.2 (*Continued*)

Target Group and Traits	Whites	Blacks	Native-Born Latinos	Foreign-Born Latinos	Native-Born Asians	Foreign-Born Asians
Latinos						
Social class disadvantage						
Poverty	5.37	5.30	4.74	5.47	5.32	5.50
Difference score	1.73	0.21	—	—	2.16	1.89
Racial stereotyping						
Unintelligent	3.98	3.93	3.87	3.55	4.04	4.59
Prefers welfare	3.96	4.19	4.29	4.41	4.15	5.25
Poor English	4.70	4.83	4.05	4.50	4.45	4.53
Drugs and gangs	4.59	4.74	4.90	4.66	4.97	4.65
Absolute rating	4.31	4.42	4.28	4.28	4.40	4.76
Difference score	1.69	0.72	—	—	1.77	1.88
Social distance						
Hard to get along with	3.69	3.40	2.83	2.72	3.27	3.76
Difference score	0.48	0.29	—	—	0.43	0.84
Discrimination						
Discriminates	4.38	4.40	4.08	3.41	4.57	3.48
Asians						
Social class disadvantage						
Poverty	3.61	3.12	3.14	2.87	3.16	3.61
Difference score	–0.02	–1.97	–1.60	–2.60	—	—
Racial stereotyping						
Unintelligent	2.88	3.30	3.13	2.75	2.67	2.85
Prefers welfare	2.30	2.72	2.67	2.87	1.88	2.36
Poor English	3.83	4.84	4.62	3.87	3.05	3.69
Drugs and gangs	3.19	3.99	3.46	3.32	2.91	2.59
Absolute rating	3.05	3.71	3.47	3.20	2.63	2.87
Difference score	0.43	0.01	–0.81	–1.08	—	—
Social distance						
Hard to get along with	3.64	4.29	4.12	4.17	2.84	2.92
Difference score	0.43	1.17	1.29	1.46	—	—
Discrimination						
Discriminates	4.33	5.19	4.69	4.51	4.45	3.53
Number of cases	739	1,075	177	737	127	917

Source: Author's compilation.
Notes: $p < .001$ except poverty for black target group ($p < .01$), drugs and gangs for Latino target group (p = not significant), and social distance difference score for white ($p < .05$) and Latino target groups ($p < .01$).

ditional racial stereotypes, and difference scores for perceived social class difference, racial stereotyping, and social distance for all respondent- and target-group pairings.

Perceived Economic Status Differences

Consider first the rich/poor trait and the corresponding perceived SES difference score, indicators of the degree to which respondents perceive racial-group differences in the economic status of groups. Unlike the other traits, the rich/poor item does not represent a personality or dispositional trait, nor does it ask about innate ability. Racial-group differences in economic status are a reality in American society; thus, perceptions of group poverty or affluence are often more objective in nature, based on media reports or scholarly research on economic inequality by race (Farley et al. 1994). In this case, it is not the knowledge that, at the aggregate level, blacks and Latinos are more likely to be poor and whites and Asians are more likely to be affluent that is problematic, since this is simply reality. Rather, it is when individuals are unable or unwilling to evaluate a racial-ethnic group member (particularly one from an economically disadvantaged group) according to his or her individual characteristics that this perception is problematic. Such a tendency is referred to as statistical discrimination because if, on average, blacks tend to be poor, then the odds are good that this categorization of a random black person will be accurate; such a judgment is said to be based on real, objective circumstances rather than prejudice. In either case, the consequences are potentially the same, to the extent that such perceptions are linked to aggregate-level residential outcomes. It is for these reasons that this particular trait is considered separately from the rest.

What stands out immediately is the high level of consistency across respondent categories in perceptions of racial-group economic status. Looking first at the mean trait-rating scores, all groups viewed blacks and Latinos as "tending to be poor" (they had the highest mean scores). Although the difference between the black and Latino scores tends to be small, all groups—except blacks and native-born Latinos—perceived Latinos as the most disadvantaged group; in practical terms, however, these differences are minor. There was an equally high level of consensus regarding the most affluent group. Except for native-born Asians, who viewed themselves as slightly better off, all respondent groups viewed whites as the most affluent of the four racial groups (the group with the lowest mean score on the trait-rating item). Asians were also generally perceived as affluent, with scores similar to those of whites.

Mean scores on the perceived SES difference score tell a similar story:

whites perceived very little difference between themselves and Asians (–.02), but viewed both blacks and Latinos as economically disadvantaged relative to their own group (1.57 and 1.73, respectively). Asians exhibited a similar pattern, perceiving little or no difference between themselves and whites (.11 and –.61 for native-born and foreign-born Asians, respectively), but comparatively large differences between themselves and both blacks and Latinos. (For native-born Asians, mean scores are 2.13 and 2.16, respectively; for foreign-born Asians, scores are 1.74 and 1.89, respectively.) Conversely, both blacks and Latinos—especially the foreign-born—tended to perceive both whites and Asians as economically advantaged compared to their own groups, while believing that they were economically no different from one another (scores are less than 1). Thus, Los Angeles County residents had a clear understanding of racial-group differences in economic status that was widely held and mutually agreed upon. In and of itself, this finding is not necessarily problematic, since how respondents perceive the poverty or affluence of groups reflects the actual economic circumstances of these groups in American society (the so-called kernel of truth in stereotypes). Again, it is when we rely too heavily on this information in evaluating individual members of groups that "tend to be poor"—particularly in the face of other, contradictory information—that our evaluations are negatively biased and illustrate negative racial stereotyping.

In-Group Racial Attitudes

Since respondents rated their own group in addition to each out-group, the results can also provide insights into how individuals rated their own group on each of the remaining dispositional traits. This is useful as an additional source of in-group perceptions aside from common fate identity and as a baseline for understanding respondents' perceptions of out-groups relative to attitudes about their own group, a subject to be taken up shortly.

Looking first at white respondents' views of themselves, the most noteworthy trend is their tendency to view themselves in a favorable light. For each of the four items gauging traditional racial stereotypes—particularly the English ability trait—scores are decidedly favorable; this is also clear from the mean overall rating value of 2.62. (Recall that low scores indicate favorable assessments of groups.) Whites also tended to perceive themselves as "easy to get along with." In fact, the only instance in which whites came close to viewing themselves unfavorably was on the "tends to discriminate against other groups" item, and even here, the mean score of 4.05 is very near the midpoint of the 1-to-7 scale and can be interpreted as a neutral response.

Asians' responses generally mirrored those of whites: both native- and foreign-born Asians tended to view themselves in favorable terms, with overall mean ratings of 2.63 and 2.87, respectively. Both groups of Asians rated themselves most favorably on the welfare dependence trait (1.88 and 2.36, respectively), which was stated as a *preference* for self-sufficiency versus a *preference* for reliance on public assistance. Across nativity-status categories, Asians perceived themselves as easy to get along with; their average in-group rating on this indicator of social distance was among the most favorable reported overall. And again like whites, the only instance of a score that approaches a negative in-group rating among Asians is a perceived tendency toward discrimination against other groups that native-born Asians saw in their own group (4.45), though their foreign-born counterparts did not.

With a mean absolute stereotype rating of 3.71, blacks also tended to see themselves in a positive light, though they were somewhat less inclined to do so than both whites and Asians. The difference in mean overall stereotyping score is due largely to blacks' tendency to view themselves less favorably on preference for welfare (4.04) and involvement in drugs and gangs (4.68), items on which average scores lean toward decidedly unfavorable perceptions. Blacks' most positive rating of themselves is on the "easy to get along with" (3.11) and English-language ability traits (2.71).

Unlike the generally favorable in-group perceptions of the groups discussed so far, Latinos tended to have the least-favorable in-group perceptions overall. Moreover, the native-born were more likely than immigrants to give negative in-group evaluations. The mean absolute stereotype rating scores are 4.28 for both the native- and foreign-born; among both groups of Latinos, three of the four stereotyping traits yield average scores greater than 4.00, with the most extreme instances being a belief that Latinos prefer welfare dependence (4.29 and 4.41, respectively) and the belief that they are involved with drugs and gangs (4.90 and 4.66, respectively). Not so surprisingly, foreign-born Latinos also rated themselves slightly negatively on average on the English ability trait (4.50).[5] Across nativity-status categories, Latinos were most likely to view themselves as easy to get along with. Finally, in a pattern similar to that of Asians, foreign-born Latinos generally perceived members of their group as tending to treat members of other groups equally, while their native-born counterparts were more likely to perceive themselves as tending to discriminate against other groups.

Out-Group Racial Attitudes

Table 4.2 also summarizes respondents' ratings of out-groups, both in absolute terms and relative to their own group. (Recall, however, that we have already discussed the rich/poor trait in the context of perceived economic disadvantage.) Immediately apparent is both the absence of extreme categorical ratings and a subtle overall tendency toward negative perceptions of racial-ethnic minority groups. Moreover, groups also exhibited a high degree of consensus regarding the rank-ordering of out-groups: whites, followed by Asians, consistently received the most favorable out-group ratings, while blacks and Latinos routinely received the most unfavorable ratings in both absolute and relative terms.

Whites' mean overall stereotype rating of Latinos strayed slightly into the negative end of the scale (4.31), while their beliefs about blacks were, on average, neutral. On the other hand, whites tended to evaluate Asians in clearly favorable terms, with a mean absolute rating of 3.05. The pattern of responses was similar for both native- and foreign-born Asians, who gave Latinos slightly more negative ratings than blacks compared to their clearly favorable ratings of whites. Blacks and Latinos were most likely to receive negative evaluations with respect to welfare preference and involvement in drugs and gangs; again, Latinos also tended to fare badly in terms of perceived English-language ability. Blacks and Latinos also tended to express negative stereotypes about each other. At 4.42, blacks had an average absolute stereotype rating of Latinos that was higher than for nearly all other out-groups (with the lone exception of foreign-born Asians). Similarly, both native- and foreign-born Latinos had overall stereotype ratings of blacks that exceeded those of all other out-groups. Both groups, however, had generally favorable ratings of both whites and Asians across the four stereotype traits.

In absolute terms, blacks and Asians were the groups most likely to be perceived as difficult to get along with. The only instance of clear, negative evaluations on this trait—scores exceeding 4—came from foreign-born Latinos and Asians rating blacks and from blacks and Latinos (both native- and foreign-born) rating Asians. Among nonwhites, interestingly, whites were the out-group rated easiest to get along with, compared to the average scores across respondent- and target-group pairings. On average, whites rated Asians the out-group easiest to get along with, with Latinos ranking a close second and blacks a slightly distant third. The pattern was similar among Asian respondents. Whites were rated as easiest to get along with, followed by Latinos and then blacks; in all instances, however, native-born Asians were more positive in their evaluations than the foreign-born were.

The last trait is the tendency for each of the racial groups to discriminate against members of other groups compared to a tendency to treat members of other groups equally. Overall, minority group members generally agreed that whites tend to discriminate against other groups; recall that this is the dimension on which whites rated themselves most negatively. There was also a high degree of consensus regarding a tendency to discriminate among Asians; in both instances, blacks led the way in negative evaluations, with mean values exceeding 5 for both groups. Minority perceptions of whites are not surprising given whites' dominant status and what is likely to be viewed as a constant stream of evidence confirming those perceptions—from media reporting of corporate behavior (Texaco, Denny's, or Abercrombie and Fitch) and heinous hate crimes (the 1999 murder of James Byrd Jr. in Jasper, Texas) to anecdotal reports from friends, family, and coworkers, to individuals' own experiences. As stated previously, perceptions of Asians as tending to be discriminatory in their treatment of other groups are probably tied to cultural differences in interaction styles. Such differences may be more salient for blacks, who have frequent interactions with the Asian merchants doing business in predominantly black neighborhoods and are aware of Asians' tendency toward extremely negative anti-black stereotypes. To some extent, these factors may also contribute to Latino perceptions of Asians as discriminatory.

It is important to move beyond these absolute evaluations, however, and examine group members' views of various out-groups relative to their own group. This may turn out to be the most important question for understanding the prevalence and strength of negative racial attitudes, since Americans are now too "politically correct" to speak of out-groups in clear, categorical terms (Bobo 2001). It is for this reason that difference scores are useful as indicators of the extent to which an out-group is perceived as similar to or different from one's own group (whether superior or inferior). We already know that LASUI respondents tended to express nontrivial levels of common fate identity and to hold generally favorable in-group attitudes. Was there a tendency to view all out-groups as similarly inferior to one's own group—a sign of ethnocentrism—or did variations emerge that were more consistent with a shared understanding of hierarchical relationships? The stereotype difference score and the social distance difference score provide comparative indicators of racial attitudes. Recall that scores range from –6 to +6; the stereotype difference score is based on the four traits representing traditional racial stereotypes, and the social distance difference score compares groups as easy or difficult to get along with socially. (The social class difference score is a similar measure that has already been considered.) The higher the score, the more unfavorably an out-group is perceived relative to one's own group, and a score of 0 indicates that there is no perceived difference between groups.

As has been the case throughout, whites and Asians exhibited similar patterns of out-group stereotyping relative to their own group. These two groups perceived extremely little difference between themselves—scores are near 0. Still, whites had a slight tendency to view themselves more favorably, while Asians were slightly inclined toward elevated evaluations of whites relative to their own group. Similarly, and consistent with their objective group statuses (at least socially if not economically), both groups tended to rate themselves as slightly superior to blacks and Latinos, with scores ranging from 1.32 to 1.41 for blacks and from 1.69 to 1.88 for Latinos. At first glance, the more negative rating that whites gave to Latinos compared to blacks is surprising: to varying degrees, both whites and Asians have histories of tense and negative relationships with blacks, the most recent being the civil unrest in L.A. in 1992. Upon closer inspection, however, it appears that the more negative rating of Latinos relative to blacks is a consequence of the English-language ability item. Owing to the large number of recent immigrants in the Latino population of Los Angeles, both whites and Asians gave Latinos a particularly negative rating on this item. When difference scores are recalculated without this item, blacks and Latinos have nearly equal scores and share the dubious distinction of being the most negatively rated out-group.

Blacks and Latinos also shared a tendency to see few differences between themselves; however, whatever differences were emphasized tended toward in-group favoritism. Like Asians, blacks perceived few stereotypic differences between themselves and whites; at the same time, they tended to favor whites over their own group on the traits of intelligence, welfare dependence, English ability, and involvement in drugs and gangs. Not only did Latinos view whites more favorably relative to their own group, but the perceived difference was larger among both the native- and (especially) the foreign-born. In this case, scores clearly favored whites: average stereotype difference values were –1.35 and –1.58 for the two groups, respectively. On average, Latinos also tended to stereotype Asians favorably compared to their own group. Blacks, on the other hand, tended to perceive virtually no difference between themselves and Asians in terms of racial stereotypes (.01).

Interestingly, whites generally perceived very little social distance between themselves and other groups, as evidenced by mean social distance difference scores that were well below 1. In each case, the actual interpretation of mean social distance difference scores was one of no perceived difference, since values for each target group were close to 0. Despite this, there is also evidence of a now-familiar rank-ordering of out-groups: whites' mean score for the black target group was 23 to 31 percent higher than the comparable scores for whites' perceived social distance from Latinos and Asians, respectively. Among Asian respondents, perceptions of social distance depended to some extent on nativity status. Foreign-born Asians were substantially more likely than their native-born counterparts to view blacks as difficult to get along with; this was also true, albeit to a lesser extent, of Asians' perceptions of both whites and Latinos. Irrespective of nativity status, however, Asians perceived whites as least socially distant from themselves, and blacks as most socially distant.

Blacks and Latinos expressed similar feelings of social distance from whites; both groups viewed whites as more difficult to get along with than members of their own groups (scores ranged from .83 to .95). These perceptions of relative social distance from whites paled in comparison, however, to the substantially greater degree of distance that blacks and Latinos perceived between themselves and Asians. Indeed, for both blacks and native-born Latinos, Asians ranked as the most socially distant out-group. This is not the case, however, for immigrant Latinos. Despite the perception of substantial social distance between themselves and Asians, they perceived the most distance between themselves and blacks, with an average social distance difference score of nearly 2. We cannot say for sure what accounts for these feelings; however, one explanation may be that recently arrived Latino migrants tend to settle in historically black communities; thus, this subset of Latinos is often in competition with blacks over neighborhood resources, which may be exacerbated by language and other cultural differences.

To what extent did respondents share common perceptions of out-groups? All out-groups agreed that whites tend to discriminate against members of other groups. Given whites' dominant-group status, this is not a surprising trend, but it does represent the only instance of a common, negative attitude toward this group. Conversely, blacks were consensually perceived as preferring welfare dependence over self-sufficiency, being involved with drugs and gangs, and tending to discriminate against others. Similarly, there was general out-group consensus that Latinos tend to speak English poorly and to be involved with drugs and gangs, and near-consensus regarding a perceived tendency in Latinos to discriminate against others (whites, blacks, and native-born Asians) and to prefer welfare dependence over self-sufficiency (blacks and both native- and foreign-born Asians). Asians, like whites, were universally perceived as tending to discriminate against others, with all out-groups giving them an unfavorable rating on this trait. Similarly, both blacks and Latinos tended to perceive Asians as slightly difficult to get along with. And unlike with Latinos, there was no consensus regarding Asians' English-language skills: whites and foreign-born Latinos tended to rate Asians favorably on this trait, while blacks and native-born Latinos rated Asians negatively on average.

To illustrate trends in racial stereotyping and social distance more clearly, figures 4.1 and 4.2 show the percentage of each respondent racial

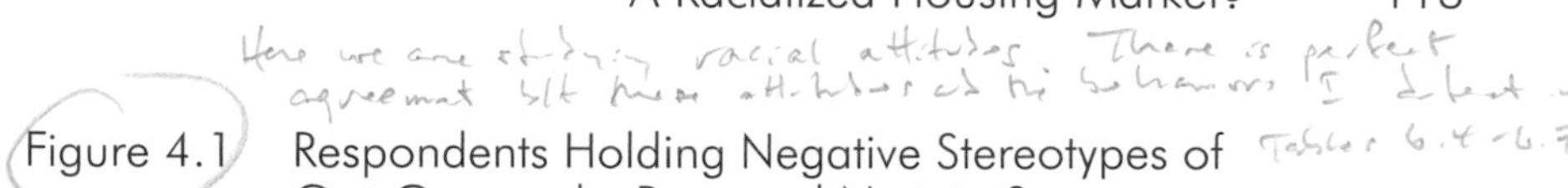

Figure 4.1 Respondents Holding Negative Stereotypes of Out-Groups, by Race and Nativity Status

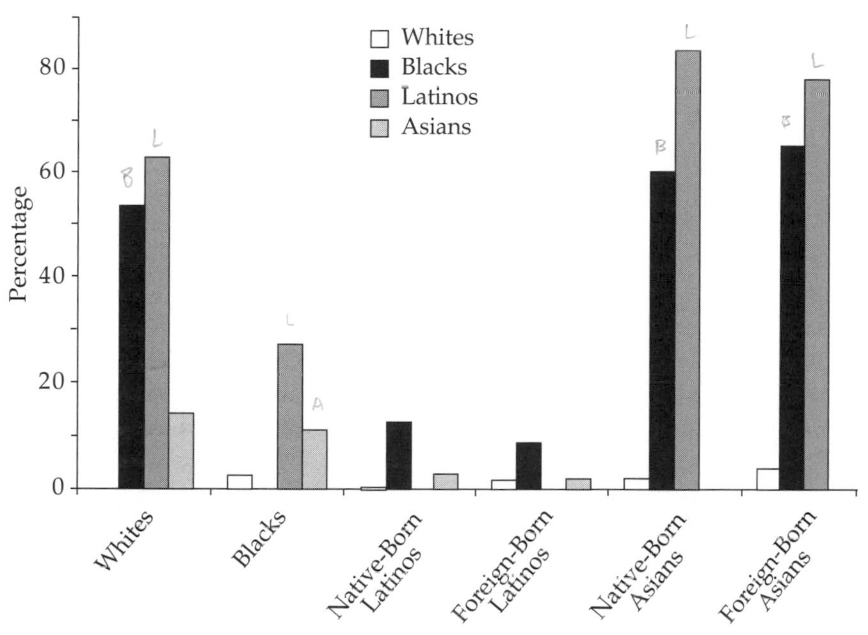

Source: Author's compilation.
Notes: Measures are stereotype difference scores greater than 1.00. $p < .001$ for all except negative stereotyping of whites ($p < .01$).

and nativity-status category reporting negative stereotypes and feelings of social distance across target groups (difference scores greater than 1). What is probably most remarkable about the results reported in these two figures is that Asians—not whites—emerge as the group most likely to adhere to negative stereotypes of blacks and Latinos. Just over 60 percent of native-born Asians and almost two-thirds of their foreign-born counterparts held negative stereotypes of blacks. Both groups of Asians were even more likely to view Latinos negatively compared to their own group. Conversely, fewer than 5 percent of both Asian categories expressed negative stereotypes of whites.

Especially compared to Asians, whites' rates of anti-black and anti-Latino stereotyping painted a more optimistic picture of dominant-group racial attitudes. In general terms, whites and Asians were similar in their

Figure 4.2 Respondents Perceiving Social Distance Between Their Own Group and Various Out-Groups, by Race and Nativity Status

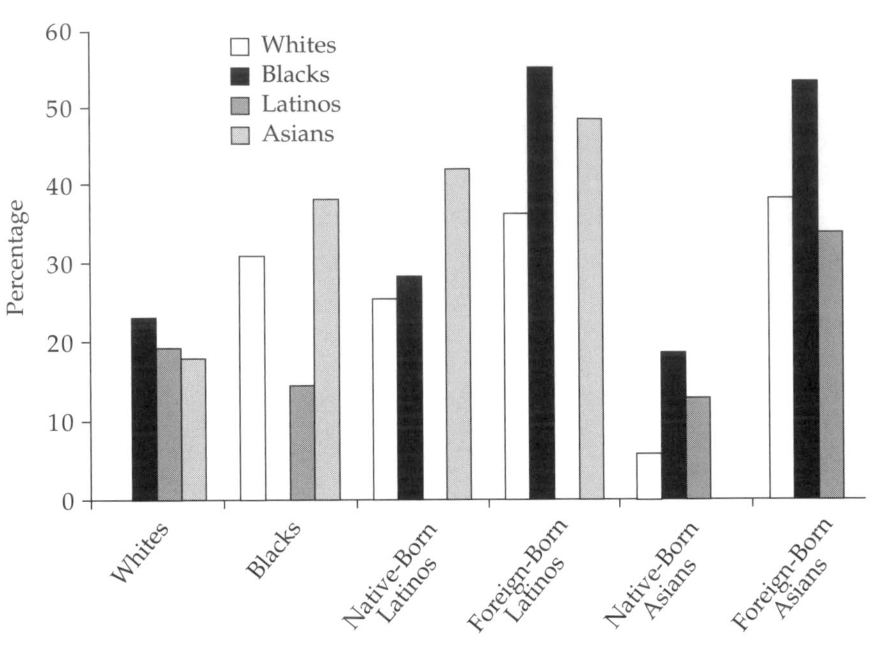

Source: Author's compilation.
Notes: Measures are social distance difference scores greater than 1.00. p < .001 for all except social distance from whites (p < .05).

ratings of out-groups relative to themselves. Like Asians, a clear majority of whites' stereotype difference scores reflected negative views of both blacks (54 percent) and Latinos (63 percent); still, whites were significantly less likely to hold negative views of these two groups than Asians were. Again, keep in mind that without the English ability item, blacks and Latinos were equally likely to be negatively stereotyped by whites and that the English ability item may have been viewed differently (and less pejoratively) in relation to Latinos than it was in reference to blacks. Whites were least likely to adhere to negative stereotypes of Asians—fewer than 15 percent of whites did so. Still, whites were two to five times more likely to adhere to negative stereotypes of Asians than vice versa.

Blacks and Latinos were least likely to adhere to negative stereotypes across target groups; nevertheless, both groups maintained a pattern that suggests a commonly accepted rank-ordering of groups: each was most likely to stereotype the other negatively, and least likely to do so with whites. (Again, bear in mind that these are difference scores, which measure stereotypes of target groups in relation to stereotypes of one's own group.) Similarly, minute percentages of both groups held anti-white stereotypes (between 2.5 and 4 percent). Here again, however, blacks were between three and five times more likely than either category of Latinos to express negative stereotypes of Asians. Finally, contrary to the pattern found among Asian respondents, native-born Latinos were more likely than their foreign-born counterparts to hold clearly negative stereotypes of out-groups.[6]

Figure 4.2 summarizes social distance difference scores greater than 1.00 (clearly negative ratings) across respondent racial and nativity-status categories and target-group categories. It is again encouraging to see that, consistent with the results presented in table 4.2, whites generally did not perceive a great deal of social distance between themselves and nonwhite groups. Overall, it appears that immigrants—both Asian and Latino—were most likely to perceive the various out-groups as difficult to get along with relative to their own group. A comparison of scores by length of time in the United States (not shown here) suggests that increasing acculturation decreases feelings of social distance, as we might expect. In all other ways, patterns of perceived social distance are consistent with those presented in table 4.2.

In sum, the racial stereotypes and related racial attitudes of Los Angeles County adults—the general consensus among groups regarding commonly held stereotypes of specific groups and the rank-ordering of out-groups, in both absolute and relative terms—appear to reflect both the relative positioning of groups in the larger social structure and American racial ideology (Bobo and Zubrinsky 1996; Eagly and Steffen 1984; Sigelman and Welch 1993; Jackman 1994). Though not large in magnitude, it is clear that these attitudes and perceptions vary in fairly predictable ways in terms of the negative traits associated with particular groups. Together, patterns of perceived social class disadvantage, racial stereotypes, and social distance among Los Angeles County residents are largely consistent with national trends and hint at potential barriers to positive intergroup relations and increased residential contact.

At the same time, however, variations in group socioeconomic resources, culture, and historical circumstances may leave some groups better equipped than others to challenge negative views about their group (Jackman and Senter 1983). Chinese-origin Asians may present the best example of this. Economically, this group tends to do well, and as with all

Asian groups, increasing socioeconomic status brings with it improved residential outcomes. Prior research suggests a cultural orientation that stresses homeownership. And finally, Chinese-origin Asians find themselves benefiting from the historical circumstance that Americans (particularly whites) tend to stereotype Asians as "model minorities" and thus direct lower levels of negative attitudes at this group.

Although there is still cause for concern regarding the clear majority of whites who adhere to anti-black and/or anti-Latino stereotypes, a substantial minority of whites—nearly one-third—perceive virtually no difference between themselves and these groups.[7] This could bode well for the future, inasmuch as it suggests that intergroup relations between the dominant group and the two groups at the bottom of the social and economic hierarchies may be open to improvement. Potentially more troubling are the substantially higher rates of anti-black and anti-Latino stereotyping found among Asians combined with the greater propensity for negative stereotyping found among the foreign-born (both Asian and Latino).

BELIEFS ABOUT THE PREVALENCE OF DISCRIMINATION

In addition to patterns of racial stereotyping—or perhaps in part *because* of persisting racial stereotypes—whites and nonwhites continue to hold decidedly different opinions about the prevalence of racial discrimination. Whites acknowledge some discrimination but tend to minimize its present-day importance, suggesting that it is largely the domain of "a few bad apples." Moreover, whites are inclined to perceive the inability of some blacks and other minority groups to succeed and get ahead as a consequence of their lack of motivation or other cultural deficiencies. Specifically, only 20 to 25 percent of whites believe that blacks and Latinos face "a lot" of employment discrimination, and even fewer—not even 10 percent—believe that this is true for Asians (Bobo 2001, 281–82).

On the other hand, blacks, Latinos, and, to a much smaller degree, Asians tend to view racial discrimination as systematic, pervasive, and consequently deeply implicated in persisting racial inequality. Fully 70 percent of blacks and 60 percent of Latinos believe this to be the case regarding their own group's structural barriers, compared to fewer than 10 percent of Asians (Bobo 2001; Bobo and Suh 2000).[8]

LASUI respondents' beliefs about the prevalence of housing market discrimination were consistent with these trends. Respondents were asked how often blacks, Latinos, and Asians miss out on good housing because (1) individual whites will not rent or sell to them, (2) real estate agents will not show or sell homes in white areas to them, and/or (3) banks and lenders will not lend money to them. Figure 4.3 shows the percentage of respondents who indicated that a target group faces one or more of these barriers "sometimes" or "very often." To balance budget constraints and an interest in gathering the best intergroup relations data possible, the LASUI researchers employed a split-ballot format in which one-third of each respondent racial category was randomly assigned a target group to consider; though this sample design allows for generalization to the full sample, sample sizes for native-born Latinos and Asians were too small to separate these groups by nativity status. When appropriate, important nativity-status distinctions are considered.

Looking first at the overall pattern of responses, note the high level of consensus regarding which groups are most likely to face housing market barriers. Across respondent racial categories, blacks were perceived as the group most likely to face each of the three types of barriers, followed by Latinos; Asians were a distant third. Other interesting patterns emerge when the focus is on racial-group differences in responses to these items. Among whites (the left-most and lightest bar in each cluster), clear or near majorities believed that blacks and Latinos face all three types of housing discrimination, while a much smaller percentage (between 20 and 42 percent, depending on the particular barrier) believed this to be true for Asians. Once again, then, a clear rank-ordering of target groups is evident. Both blacks and Latinos exhibited a similar pattern: consistent with prior research, these groups were much more likely to perceive significant housing market barriers of all types. Conversely, Asians were least likely to sense the presence of significant housing market discrimination, especially in regard to their own housing market experiences.

Note too that while all groups were more inclined to agree that individual whites discriminate—consistent with the "few bad apples" hypothesis—within-respondent-group disparities in perceptions of each type of discrimination were most stark for whites and Asians. Specifically, for these two groups bad behavior by individual whites was the most prevalent barrier to good housing: both groups were between 12 and 20 percent less likely to believe that real estate and lending discrimination are meaningful housing market barriers for minority home-seekers. These patterns persisted across target groups. This tendency among whites to privilege the "few bad apples" explanation over institutional-level discrimination is consistent with national trends (Bobo 2001); compared to the much lower percentage of Asians who perceived any kind of housing market barriers, however, Los Angeles–area whites once again appeared quite liberal in their thinking on this issue.

As expected, blacks and Latinos in Los Angeles saw housing market

Figure 4.3 Perception That Blacks, Latinos, and Asians Face Various Housing Market Barriers "Sometimes" or "Very Often," by Respondent Race: Summary Statistics

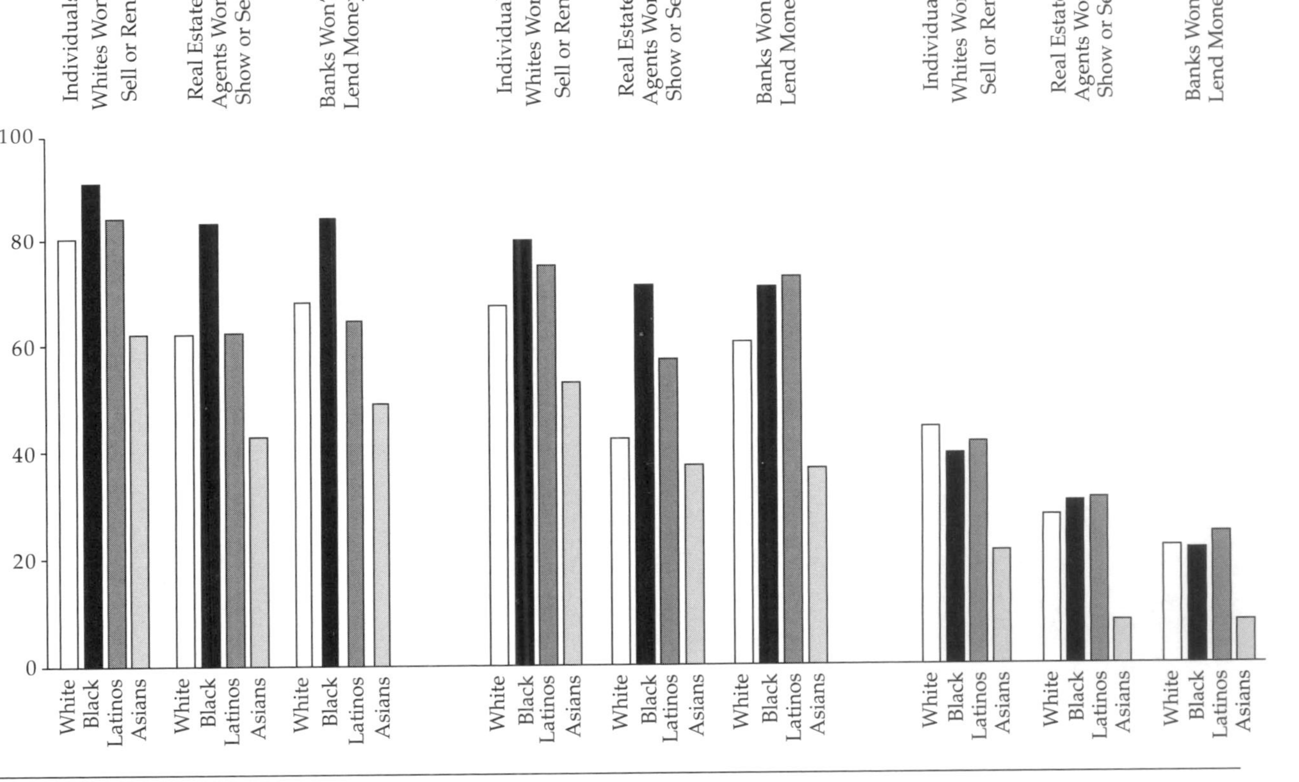

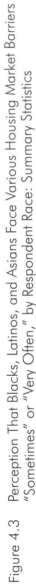

Source: Author's compilation.

Notes: For black target group, $p < .001$ for individual whites won't sell or rent and banks won't lend money; $p < .01$ for real estate agents won't show or sell. For Latino target group, $p < .001$ except for individual whites won't sell or rent ($p < .01$). For Asian target group, $p < .001$ for individual whites won't sell or rent; $p < .01$ for real estate agents won't show or sell; $p < .05$ for banks won't lend money.

discrimination as a more substantial and pervasive obstacle to obtaining housing—for their own group, for one another, and for Asians—than either whites or Asians did. This was most true for blacks, who were more likely to believe that Latinos face substantial barriers than Latinos themselves were. Thus, when considering their own experiences, between 80 and 90 percent of blacks believed that they face discriminatory barriers at least sometimes, compared with 56 to 74 percent of Latinos reflecting on their housing market experiences.

These patterns are further highlighted by an index item summarized in table 4.3 for all respondent- and target-group pairings. This measure captures respondents' beliefs about the prevalence of housing market discrimination across all three domains—individual whites, real estate agents, and banks—for each target group. Values are simply the average of responses to the three items; they range from 1 (the target group "almost never" experiences any discrimination) to 4 (the target group experiences all three types of barriers "very often").[9] Mean values reinforce the patterns presented in figure 4.3 and illustrate the high degree of consensus regarding beliefs about the existence of housing market barriers and about which groups are most (and least) likely to face one or more barriers among Los Angeles County residents. Finally, nativity-status comparisons indicate that foreign-born Asians and Latinos tended to perceive less housing market discrimination across target groups. The single ex-

Table 4.3 Overall Belief That Blacks, Latinos, and Asians Face Housing Market Barriers, by Respondent Race: Summary Statistics

	Whites	Blacks	Latinos	Asians
Housing market barriers faced by:				
Blacks	2.76	3.20†††	2.79	2.40††
Latinos	2.51	2.87†††	2.81††	2.23†
Asians	2.01	2.14	2.14	1.74††

Source: Author's compilation.

Notes: Comparisons are by respondent race, within target group. Overall index measure is the average of the three individual items. Scores range from 1 (almost never) to 4 (very often). Cronbach's alpha is .79 for the black and Latino target groups and .81 for the Asian target group.

*** $p < .001$; where mean values differ significantly from whites, ††† $p < .001$, †† $p < .01$, and † $p < .05$

ception is foreign-born Latinos, who perceived slightly more discrimination against their own group than their native-born counterparts did; in general, however, nativity-status differences were slight.[10]

In a related question, all LASUI respondents were asked whether they themselves had experienced discrimination while trying to rent or purchase a home; this question tapped a slightly different dimension of beliefs about the prevalence of racial discrimination in housing, focusing on the respondent's own personal experience of discrimination rather than on his or her idea of what was likely to happen to group members generally. The results are summarized in figure 4.4. Most striking is that blacks were three to five times more likely than any other group to report having experienced housing market discrimination during their own housing search (30.67 percent, $p < .001$). Latinos were a very distant second, with just under 10 percent of both the native- and foreign-born indicating that they had experienced housing market discrimination. Consistent with the patterns of response detailed earlier, Asians were least likely to report personal experiences of housing discrimination, and there were no meaningful nativity-status differences between Asians or Latinos. Whites were in between Latinos and Asians, with roughly 8 percent stating that they had been victims of housing market discrimination.

Finally, contrary to suggestions that minority-group members—particularly blacks—are paranoid or oversensitive, recent studies of the Los Angeles–area housing and lending markets suggest that blacks may be justified in their concerns and that both Latinos and Asians may not be concerned enough. Results from the 2000 Housing Discrimination Study show that both blacks and Latinos continue to face substantial mistreatment and that Chinese and Korean home-seekers face unfavorable treatment similar to the experiences of blacks and Latinos (Turner et al. 2002). Moreover, another study concludes that, compared to whites, blacks are more than twice as likely to be denied a conventional mortgage loan, and Latinos more than one and a half times as likely (ACORN 2003).

The greater tendency for whites to believe that racial discrimination in housing (especially the institutional variety) is a thing of the past leads easily to a tendency to blame minority-group disadvantage on their own supposed cultural deficiencies, a line of argument that often invokes negative racial stereotypes. Thus, if African Americans and Latinos are inadequately prepared for college admission relative to whites and Asians (for example, by scoring lower on college entrance exams, earning lower grade point averages, and taking fewer advanced placement courses), whites are more inclined to believe that these groups lacked motivation or did not value education. On the other hand, blacks, Lati-

Figure 4.4 The Belief Among LASUI Respondents That They Experienced Housing Market Discrimination, by Respondent Race and Nativity Status

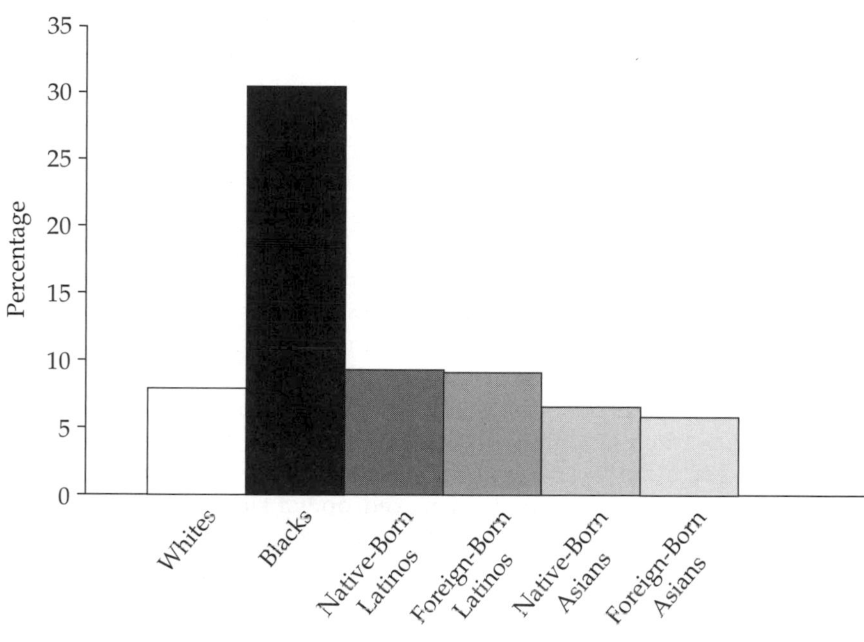

Source: Author's compilation.
Notes: $p < .001$.

nos, and, to a far lesser extent, Asians are more inclined to invoke explanations rooted in structural barriers, such as the persistence of racial discrimination in society or a lack of opportunity to receive a good education (Bobo 2001).

Another natural outgrowth of persisting antiminority stereotypes and clear-cut differences in opinions about racial discrimination and inequality is their impact on political attitudes, including support for progressive social policies like affirmative action. James Kluegel and Elliot Smith (1982, 1986) conclude, for instance, that the more whites' explanations for inequality are rooted in cultural or volitional deficiencies rather than structural barriers, the less likely they are to support government intervention, such as affirmative action. Thus, whites' support for affirmative action depends on the type of policy proposed: those policies intended to increase the human capital attributes of disadvantaged groups garner more support than those that extend preferential treatment (Bobo and Kluegel 1993; Bobo and Smith 1994; Kluegel and Smith 1986; Lipset and Schneider 1978; Schuman et al. 1997). Alternatively, blacks, Latinos, and, to a lesser degree, Asians express greater support for a variety of affirmative action policies, either because they represent compensation for past wrongs or because they are viewed as necessary strategies for combating present-day discrimination (Bobo and Johnson 2000; Schuman et al. 1997).[11] For all groups, however, support for progressive social policies is also influenced by the degree to which targeted groups are perceived to be competitive threats to their own economic and political well-being (Bobo and Johnson 2000)—another racial attitude with implications for neighborhood outcomes.

PERCEIVED RACIAL GROUP COMPETITION

Even as racial-ethnic diversity is part of what makes Los Angeles such a fascinating place for studying racial residential segregation, its spread and the speed with which it has increased may foster feelings of group-level competition over coveted social resources like jobs and political influence. By extension, the perception of particular out-groups as competitive threats to one's own status (or that of one's group) may give rise to race-based antagonism and conflict that "colors" other racial attitudes, particularly preferences for racially integrated neighborhoods. In short, prejudice is more than simple out-group hostility; it also animates the collective defense of a relative group position and the perceived status advantages associated with that position (Blumer 1958; Bobo 1999; Bobo and Kluegel 1996; Charles 2000a).

Quite often, feelings of group competition are expressed in zero-sum terms; for instance, LASUI respondents were asked how much they agreed with the assertions that "more good jobs for (blacks/Latinos/Asians) mean fewer good jobs for [the respondent's racial group]" and that "the more political influence (blacks/Latinos/Asians) have in local politics, the less influence [the respondent's racial group] will have in local politics." Scores on each item ranged from 0 ("strongly disagree") to 4 ("strongly agree"); to assess the overall intensity of feelings of group threat, these items are summed and presented as an index of racial-group competition for each target-group.[12] These questions employed a three-way split-ballot experiment comparable to the one used in the prevalence-of-discrimination items. The percentage of respondents expressing either general or strong agreement with each statement, organized by re-

Table 4.4 Perceptions of Blacks, Latinos, and Asians as Competitive Threats to Economic Opportunities and Political Influence, by Respondent Race and Nativity Status: Summary Statistics

Target Group	Whites	Blacks	Native-Born Latinos	Foreign-Born Latinos	Native-Born Asians	Foreign-Born Asians
Blacks						
Job threat	26.61%	—	27.58%	30.57%	13.96%	25.96%
Political threat	30.47	—	26.46	42.10	11.59	36.34
Mean overall threat	3.51	—	3.63	4.51†††	2.66	3.81
Latinos						
Job threat	26.59%	52.37%	—	—	10.13%	32.20%
Political threat	34.56	44.56	—	—	18.68	48.01
Mean overall threat	3.67	4.65†††	—	—	2.35	4.26†
Asians						
Job threat	31.89%	63.67%	41.99%	49.92%	—	—
Political threat	31.99	54.10	46.88	58.20	—	—
Mean overall threat	3.74	5.31†††	4.32	6.02†††	—	—

Source: Author's compilation.
Notes: Percentages are for respondents reporting that they "generally" or "strongly" agreed that the group posed a threat. Mean overall threat is the combined average of respondents' scores on individual items, measured as a 1–5 scale where 1 indicates no perceived threat, 5 indicates strong perceived threat, and 3 is a neutral category. Cronbach's alpha is .78 for blacks, .76 for Latinos, and .80 for Asians. For percentages, $p < .001$ except black political threat ($p < .01$). For mean overall threat values significantly different from whites, ††† $p < .001$, †† $p < .01$, and † $p < .05$.

spondent race and nativity status and target-group race, is presented in table 4.4; the bottom row of each target-group block reports a mean overall threat index score, which is the average of responses to both items.

In general, perceptions of racial-group competition were moderate to substantial, ranging from 24 to 64 percent of respondents depending on respondent race, target-group race, and type of threat. Whites, interestingly, tended to express the lowest levels of perceived racial-group competition and appeared slightly more concerned about a loss of political influence than about shrinking economic opportunities. And though it appears that whites viewed Asians as more of a threat than either blacks or Latinos, target-group differences on the overall threat measures are not statistically significant for white respondents. These patterns are consistent with whites' dominant-group status: despite the changing demographic composition of Los Angeles—now a "majority-minority" city—whites appear fairly confident in their ability to maintain their relative status advantages, both economic and political.

Blacks stood out as being most concerned about their economic opportunities. Just over half of blacks perceived Latinos as economic threats; nearly two-thirds of blacks viewed Asians as such. Blacks also expressed serious concern about political competition from other groups: nearly 45 percent said that Latinos pose a political threat, and 54 percent said that Asians threaten their own group's local political power. Heightened concerns regarding economic opportunities and, to a slightly lesser extent, local political influence are consistent with blacks' lower average economic status (especially relative to whites), their beliefs about the prevalence of racial discrimination, and the common belief that continued immigration threatens their economic opportunities and political power. The recent election of Antonio Villaraigosa as mayor of Los Angeles—the first Latino mayor in over a century—after a close primary victory over the African American candidate Bernard Parks no doubt has fueled blacks' concerns about loss of political power.

Perceptions of racial-group competition among Latinos and Asians vary substantially by nativity status. As we might expect, the foreign-born of both groups expressed greater perceived vulnerability compared to their native-born counterparts, whether the issue was economic or political; at times, these differences were striking. Overall, both native- and foreign-born Latinos perceived blacks as a greater competitive threat than either whites or Asians did; like blacks, however, all Latinos perceived Asians as the bigger threat, both economically and especially politically. Native-born Latinos, moreover, did not differ significantly from whites in their overall perceptions of out-groups as competitive threats; however, foreign-born Latinos perceived both blacks and Asians as significantly bigger threats than whites did. That foreign-born Latinos feel more threatened by other racial groups may reflect not only their considerably lower SES levels and English-language proficiency relative to other groups but also the vulnerability they experience from immigration flows and methods of entry that set them up for labor market exploitation and exclude them from formal politics.

Finally, differences between native- and foreign-born Asians are particularly striking. First, native-born Asians expressed the absolute lowest levels of perceived racial competition. The percentage of those who agreed that other groups pose a threat to their own position exceeded 15 percent in only one instance—roughly 19 percent thought that Latinos threaten their political influence. Feelings of competitive threat from blacks were especially low among native-born Asians, and for both target groups levels of overall threat were lower but not significantly different from those of whites. Foreign-born Asians expressed marginally more concern about competitive threat from Latinos than whites did, as well as roughly equivalent levels of competition from blacks. Overall, Asians' patterns of perceived racial-group competition were fairly consistent with the relatively advantaged position of this group, especially compared to blacks and Latinos.

NEIGHBORHOOD RACIAL COMPOSITION PREFERENCES

A final troubling trend in racial attitudes is particularly relevant to discussions of residential segregation by race and the likelihood of increasing and sustaining residential integration: despite some improvement, substantial differences remain in both the meaning and preferred levels of racial integration across racial categories. For many whites, a racially integrated neighborhood is one that is majority-white. To put it plainly, whites are *willing* to live with a small number of blacks, Latinos, and/or Asians but *prefer* to live in predominantly same-race neighborhoods. Blacks, Latinos, and Asians, on the other hand, all prefer substantially more racial integration and are more comfortable than whites as numerical minorities. Still, each group's preference for same-race neighbors exceeds whites' preferences for integration. And consistent with the patterns associated with the various racial attitudes examined to this point, patterns of neighborhood racial composition preferences follow a now-predictable racial hierarchy: whites are always the most preferred out-group and blacks the least preferred; Asians and Latinos, in that order, are located in between these two extremes (Bobo 2001; Bobo and Zubrinsky 1996; Charles 2000a, 2001b; Farley et al. 1978, 1993).

An important task in the development of the LASUI project was determining how to tap attitudes toward residential integration in a truly multiracial-multiethnic environment. To accomplish this goal, we presented all respondents with a blank neighborhood showcard (similar to figure 4.5) and asked them to specify the racial composition of their ideal neighborhood:

> Now I'd like you to imagine an ideal neighborhood that had the ethnic and racial mix you, personally, would feel most comfortable in. Here is a blank neighborhood card. . . . Using the letters A for Asian, B for Black, H for Hispanic, and W for White, please put a letter in each of these houses to represent your ideal neighborhood, where you would most like to live. Please be sure to fill in all of the houses.

Figure 4.5 Multiethnic Neighborhood Experiment Showcard

Source: 1993–94 Los Angeles Survey of Urban Inequality.

The measures of neighborhood racial composition preferences presented here—percentage white, percentage black, and so on—are simply the sum of each group represented on a respondent's completed card, divided by the total number of houses (including the respondent's own), and then multiplied by 100.

Table 4.5 offers summary information for all respondent- and target-group pairings. The first row of each target-group panel provides the mean percentage of that group in each respondent's ideal neighborhood, and the second row provides the percentage in each respondent category who preferred a neighborhood without any target-group members. For ease of interpretation and comparison, preferences for same-race neighbors are located in the bottom panel of the table; the first row of the panel shows the mean percentage of same-race neighbors, and the second row is the percentage in each respondent category who preferred an entirely same-race neighborhood.[13]

This experiment reveals patterns of preferences that reflect decidedly more aversion to integration among Los Angeles–area residents than was previously thought, while at the same time suggesting that they would be more tolerant of greater interracial residential contact than currently exists.[14] All of the racial and nativity-status groups tended to prefer substantially integrated neighborhoods, but ones in which in-group representation always exceeded that of any single out-group. A number of other distinct patterns are also apparent. First, though all groups preferred neighborhoods dominated by coethnics, this preference was strongest for whites: their average ideal neighborhood was over half same-race (53 percent). Following just behind whites, however, were foreign-born Latinos and foreign-born Asians, whose mean same-race preferences neared the 50 percent mark (48 percent and 46 percent, respectively). The ideal neighborhoods of blacks and native-born Latinos were just over 42 percent same-race; native-born Asians appeared least inter-

Table 4.5 Neighborhood Racial Composition Preferences, by Respondent and Target-Group Race: Summary Statistics

Target-Group Race	Whites	Blacks	Native-Born Latinos	Foreign-Born Latinos	Native-Born Asians	Foreign-Born Asians
White neighbors						
Mean percentage	—	21.52%	26.18%	24.50%	27.52%	30.62%
No whites	—	8.71	5.67	15.81	0.74	8.34
Black neighbors						
Mean percentage	14.91%	—	15.39	11.74	16.29	9.38
No blacks	20.04	—	18.97	38.07	14.83	44.44
Latino neighbors						
Mean percentage	15.82	19.83	—	—	19.76	13.54
No Latinos	18.46	9.36	—	—	8.76	29.38
Asian neighbors						
Mean percentage	16.29	16.25	16.05	15.71	—	—
No Asians	17.78	16.78	18.61	25.12	—	—
Same-race neighbors						
Mean percentage	52.97	42.39	42.37	48.04	36.43	46.46
All same-race	12.35	3.02	3.84	8.39	0.74	8.13

Source: Author's compilation.
Notes: $p < .001$.

ested in coethnic neighborhoods, expressing a preference for an average ideal neighborhood that was just over one-third same-race. Whites were also the group most likely to prefer entirely same-race neighborhoods (12 percent)—a rate three to four times that of native-born Latinos (4 percent) and African Americans (3 percent) and more than sixteen times that of native-born Asians (1 percent). Indeed, only the foreign-born groups came close to having same-race preferences similar to those of whites, and their preference for same-race neighbors may have had more to do with an immigrant-specific need for the comfort and familiarity of compatriots than with anti-out-group sentiments.

Another noteworthy pattern is that blacks were always the least preferred out-group neighbors. This is seen in two ways. First, blacks were the most likely to be completely excluded from the ideal neighborhoods of other groups. One-fifth of whites and nearly as many native-born Latinos preferred neighborhoods with no black households; native-born Asians were least likely to exclude blacks from their ideal neighborhoods, yet nearly 15 percent of this group would completely avoid blacks as neighbors. Still, this is not nearly as startling as the preferences of foreign-born Latinos and Asians: 38 percent of the former and 44 percent of the latter preferred neighborhoods without a single black neighbor. Latinos also suffered a great deal of exclusion by whites and especially by foreign-born Asians: more than 18 percent of the former and 29 percent of the latter excluded this group entirely, compared to approximately 9 percent of both blacks and native-born Asians. Despite their status as least preferred neighbors, blacks were among the most open to integration with all other groups, rivaled only by native-born Asians. Finally, all non-white groups—both native- and foreign-born—preferred integration with whites to other-race minorities.[15]

Again, it is important to highlight the optimistic elements of these results: in absolute terms, and at least relative to actual levels of racial residential segregation, the patterns of preferences detailed here suggest substantial openness to residential integration across racial and nativity-status categories.[16] Respondents did not give unreflective pro-integration responses. It is immediately apparent that members of each racial and nativity-status group reacted differently to each potential out-group neighbor. Indeed, the clear-cut racial rank-ordering of out-groups as potential neighbors and the consensus across groups regarding the top (whites) and bottom (blacks) positions easily outweighed much of the optimism generated by the high degree of openness to integration expressed by LASUI respondents.

This is especially true for foreign-born respondents, who expressed remarkably high aversion to residential contact with blacks and with one another. There are at least two ways to interpret patterns of minority-group exclusion among foreign-born Latinos and Asians. One possibility is that the globalized media have reinforced negative attitudes, particularly about blacks, among immigrants who come to the United States; an alternative interpretation is that immigrants are a self-selected group of extremely mobility-conscious individuals assimilating into a racially stratified environment. Focused on attaining their own American Dream, these individuals are motivated to put as much distance as possible between themselves and the group at the bottom of the status hierarchy. In fact, both of these mechanisms may be at play, with the former intensifying the expression of the latter.

Further complicating the interpretation of these results is the much more subtle rank-ordering of groups by white respondents, whose means for black, Latino, and Asian neighbors and rates of complete exclusion of these groups do not differ very much, especially when compared to the means and exclusion rates of foreign-born respondents. Indeed, we could interpret these results much more optimistically, minimally suggesting that whites perceive all out-groups similarly—that is, as an undifferentiated mass. Further investigation of whites' preferences (analysis not shown here) adds evidence of the salience of race among whites regarding their preferences for neighborhood racial integration. Across target groups, the majority of whites would have no more than 20 percent of any target group in their ideal neighborhood. Still, nearly one-quarter of whites preferred a neighborhood that was more than 20 percent Latino or Asian, compared to fewer than one-fifth of whites having an ideal neighborhood that was over 20 percent black. When these results are put into the context of whites' racial attitudes more broadly, then, it is more difficult to conclude that all out-groups are perceived similarly by whites.

The awareness of a widely shared perception of blacks as the least desirable neighbors may be more consequential for individual housing choices and location than a deeply held *personal* aversion. For example, blacks (and increasingly Latinos) may be discouraged from moving into predominantly white neighborhoods because they want to avoid negative reactions from even just a few potentially hostile white residents, who are not necessarily easy to distinguish from their less intolerant neighbors. Minimally, and however subtly or obviously, this hierarchical pattern of preferences closely mirrors the findings from more objective measures of residential segregation by race and is consistent with each group's social and economic position in contemporary American society (Bobo and Zubrinsky 1996; Farley 1996a; Jaynes and Williams 1989; Massey and Denton 1993). In short, these bivariate patterns offer clear evidence that race is consequential for residential decisionmaking. But exactly *how* does race matter?

There is good reason to believe that the "bad news" trends detailed in this chapter are driving forces in neighborhood racial composition preferences. A growing body of research points to the direct effects of negative racial stereotypes on preferences for integration. As expected, the more negatively a particular racial group is perceived, the less desirable members of that group are as potential neighbors, and this is especially true for whites' perceptions. Though limited, some evidence also indicates that when whites perceive blacks as competitive threats, they also view blacks as less desirable neighbors (Timberlake 2000). Whites' perceptions of neighborhood desirability also appear to be influenced by racial composition: as the number of minorities in a neighborhood increases, it becomes increasingly undesirable to whites, particularly if the minority residents are black or Latino. This is true even in "structurally strong" neighborhoods—safe, middle-class or affluent neighborhoods of owner-occupied houses with high property values (Ellen 2000). For minority-group members, neighborhood desirability is tied to their perceptions of racial tolerance: understandably, those communities perceived by minorities as hostile toward them are less desirable than those they perceive as welcoming. As a result, minority-group members tend to find integrated neighborhoods more attractive and to view overwhelmingly white neighborhoods with suspicion or trepidation (Charles 2001b; Farley et al. 1993; Krysan and Farley 2002; Zubrinsky and Bobo 1996).

Various racial attitudes have been documented here: the persistent adherence to negative racial stereotypes, particularly but not exclusively among whites; often severely divergent views regarding perceptions (and experiences) of discrimination; perceptions of racial-group competition for valued societal resources; and preferences for residential integration with various out-groups. Trends in these attitudes paint a clear picture of a well-defined, widely understood racial rank-ordering of groups in which, as in society more generally, whites are clearly situated at the top, in the most advantaged position, while blacks are found just as obviously at the bottom, in the most disadvantaged position. Asians and Latinos are located in between these two extremes, with Asians faring more like whites and Latinos having more in common with blacks. This ordering of groups and the accompanying status advantages or disadvantages contribute to interracial interactions "rife with the potential for missteps, misunderstanding, and insult" and a fair amount of mistrust (Bobo 2001, 279); that mistrust creates a sense of interracial awkwardness that no doubt factors into our preferences about where we live, who lives around us, and how we search for housing. The following chapter confronts these issues more directly by examining the degree to which the various racial attitudes considered to this point are implicated in our preferences for racial residential contact.

Chapter Five | From Racial Attitudes to Neighborhood Racial Composition Preferences

A VARIETY OF factors shape residential decisionmaking: cost and affordability, the quality of the housing stock, preferences for particular dwelling amenities, proximity to work or other important destinations, stage in the life course, the quality of the public schools (Ellen 2000; Galster 1988). Consequently, aggregate-level residential outcomes are the result of a multitude of individual-level attitudes and behaviors. In analyses of patterns of *racial* residential preferences, however, three hypotheses are typically considered:

1. Perceived differences in socioeconomic status that heavily coincide with racial-ethnic boundaries contribute to racial residential preferences.
2. Members of all social groups tend to be ethnocentric, that is, to prefer to associate with coethnics.
3. More active out-group avoidance is at the root of neighborhood racial composition preferences.

The expression of prejudice can take a variety of forms, including negative racial stereotypes, perceptions of social distance, and the belief that one or more groups pose a competitive threat to one's own group. Also relevant, though not typically considered, are minority-group beliefs about the prevalence of discrimination; these beliefs may influence the preferences of minority-group members for white or same-race neighbors (for important exceptions, see Krysan 2002 and Timberlake 2000). The goal of this chapter is to examine the associations between this broader range of racial attitudes and neighborhood racial composition preferences.

Studies of neighborhood racial preferences have only recently begun to include Latinos and Asians, having historically focused on the extreme levels of black-white residential segregation (see, for example, Emerson et al. 2001; Farley et al. 1978, 1993, 1994; Krysan and Farley 2002; Krysan 2002; Timberlake 2000). We know comparatively little, however, about the racial preferences of Latinos and Asians, and less still about the impact on their preferences of immigrant adaptation. The few existing analyses of Latino and Asian preferences shed little light on the effects of generation and assimilation, rely on only a crude measure of nativity status (native- versus foreign-born), and ignore the potentially important roles of national origin, English-language proficiency, and finer distinctions among the foreign-born (such as length of time in the United States). A thoroughgoing analysis of the racial preferences of all groups is essential for understanding both neighborhood outcomes and intergroup relations in a country where racial diversity continues to grow—owing in large part to immigration from Latin American and Asian countries.

As part of a detailed analysis of the relationship between various racial attitudes and neighborhood racial preferences, this chapter examines both the direct and interactive effects of immigration-related characteristics among Latinos and Asians. There is substantial variation within the statistically convenient categories of "Latino" and "Asian," and so the analysis also accounts for national-origin differences. Although we have no reason to expect that racial preferences differ according to national origin (that is, that something about being Korean or Mexican forms certain preferences), it is also undoubtedly true that circumstances in immigrants' home countries play some role in their racial preferences; for example, nearly all of the Central American respondents are refugees, but none of the Mexican respondents are. The nature of intergroup relations may also vary by national-origin group: Koreans, for instance, are often characterized as having tense relations with blacks, but this may not be an issue at all for Japanese.

In an initial examination of the influence of racial attitudes on neighborhood racial preferences, table 5.1 presents bivariate correlations between neighborhood racial composition preferences and racial attitudes for each respondent- and target-group combination. The perception of an out-group's social class position relative to a respondent's own group is measured with the perceived social class difference (listed here as social class disadvantage) score (introduced in the previous chapter). Scores range from –6 to +6: negative scores indicate more favorable ratings of out-groups relative to one's own group; positive scores indicate unfavor-

Table 5.1 Racial Attitudes and Neighborhood Racial Composition Preferences, by Respondent Race: Correlations

Target-Group Race	Whites	Blacks	Latinos	Asians
White neighbors				
Social class disadvantage	—	0.140***	0.035	0.039
In-group attachment	—	–0.145***	–0.088**	0.091**
Racial stereotyping	—	–0.079*	–0.069*	0.033
Social distance	—	–0.276***	–0.211***	–0.180***
White discrimination	—	–0.216***	–0.110**	0.031
Black neighbors				
Social class disadvantage	–0.051	—	0.034	–0.227***
In-group attachment	0.004	—	–0.046	0.002
Racial stereotyping	–0.360***	—	–0.051	–0.115***
Social distance	–0.270***	—	–0.182***	–0.102**
Racial-group threat (blacks)[a]	–0.213***	—	–0.034	–0.309***
Latino neighbors				
Social class disadvantage	–0.035	0.014	—	–0.179***
In-group attachment	–0.062	0.021	—	–0.092**
Racial stereotyping	–0.248***	–0.057	—	–0.193***
Social distance	–0.186	–0.043	—	–0.051
Racial-group threat (Latinos)[a]	–0.280***	–0.022	—	–0.092*
Asian neighbors				
Social class disadvantage	–0.103**	0.109***	–0.009	—
In-group attachment	–0.053	–0.066*	–0.039	—
Racial stereotyping	–0.261***	–0.078*	–0.016	—
Social distance	–0.202***	–0.263***	–0.130***	—
Racial-group threat (Asians)[a]	–0.303***	–0.192***	–0.122**	—
Same-race neighbors[b]				
Social class disadvantage	0.080*	–0.045	–0.080*	0.073*
In-group attachment	0.049	0.124***	0.112***	0.022
Racial stereotyping	0.343***	0.090**	–0.006	0.032
Social distance	0.245***	0.236***	0.233***	0.049
Racial group threat	0.317***	0.146***	0.112***	0.167***
White discrimination	—	0.093**	0.111***	–0.040

Source: Author's compilation.

a. Competitive threat items also relied on an experimental ballot, such that roughly one-third of whites considered blacks (N = 234), Latinos (N = 241), and Asians (N = 228); about half of each nonwhite group considered group competition from the remaining two groups (for blacks, 512 got the Latino ballot and 523 the Asian ballot; 441 Latinos considered blacks, and 467 responded to Asians as competitive threats; among Asian respondents, 505 considered whether or not blacks pose a competitive threat, while 509 responded to the Latino items).

b. For same-race neighbors, racial attitudes combine responses for all out-groups (for example, for white respondents, attitudes toward blacks, Latinos, and Asians are combined for perceived SES, stereotype, and social distance measures and for competitive threat).

*** $p < .001$; ** $p < .01$; * $p < .05$

able ratings of out-groups relative to one's own group; and a score of 0 suggests that a respondent does not perceive any difference in socioeconomic status between the two groups. In-group attachment (or ethnocentrism) is measured with the common fate identity item (also presented in the previous chapter); scores range from 0 (no sense of common fate identity) to 3 (a strong sense of common fate identity).

The battery of racial stereotype items presented in the previous chapter is helpful for understanding the roles of both the traditional and group-position variants of the prejudice hypothesis. Racial stereotyping is an important aspect of the traditional prejudice hypothesis; in this chapter, I employ the four-trait measure presented in the previous chapter—intelligence, welfare dependence, English-language ability, and involvement in drugs and gangs—as representative of traditional racial stereotypes and prejudice as simple out-group antipathy. The "difficult to get along with" trait taps perceptions of social distance. Recall that both the racial stereotyping and social distance measures are difference scores similar to the perceived social class disadvantage item (on a scale of –6 to +6, with positive values reflecting unfavorable attitudes toward out-groups). By tapping attitudes and perceptions of out-groups relative to the respondent's own group, these measures also capture elements of the group-position variant of prejudice, which is fueled by a commitment to a specific group status or relative group position rather than by simple out-group hostility. What matters most is the magnitude or degree of difference from particular out-groups that in-group members have socially learned to expect and maintain.

Also considered here are beliefs about racial-group competition, which offer another lens through which to examine feelings of racial hostility; the racial-group threat item ranges from 0 ("no threat") to 8 ("substantial threat"). The remaining area of racial attitudes taken up here relates to minority-group members' beliefs about the prevalence of racial discrimination and captures a general perception of whites as "tending to discriminate" against minority groups. This is an absolute measure, ranging from 1 ("whites tend to treat members of other groups equally") to 7 ("whites tend to discriminate against members of other groups").

Bivariate correlations clearly point to prejudice as most influential in the formation of neighborhood racial composition preferences. Looking first at whites, note that their beliefs about minority-group economic disadvantage have little or no correlation with their neighborhood racial composition preferences; moreover, their levels of in-group attachment are never significantly correlated with neighborhood preferences, irrespective of the race of the target group. Of the racial attitude measures, negative racial stereotyping and the perception of racial-group competition stand out as most strongly associated with whites' preferences for neighborhood integration. As expected, the more negative the stereotypes whites held of out-groups (relative to their ratings of their own group), the less they expressed a preference for integration with those groups and the more they preferred same-race neighbors. This was most true when potential neighbors were black (–.360) or same-race (.343), and least so when potential neighbors were Latino (–0.248) or Asian (–0.261).

Perceptions of social distance were also most influential when potential neighbors were black. Whites' preferences for Asian and Latino neighbors appeared to be influenced more by their concerns about perceived racial-group competition than by negative stereotypes or social distance; this was true in both absolute terms and relative to blacks as potential neighbors.[1] This pattern persists when we consider white preferences for same-race neighbors: racial attitudes were more important than either class attitudes or ethnocentrism, and stereotyping and perceptions of racial-group threat outweighed social distance. That racial stereotyping was always more strongly associated with whites' preferences than perceived social distance suggests that whites discount their actual experiences with out-group members—which presumably inform their social distance attitudes—in favor of global beliefs about a group's tendency to have "undesirable" characteristics.

Racial attitudes are also the most important correlates of the neighborhood racial composition preferences of minority groups, though they tend to be less influential for these groups compared to whites. Blacks provided the most striking example of the more varied role of racial attitudes for minority-group preferences: none of the attitudinal measures was significantly correlated with preferences for Latino neighbors. Unlike with whites, social distance attitudes were often among the strongest correlates of minority preferences, especially those for white, Asian, and same-race neighbors. The belief that whites tend to discriminate against members of other groups was strongly associated with blacks' preference for white neighbors; however, this correlation was much weaker among Latinos and virtually nonexistent for Asians. As with whites, racial-group competition appears to be important for understanding Asians' preferences. For blacks and Latinos, however, correlations between perceived racial-group competition and preferences were quite modest.

Minority groups also differed from whites to the extent that both in-group attachment and perceived social class disadvantage were sometimes associated with neighborhood racial composition preferences. Among blacks and Latinos, in-group attachment was negatively associated with preferences for white neighbors and positively associated with preferences for same-race neighbors; in-group attachment was also negatively associated with black preferences for Asian neighbors. These patterns are consistent with black and Latino perceptions of whites (and black perceptions of Asians) as discriminatory or difficult to get along with. The tendency for in-group attachment to increase preferences for same-race neighbors, on the other hand, is in keeping with the assertion that preferences are largely a function of a neutrally expressed ethnocentrism. Still, correlations between in-group attachment and preferences were always weaker than for the various out-group-directed racial attitudes, and the inconsistency of the associations between in-group attachment and neighborhood racial preferences casts doubt on the idea that minority preferences are either neutral or primarily about in-group solidarity.[2]

Asians stand out as the only group to show consistent associations between perceived social class disadvantage and neighborhood racial preferences. This tendency was strongest when potential neighbors were black, suggesting that concerns about economic position are more important than either racial stereotypes or social distance. Indeed, only a perception of blacks as competitive threats (–.31) outweighed clearly class-based concerns. Correlations between negative stereotypes of and social distance from blacks, on the other hand, were roughly half as influential as social class concerns. Perceived social class disadvantage and racial stereotyping were nearly equivalent in their association with Asian preferences for Latino neighbors as well; however, economic concerns had only a modest impact on Asian preferences for same-race neighbors, where racial-group competition is most critical (though even this correlation was a very modest .17). Only when Asians considered Latinos as neighbors did in-group attachment have the hypothesized association with preferences (albeit an extremely weak one); the association between in-group attachment and preferences was roughly the same size when Asians considered whites as neighbors, but it was positive, suggesting that greater in-group solidarity increases their preferences for white neighbors. To the extent that whites and white neighborhoods are associated with upward social mobility, however, this too is consistent with heightened socioeconomic class status concerns.[3]

In short, the bivariate evidence presented to this point suggests that perceived economic disadvantage and ethnocentrism play at best marginal roles in individuals' residential decisionmaking—with the clear exception of Asians, but even for this group class concerns appear to be much more salient for immigrants than for the native-born. In most cases, any evidence that supports these explanations pales in comparison to evidence that supports explanations rooted in the three forms of racial prejudice (traditional, sense of group position, and competitive threat). Nonetheless, this first-cut analysis of the association between racial attitudes and preferences does not account for other individual-level characteristics known to influence both neighborhood racial composition preferences and the racial attitudes believed to be associated with them; bivariate correlations are also inadequate for addressing the relative importance of the various race-associated and racial attitudes on preferences.

To address these issues, we turn to multivariate analysis aimed at assessing the relative importance of the various racial attitudes considered to this point, after controlling for other relevant individual and contextual factors. There are important differences among respondents and across groups in educational attainment, income and sex distributions, family structure, homeownership rates, and immigration-related characteristics. In the following sections, I present a series of OLS regression analyses that control for these factors in addition to two other factors that may be important for understanding neighborhood racial composition preferences: experience in public housing and the presence of target-group members in the respondent's own neighborhood. These two characteristics reflect both socioeconomic status and opportunities for intergroup contact.

In addition to these controls, models of preferences for various out-group and same-race neighbors include (1) the social class disadvantage measure; (2) the in-group attachment measure; (3) the racial stereotyping measure; (4) the social distance measure; (5) when applicable, measures of perceived white discrimination (minority-group preferences for white neighbors); and (6) perceived racial-group competition (preferences for black, Latino, or Asian neighbors).[4] Note that, for this analysis, in-group attachment has been recoded to a series of dummy variables that distinguish those with moderate ("some") or high ("a lot") in-group attachment from those with no such attachment. For models predicting preferences for same-race neighbors, out-group-directed racial attitudes—social class disadvantage, racial stereotyping, social distance, and racial-group threat—are pooled for all relevant out-groups.[5] Models are presented separately by respondent race and discussed in turn in the following sections. That discussion is limited to the effects of the various racial attitudes and, in the case of Latino and Asian respondents, immigration-related characteristics; all tables include standardized coefficients in addition to slope coefficients to facilitate discussion of the relative impact of each measure. Full results for all final models are located in the appendix (tables A2 through A5).[6]

WHITES' NEIGHBORHOOD RACIAL COMPOSITION PREFERENCES

Table 5.2 summarizes racial-attitude-specific results for the full models of whites' preferences for black, Latino, Asian, or same-race neighbors, testing the relative importance of perceived social class disadvantage, in-

Table 5.2 Effects of Various Racial Attitudes on Whites' Preferences for Black, Latino, Asian, and Same-Race Neighbors: Selected OLS Regression Coefficients

	Black Neighbors			Latino Neighbors			Asian Neighbors			Same-Race Neighbors		
	B	SE	Beta	B	SE	Beta	B	SE	Beta	B	SE	Beta
Racial attitudes												
Social class disadvantage	0.44	0.30	0.05	–0.14	0.28	–0.02	–0.42	0.47	–0.04	0.35	0.89	0.02
In-group attachment												
None or low (ref)	—	—	—	—	—	—	—	—	—	—	—	—
Medium	0.17	0.89	0.01	0.68	0.39	–0.03	–0.89	0.83	–0.04	0.66	2.00	0.01
High	0.30	0.85	0.01	–1.19	0.85	–0.05	–0.89	0.74	–0.04	1.66	1.61	0.03
Racial stereotyping	–1.92***	0.46	–0.19	–1.36***	0.34	–0.15	–2.23**	0.71	–0.15	5.00***	1.11	0.18
Social distance	–0.75**	0.27	–0.11	–0.69*	0.31	–0.10	–1.15**	0.36	–0.15	1.95**	0.68	0.11
Racial group threat	–0.56*	0.22	–0.10	–0.62**	0.18	–0.12	–0.61**	0.21	–0.11	1.83***	0.40	0.16
Constant	25.12***	2.87		18.53***	2.72		18.67***	2.56		28.63***	5.23	
R-squared		0.28***			0.16***			0.16***			0.23***	

Source: Author's compilation.

Notes: N = 705. Models control for sex, age, education, income, political ideology, homeownership status, public housing experience, household structure, and the presence of target-group members in actual neighborhoods.

*** $p < .001$; ** $p < .01$; * $p < .05$

group attachment, and the three measures of racial hostility. These results illustrate two main points with particular clarity. First, class-related attitudes and in-group attachment played no meaningful role in the neighborhood racial composition preferences of whites. This was true irrespective of the race of potential neighbors, whether out-group or same-race. Second, patently negative racial attitudes exerted consistently significant effects on preferences, and in the anticipated direction—reducing preferences for residential integration and increasing preferences for residential isolation. Moreover, the salience of each of these attitudes persisted when considered simultaneously. Controlling for basic social background characteristics and potential contact with target-group members, whites' preferences for neighborhood racial integration are best understood as the result of anti-out-group sentiment, not concerns about avoiding poverty or a neutral in-group favoritism.

Other results are noteworthy as well. For example, consistent with the bivariate correlations detailed previously, traditional out-group racial stereotypes remained the most influential racial attitude. (Standardized coefficients ranged from –.15 to –.19 for out-group preferences; the standardized coefficient for same-race preference was .18.) Given the long and often sordid history of race relations between whites and blacks, not to mention that between whites and both Latinos and Asians (especially in California), the salience of stereotypes is not necessarily surprising—such beliefs are a stable aspect of the cultural landscape. The lone exception is whites' preference for Asian neighbors: here racial stereotypes and perceived social distance were equally influential (betas were 0.15 and $p < .01$).

Indeed, the importance of perceived social distance varied with the race of the target group in interesting ways. When potential neighbors were black or Asian, this attitude was more important than the extent to which whites viewed these groups as competitive threats to valued resources. Alternatively, when whites thought about residential integration with Latinos, perceived threat outweighed social distance. Recall that Latinos are the single-largest and fastest-growing group in Los Angeles, while blacks and Asians represent roughly equal and much smaller percentages of the total population. As such, the pattern of results documented for whites is consistent with prior research indicating that increased minority presence in a metropolitan area is tied to both greater perceptions of group threat and resistance to residential integration (Fossett and Kiecolt 1989). Finally, note the racial rank-ordering of overall explanatory power: when potential neighbors were black, this collection of attitudes explained nearly 30 percent of the variation in whites' preferences and almost one-quarter of the variation in their preferences for same-race neighbors. Alternatively, similar models explained 16 percent of whites' preferences for Latino or Asian neighbors.

Across the board, then, racial attitudes are essential for understanding whites' neighborhood racial composition preferences. Perceived social class disadvantage and in-group attachment had no meaningful impact on their out-group or same-race preferences; this casts strong doubts on claims that whites avoid minority-group neighbors—especially black neighbors—because they want either to avoid poor people or to exercise some race-neutral, ethnocentric tendency. Although whites may have perceived minority groups as economically disadvantaged, that perception had virtually no effect on their neighborhood racial preferences, no matter how accurate it might have been; feelings of in-group solidarity had equally little effect. It should also be noted that almost none of the social background characteristics exerted any consistent impact on white preferences, and when they did matter, it was often in ways that decreased the likelihood of racial residential integration.[7]

Alternatively, when whites (1) viewed racial minority groups as relatively socially distant, (2) deemed them culturally or intellectually inferior (because they preferred welfare, were less intelligent, and so on), or (3) perceived them as competitive threats to valued resources that had long been the purview of whites, their preferences for integration declined and desire for residential isolation increased. The impact of racial stereotyping offers support for a traditional prejudice interpretation; however, the overall impact of racial attitudes lends strong support to the impact of the group-position variant of prejudice, given that both the stereotyping and social distance measures are difference scores: out-groups were rated relative to the respondent's own group, and the racial-group threat measure was a direct instance of concern about one's own racial group status.

BLACKS' NEIGHBORHOOD RACIAL COMPOSITION PREFERENCES

Table 5.3 presents selected results of models predicting black preferences for white, Latino, Asian, and same-race neighbors. Here too results offer little support for the influence of perceived social class disadvantage and in-group attachment. Class attitudes are very marginally significant with respect to blacks' preference for white neighbors, though more strongly associated with preference for Asian and same-race neighbors; in each case, however, the impact of perceived social class disadvantage contradicts the hypothesized association. Thus, when blacks viewed whites and Asians as relatively disadvantaged economically, this perception did not

Table 5.3 Effects of Various Racial Attitudes on Blacks' Preferences for White, Latino, Asian, and Same-Race Neighbors: Selected OLS Regression Coefficients

	White Neighbors			Latino Neighbors			Asian Neighbors			Same-Race Neighbors		
	B	SE	Beta	B	SE	Beta	B	SE	Beta	B	SE	Beta
Racial attitudes												
Social class disadvantage	0.33†	0.19	0.06	–0.09	0.35	–0.01	0.51**	0.15	0.10	–1.11**	0.33	–0.09
In-group attachment												
None or low (ref)	—	—	—	—	—	—	—	—	—	—	—	—
Medium	1.82**	0.60	0.08	–0.14	0.65	0.01	–0.00	0.56	–0.00	–1.97*	0.97	–0.05
High	–1.20	0.76	–0.05	–0.60	0.88	–0.02	–0.50	0.82	–0.02	2.47†	1.61	0.06
Racial stereotyping	–0.72*	0.35	–0.08	–1.06*	0.46	–0.09	–0.53*	0.26	–0.06	2.68***	0.60	0.13
Social distance	–0.73***	0.19	–0.14	–0.32	0.20	–0.05	–0.54**	0.14	–0.12	1.11**	0.34	0.11
White discrimination	–0.50*	0.26	–0.07	—	—	—	—	—	—	0.26	0.34	0.02
Racial-group threat	—	—	—	–0.16	0.13	–0.04	–0.28†	0.15	–0.07	0.45†	0.24	0.06
Constant	20.37***	2.02		19.00***	2.15		13.97***	1.47		43.92***	4.33	
R-squared		0.12***			0.06***			0.09***			0.13***	

Source: Author's compilation.

Notes: N = 1,038. Models control for sex, age, education, income, political ideology, homeownership status, public housing experience, household structure, and the presence of target-group members in actual neighborhoods.

*** $p < .001$; ** $p < .01$; * $p < .05$; † $p < .10$

have a negative impact on their preferences for residential integration but rather increased their preferences for integration with these groups and decreased their preferences for same-race neighbors. In-group attachment also had a counterintuitive impact on blacks' preferences for both white and same-race neighbors: a moderate amount of in-group attachment significantly increased preferences for white neighbors and decreased preferences for same-race neighbors.

The out-group-directed racial attitudes—stereotyping, social distance, perceptions of white discrimination, and racial-group competitive threat—were variously influential on blacks' neighborhood racial composition preferences. This was especially true when potential neighbors were white, Asian, or same-race, but far less so when those neighbors were Latino. As with whites, moreover, many of these attitudes among blacks were simultaneously important. For instance, note that each of the three measures of anti-white attitudes had a significant impact on blacks' preferences with regard to residential integration with whites. Unlike with white respondents, however, social distance emerged as the most influential attitude: it was roughly twice as important as both racial stereotyping and perceptions of whites as discriminatory, which were about equally influential.

Racial attitudes were much more consistent and reliable indicators of blacks' desire for (or avoidance of) Asian neighbors than for Latino neighbors. Relative perceived social distance from Asian neighbors, once again, was the most influential racial attitude. A comparison of standardized coefficients (betas) shows that this attitude was about twice as important as both stereotypes and perceived threat, which were about equally influential. The pattern of influence for perceived racial-group competition is also interesting. Despite the reality that Latinos are both a larger share of the population and more likely to be direct competitors for jobs and political power, racial-group competition had no significant impact on blacks' preference for Latino neighbors. Conversely, the perception of Asians as competitive threats to black economic and political power was associated with a tendency to prefer fewer Asian neighbors, net of other factors.

There are two ways to interpret this. First, blacks quite often come into contact with Asians—particularly Koreans—who own and operate small retail businesses in black communities that were previously owned by Jewish merchants (see Lee 2002). Many blacks have come to believe that the Asians moving into these businesses (much like the previous non-black owners) are thwarting potential entrepreneurial opportunities that would benefit their own group. To the extent that this perception prevails, competition with Asians may be more salient and more influential. Alternatively, blacks may perceive Asians as greater threats to their own economic and political opportunities because Asians not only have higher average levels of educational attainment (in absolute terms as well as compared to both Latinos and blacks) but also enjoy higher standing in the racial hierarchy; the more favorable attitudes that whites tend to have toward Asians, seemingly irrespective of immigrant status, may be particularly salient to blacks. This "model minority" status may combine with already tense relations between the two groups and resentment over "stolen" opportunities to explain the racial-group threat that blacks perceive when potential neighbors are Asian but not when they are Latino.

Nearly all of the attitudes of interest significantly influence blacks' preferences for same-race neighbors. The counterintuitive impacts of perceived social class disadvantage and moderate in-group attachment have already been considered. Also noteworthy is that a high degree of in-group attachment was modestly associated with black respondents' preference for same-race neighbors, net of other factors. Such a pattern is consistent with claims by Orlando Patterson (1997), Stephen and Abigail Thernstrom (1997), and others (Clark 1992) that persisting black-white residential segregation is largely a consequence of the voluntary preferences of blacks themselves; however, in light of the larger impact of other, clearly out-group-directed racial attitudes, we can safely conclude that in-group solidarity plays a minimal role at best.

This conclusion is best understood in terms of the substantially larger (and more statistically powerful) impact that both racial stereotyping and perceived social distance had on black preferences for same-race neighbors. In each case, the magnitude of the impact was roughly twice that of in-group attachment or perceptions of out-group racial competition; perceptions of whites as discriminatory, interestingly, were not significant predictors of preferences for same-race neighbors. It is possible that high in-group solidarity and perceptions of whites as discriminatory are correlated with each other and that such a correlation captures a related sentiment that whites have something to do with blocking blacks' opportunities. To the extent that this is the case, the positive association between high in-group attachment and preference for same-race neighbors may simply indicate a preference to avoid those perceived as responsible.[8]

The factors considered here—both racial attitudes and social background characteristics—were admittedly far less telling of the total variation in black respondents' neighborhood racial composition preferences. The total variation in blacks' preferences for any target group never exceeded 13 percent—far less than what models predicted for whites' preferences. Bear in mind, however, that regression is useful not only for explaining the total variation in an outcome of interest but also for understanding how and to what extent particular characteristics or factors influence that outcome. Results from the analysis of black respondents may be less helpful in terms of the former goal; however, this should not take away from their utility in identifying and understanding the relative importance of the factors associated with neighborhood preferences.

As was the case for white respondents, social background characteristics had few statistically significant effects on blacks' preferences for integration (for full results, see the appendix, table A3). Age was inconsistently a negative predictor of preferences for same-race neighbors; better-educated blacks—those with at least a four-year college degree—preferred Asian neighbors significantly more compared to those with less than a high school diploma, and married blacks with children preferred about 3.5 percent fewer same-race neighbors than those with other family structures. What is noteworthy, however, is the impact of public housing residence on blacks' preferences with respect to white and same-race neighbors: current public housing residents preferred white neighbors roughly 4 percent more and same-race neighbors nearly 5 percent less than those with no public housing experience, net of other factors. Such preferences are consistent with a tendency to use neighborhood racial composition as a proxy for other neighborhood characteristics. Interestingly, it is often argued that whites are the ones who use race as a proxy to avoid poor neighbors (Harris 1997; Ellen 2000); results from the previous section, however, clearly contradict this assertion. These results suggest that it is blacks themselves—at least this particular subset of blacks—who may be using race as a proxy for other neighborhood characteristics.[9]

How then should this result be interpreted? One obvious interpretation is that it is blacks themselves who use race as a proxy for the deleterious neighborhood conditions they associate with members of their own group. This may be the case for poor blacks living in public housing. Many of the negative stereotypes of blacks—that they engage in criminal behavior, that they are dependent on welfare, that they drop out of school—have class-specific undertones: these stereotypes correspond with traits exhibited by poor people, and statistically blacks are more likely to be poor. Black public housing residents, who are poor themselves and surrounded by other, similarly situated coethnics, may find it more difficult to disentangle correlates of poverty from racial-group membership; indeed, it is this subset of the overall population for whom precisely the most negative anti-black stereotypes are reinforced on a daily basis.

Moreover, and for a variety of reasons, the American Dream for many blacks includes moving up and out of predominantly black, often poor communities into more affluent, predominantly white neighborhoods thought to be safer and to offer better-quality schools, services, and other amenities. Taken together, this may explain why it is only among this particular group of blacks—and not for other racial-ethnic groups—that residence in public housing depresses preferences for same-race neighbors and increases desires for coresidence with whites. Whatever the reason for this unanticipated result, we can conclude from it that, as with whites, blacks' preference for neighborhood racial integration or isolation is much more closely connected to their attitudes about and perceptions of out-groups than to class-related concerns or in-group favoritism.

LATINOS' NEIGHBORHOOD RACIAL COMPOSITION PREFERENCES

To understand the factors that influence neighborhood racial composition preferences among Latinos, it is essential to account not only for variations in racial attitudes but also for characteristics specific to groups with large numbers of immigrants. The importance of the length of time immigrants have spent in the United States, English-language proficiency, and national origin, as well as various racial attitudes, is clearly illustrated in table 5.4, which summarizes the factors that influence Latino respondents' neighborhood racial composition preferences. The results for Latinos also highlight the complexity of the immigrant experience: racial attitudes and immigration-related characteristics exert both direct and interactive effects on preferences, and the influence of these factors varies substantially by target-group race.

Looking first at immigration-related characteristics, recall that English-language proficiency (measured on a 0-to-4 scale) was expected to have an impact on preferences similar to its impact on actual neighborhood outcomes: increasing preferences for out-group neighbors (especially, but not only, for whites) and decreasing preferences for same-race neighbors. As it turns out, however, a direct association between English ability and Latino preferences occurred only when potential neighbors were black. When potential neighbors were white or same-race, the importance of English ability was mediated by time in the United States. Specifically, English ability was important only among the most recent immigrants when potential integration was with whites, and the effect was positive: each one-unit increase in English proficiency increased preferences for white neighbors by about 4 percent. As anticipated, English proficiency de-

Table 5.4 Effects of Immigration-Related Characteristics and Various Racial Attitudes on Latinos' Preferences for White, Black, Asian, and Same-Race Neighbors: Selected OLS Regression Coefficients

	White Neighbors		
	B	SE	Beta
Immigration-related characteristics			
Mexican (ref)	—	—	—
Central American	3.53*	1.42	0.09
U.S.-born (ref)	—	—	—
Foreign-born: five years or less in the U.S.	6.28*	2.84	0.14
Foreign-born: six to ten years in the U.S.	5.33*	2.05	0.12
Foreign-born: over ten years in the U.S.	4.59**	1.40	0.14
English proficiency	0.89	0.52	0.08
Racial attitudes			
Social class disadvantage	0.18	0.29	0.02
In-group attachment			
None or low (ref)	—	—	—
Medium	0.00	1.18	0.00
High	–0.63	1.05	–0.02
Racial stereotyping	–1.40**	0.49	–0.11
Social distance	–0.72***	0.21	–0.11
White discrimination	–0.66*	0.27	–0.08
Racial-group threat	—	—	—
Interactions			
Five years or less in the U.S. × English	2.82*	1.35	0.09
More than ten years in the U.S. × English	—	—	—
Five years or less in the U.S. × stereotyping	3.21***	0.91	0.17
Five years or less in the U.S. × class disadvantage	—	—	—
Five years or less in the U.S. × high in-group	—	—	—
Five years or less in the U.S. × social distance	—	—	—
Constant	13.27***	3.91	
R-squared		0.19***	

creased preferences for same-race neighbors; however, this was again only true among immigrants—especially the most recently arrived, but also the longest-term migrants. In each case, the impact of English ability was consistent with immigrant acculturation—that is, the impact of language acquisition was generally greatest for those with the shortest time

Table 5.4 *(Continued)*

Black Neighbors			Asian Neighbors			Same-Race Neighbors		
B	SE	Beta	B	SE	Beta	B	SE	Beta
—	—	—	—	—	—	—	—	—
0.89	0.78	0.03	−0.34	1.00	−0.01	−3.74*	1.44	−0.07
—	—	—	—	—	—	—	—	—
−0.78	1.96	−0.02	−3.68*	1.65	−0.11	13.97***	3.40	0.24
−2.65	1.85	−0.08	−0.02	1.76	−0.00	2.46	3.13	0.04
−2.92*	1.24	−0.12	0.44	1.38	0.02	6.65	3.77	0.15
0.94**	0.33	0.11	0.10	0.43	0.01	−0.26	1.06	−0.02
−0.65*	0.32	−0.07	−0.21	0.21	−0.03	−0.18	0.47	−0.01
—	—	—	—	—	—	—	—	—
0.19	0.89	0.01	2.35*	0.33	0.09	−2.79†	1.46	−0.06
0.36	0.86	0.01	−0.96	0.92	−0.04	2.63†	1.46	0.06
−0.50	0.34	−0.04	−0.81*	0.36	−0.07	0.65	0.52	0.03
−0.90***	0.22	−0.18	−0.44**	0.18	−0.08	1.17***	0.32	0.10
—	—	—	—	—	—	0.74*	0.33	0.06
0.06	0.20	0.01	−0.32	0.24	−0.05	0.31	0.44	0.03
—	—	—	—	—	—	−5.61***	1.08	−0.13
—	—	—	—	—	—	−2.80**	1.06	−0.15
—	—	—	—	—	—	—	—	—
1.55*	0.61	0.09	—	—	—	—	—	—
−5.60**	1.80	−0.15	—	—	—	—	—	—
0.98*	0.44	0.11	—	—	—	—	—	—
13.15***	2.58		10.43***	2.59		41.62***	6.95	
	0.15***			0.14***			0.23***	

Source: Author's compilation.
Notes: N = 908. Models control for sex, age, education, income, political ideology, homeownership status, public housing experience, household structure, and the presence of target-group members in actual neighborhoods.
*** p < .001; ** p < .01; * p < .05; † p < .10

in the United States, and this group was the most likely to have low English ability.

The effects for time in the United States were also often modest and not so obviously consistent with the hypothesized impact of immigrant acculturation. The best example of this is the clear tendency for all categories of immigrants to prefer more white neighbors relative to their native-born counterparts, controlling for other factors. Interestingly, however, native- and foreign-born differences were greatest for the most recent arrivals, declining as time in the United States increased. When Latinos considered integration with blacks or Asians, on the other hand, immigrants showed little difference from their native-born counterparts. Foreign-born Latinos with over ten years in the United States preferred significantly less integration; when potential neighbors were Asian, the most recent arrivals tended to express less interest in coresidence. In both instances, the results offer only modest support for the role of immigrant adaptation, since the expectation is that preferences for out-group neighbors will increase with the accumulation of time in the United States. (This was the pattern for Latino preferences for Asian neighbors, but not for black neighbors.)

Patterns of immigrant versus native-born preferences for white neighbors could reflect a heightened concern with upward social mobility among immigrant Latinos, who migrated largely to improve their economic position. Symbolically at least, close proximity to whites in residential areas reflects successful mobility. At the same time, however, the accumulation of time in the United States increases opportunities to experience prejudice and discrimination; this could to some extent dull immigrant desires for residential contact with whites in spite of its symbolic meaning, and it may account for the reverse-ordering of immigrant differences in preference for white neighbors. A similar, though more circuitous, process may be at work in Latino preferences for black neighbors. Newly arriving Latino immigrants often begin their lives in America in what have been historically black neighborhoods. That early experience may reduce immigrant-native differences in the desire to avoid blacks. Over time, however, Latino migrants may come to associate neighborhood contact with blacks with stalled mobility. In each instance, immigrant Latinos are, to varying degrees, using the presence of both groups in their neighborhoods as a proxy for social class status.

Alternatively, the clearest support for an assimilationist view of preferences occurs in the model predicting that the most recent Latino arrivals will prefer substantially more coethnics compared to the native-born; moreover, longer-term migrants did not differ significantly from the native-born in their preference for same-race neighbors. Similarly, the only association between immigration and Latino preferences for Asian neighbors was that recent arrivals preferred significantly fewer Asian neighbors, net of other factors, while longer-term immigrant Latinos did not differ from the native-born. This clear difference between recent arrivals and other nativity statuses supports the possibility that newcomers have different needs that require increased proximity to coethnics and that over time these differences decline or disappear. Finally, only two instances of national-origin differences emerged: Central Americans preferred 3.5 percent more white neighbors and 3.75 percent fewer same-race neighbors than their Mexican counterparts, net of other factors.

Racial attitudes were also influential for Latinos' neighborhood racial composition preferences. Here too, however, both target-group race and nativity status were sometimes relevant. Beginning with Latino preferences for white neighbors, note that each of the three racial attitudes—stereotyping, social distance, and the belief that whites tend to discriminate against other groups—was influential. Perceptions of social distance and white discrimination did not vary along immigrant lines. Negative racial stereotypes had the anticipated effect for all Latinos except for those with five years or less in the United States, for whom the effect of stereotyping was inexplicably *positive*. Looking at the standardized coefficients, however, it appears that time in the United States was usually equally or slightly more influential than racial attitudes for understanding Latinos' desires for residential contact with whites, controlling for other factors.

The picture was somewhat different with regard to Latino preferences for other out-group neighbors. First, beliefs about an out-group's relative economic position were important only in one instance: when potential neighbors were black. This exception to the overall ineffectualness of class-based attitudes offers additional evidence that for Latinos—as a group with not only a high concentration of immigrants who may be overly concerned with economic mobility but a position low on the social and economic hierarchies irrespective of immigrant status—race, and specifically "blackness," serves as a proxy for class correlates or concern about distancing themselves from the lower rungs of the social hierarchy. What is interesting about this, however, is that perceptions about blacks' relative economic position had the opposite effect among immigrants with less than five years in the United States.

Recent immigrants also differed from other nativity statuses in terms of the impact that both in-group attachment and social distance had on their preferences for black neighbors. First, Latinos who had been in the United States five years or less and who expressed a high level of in-group attachment preferred significantly fewer black neighbors on average (−5.60, $p < .01$). Furthermore, the effect of perceived social distance for recent arrivals was near 0 (and positive [−.90 + .98 = .08, $p < .05$]). Conversely, the impact of racial attitudes on preferences for Asian neighbors did not vary at all by nativity status: anti-Asian stereotypes and the perception of Asians as relatively difficult to get along with significantly reduced preferences for neighborhood contact with this group. Potentially telling too was that concerns about either blacks or Asians as competitive threats did not influence Latino preferences in any meaningful way. The relative importance of nativity-status characteristics and racial attitudes for both target groups was similar to that observed in the model predicting Latinos' preferences for white neighbors (though being a recent immigrant was a bit more influential than any of the racial attitudes for predicting preferences for Asian neighbors).

Racial attitudes directly influenced Latino preferences for same-race neighborhoods, yet no single attitude emerged that was as critical as immigrant status and English proficiency. In-group attachment was only modestly significant, and as with blacks, moderate in-group solidarity actually depressed preferences for same-race neighbors; strong attachment had the anticipated positive effect. Of the racial attitudes, social distance was the strongest predictor of same-race preferences, followed by perceptions of whites as discriminating against other groups. Negative out-group stereotypes were not significantly associated with same-race preferences, nor were perceptions about out-groups' relative economic position. In short, Latino preferences for same-race neighbors provided the most straightforward and consistent support for the primary importance of something approaching ethnocentrism. That is, despite the influence of racial attitudes, proximity to coethnics seems to be of utmost importance for those who are new to the country or do not speak English well. The accumulation of time in the United States brings with it familiarity—with the language and with the workings of society—and with that familiarity comes a declining need to be surrounded by coethnics.

The preferred racial composition of Latinos' neighborhoods was intricately linked to their immigration-related characteristics. Among the foreign-born, both the accumulation of time in the United States and the acquisition of English-language skills increased preferences for integration with whites and diminished desires for close residential proximity to coethnics; this was particularly true for the most recent arrivals. In addition to these important immigration-related distinctions, racial attitudes were also influential. In some instances, moreover, the impact of racial attitudes was mediated by immigration-related characteristics. The most striking example of this was the tendency for racial attitudes to operate differently for recent immigrants—negative attitudes tended to be less influential, and in-group attachment was more so. These patterns were consistent with the models of immigrant adaptation used to explain the spatial assimilation of Latinos, and they were also consistent with the notion that the internalization of a U.S.-specific racial ideology is a critical component of immigrant adaptation. For Latinos, at least, it appears that the five-year mark is an important one: at that point, immigrant and native-born Latinos are similar with respect to associations between racial attitudes and preferences. Finally, it is also evident that, despite the importance of immigration, Latinos also share some things in common with blacks, particularly when potential neighbors are white or of the same race.

ASIANS' NEIGHBORHOOD RACIAL COMPOSITION PREFERENCES

Immigration-related characteristics are also essential aspects of Asian respondents' preferences for neighborhood racial integration. The results summarized in table 5.5 show us, however, that the influence of these factors is often more complicated than is the case with Latinos. Possibly the most striking difference between the two largely immigrant populations is that Asian respondents' preferences consistently differed across national-origin groups as well as along nativity-status lines. To simplify the discussion of these results, table 5.6 summarizes the effects of national origin and nativity status on Asian respondents' preferences for white, black, Latino, or same-race neighbors. These coefficients are simply the sum of the relevant coefficients presented in table 5.5 for various national-origin and nativity-status effects and interactions. For example, the effect of recent immigration on Koreans' preferences for black neighbors (–2.45, see table 5.6) is the sum of the Korean coefficient (–9.44, $p < .001$), the recent-immigrant coefficient (–3.42, $p < .05$), and the coefficient for the interaction between Korean national origin and recent immigration (10.41, $p < .001$).

Looking first at the national-origin and nativity-status differences in table 5.6, we see that foreign-born Asians tended to prefer significantly more white neighbors compared to the reference group, U.S.-born Japanese.[10] In absolute terms, however, native-born Koreans prefer more white neighbors than any other national-origin/nativity-status group, net of other factors (nearly 17 percent more whites than native-born Japanese, which is also substantially more than any of the foreign-born categories). Also noteworthy is that Japanese and Chinese immigrants with five years or less in the United States expressed preferences for neighborhood

Table 5.5 Effects of Immigration-Related Characteristics and Various Racial Attitudes on Asians' Preferences for White, Black, Latino, and Same-Race Neighbors: Selected OLS Regression Coefficients

	White Neighbors		
	B	SE	Beta
Immigration-related characteristics			
Japanese (ref)	—	—	—
Chinese	–2.92	2.16	–0.08
Korean	16.68*	6.74	0.43
U.S.-born (ref)	—	—	—
Foreign-born: Five years or less in the U.S.	0.79	4.37	0.02
Foreign-born: six to ten years in the U.S.	8.35**	3.16	0.18
Foreign-born: over ten years in the U.S.	6.62**	2.30	0.18
English proficiency	0.82	0.81	0.06
Racial attitudes			
Social class disadvantage	0.47	0.57	0.03
In-group attachment			
None or low (ref)	—	—	—
Medium	1.40	1.23	0.04
High	–2.78†	1.46	–0.07
Racial stereotyping	–0.15	0.78	–0.01
Social distance	–0.70†	0.38	–0.07
White discrimination	–0.83†	0.45	–0.07
Racial-group threat	—	—	—
Interactions			
Korean × five years or less in the U.S.	–15.56*	7.34	–0.23
Korean × six to ten years in the U.S.	–20.66**	7.59	–0.34
Korean × more than ten years in the U.S.	–19.72**	7.11	–0.39
Chinese × more than ten years in the U.S.	—	—	—
Five years or less in the U.S. × English ability	3.61*	1.47	0.17
Six to ten years in the U.S. × high in-group	—	—	—
Six to ten years in the U.S. × social distance	—	—	—
More than ten years in the U.S. × social distance	—	—	—
Constant	27.51***	4.93	
R-squared		0.22***	

Table 5.5 *(Continued)*

Black Neighbors			Latino Neighbors			Same-Race Neighbors		
B	SE	Beta	B	SE	Beta	B	SE	Beta
—	—	—	—	—	—	—	—	—
−1.42	1.02	−0.08	−2.31*	1.07	−0.11	2.70	2.15	0.06
−9.44***	2.56	−0.49	−11.86**	4.21	−0.54	6.97*	2.95	0.14
—	—	—	—	—	—	—	—	—
−3.42*	1.54	−0.15	−2.76†	1.49	−0.10	7.91†	4.73	0.14
−3.34*	1.62	−0.14	−6.08***	1.75	−0.23	5.42	3.40	0.09
−4.05**	1.33	−0.22	−3.62**	1.35	−0.17	−4.25	2.92	−0.09
0.38	0.39	0.06	0.73	0.40	0.10	−1.94*	0.87	−0.12
−0.82***	0.23	−0.12	−0.44†	0.25	−0.05	1.21**	0.48	0.05
—	—	—	—	—	—	—	—	—
−1.02†	0.57	−0.05	0.05	0.82	0.00	−0.13	1.51	−0.00
1.09	0.67	0.06	−0.81	0.70	−0.04	3.40*	1.31	0.07
−0.79**	0.29	−0.08	−0.89*	0.39	−0.08	0.53	0.90	0.02
−0.41**	0.14	−0.08	−0.96**	0.31	−0.16	0.36	0.53	0.02
—	—	—	—	—	—	0.70	0.46	0.04
−0.25	0.18	−0.05	−0.08	0.22	−0.01	0.05	0.35	0.00
10.41***	2.81	0.30	11.31*	4.41	0.29	−8.98*	4.18	−0.10
12.87***	2.47	0.42	15.64***	4.37	0.45	−11.10**	4.27	−0.15
9.92***	2.75	0.40	12.02**	4.36	0.42	—	—	—
—	—	—	—	—	—	8.03*	3.10	0.15
—	—	—	—	—	—	−4.16**	1.46	−0.15
−4.25**	1.35	−0.16	—	—	—	—	—	—
—	—	—	1.00*	0.47	0.08	—	—	—
—	—	—	0.91*	0.46	0.11	—	—	—
18.41***	2.54		17.58***	2.82		34.26***	6.02	
	0.20***			0.15***			0.31***	

Source: Author's compilation.

Notes: N = 1,014. Models control for sex, age, education, income, political ideology, homeownership status, public housing experience, household structure, and the presence of target-group members in actual neighborhoods.

*** $p < .001$; ** $p < .01$; * $p < .05$; † $p < .10$

Table 5.6 Impact of National Origin and Nativity Status on Asian Respondents' Preferences for White, Black, Latino and Same-Race Neighbors: Selected Coefficients

	White Neighbors	Black Neighbors	Latino Neighbors	Same-Race Neighbors
Japanese				
Five years or less in the U.S.	0.79	–3.42*	–2.76†	7.91†
Six to ten years in the U.S.	8.35**	–3.34*	–6.08***	5.42
Over ten years in the U.S.	6.62**	–4.05**	–3.62**	–4.25
U.S.-born	(ref.)	(ref.)	(ref.)	(ref.)
Chinese				
Five years or less in the U.S.	–2.13	–4.84*	–5.07†	10.61†
Six to ten years in the U.S.	5.43**	–4.76*	–8.39***	8.12
Over ten years in the U.S.	3.70**	–5.47**	–5.93**	6.48*
U.S.-born	–2.92	–1.42	–2.31*	2.70
Korean				
Five years or less in the U.S.	1.91*	–2.45***	–3.31*	5.90*
Six to ten years in the U.S.	4.37**	0.09***	–2.30***	1.29**
Over ten years in the U.S.	3.58**	–3.57***	–3.46**	2.72
U.S.-born	16.68*	–9.44***	–11.86**	6.97*

Source: Author's compilation.
Notes: N = 1,014. Coefficients are the sum of relevant results from table 5.5. The reference category is U.S.-born Japanese.
*** p < .001; ** p < .01; * p < .05; † p < .10

contact with whites similar to those of their U.S.-born counterparts.[11] Across national-origin categories, nativity-status groups tended to express relatively similar preferences for integration with whites; these were highest among Japanese and lowest among Koreans (with the exception of native-born Koreans). In absolute terms, these differences are quite modest; however, they also run counter to traditional acculturation models, which posit that immigrants tend to prefer fewer white (or any other out-group) neighbors than their native-born counterparts. Under the traditional scenario, then, we would expect all national-origin groups to look like Koreans, among whom the native-born preferred substantially more white neighbors than the foreign-born. English-language ability matters only among the most recent immigrants, for whom, as hypothesized, increased proficiency strengthens desires for neighborhood integration with whites (see table 5.5).

Asians' preferences for same-race neighbors also show only modest differences across national-origin and nativity-status groups. The clearest pattern of difference emerges once again among Koreans, most of whom preferred significantly more same-race neighbors than native-born Japanese did. Differences were both fewer and likely to be only marginally significant among Japanese- and Chinese-origin respondents; nonetheless, there did appear to be an overall tendency for the most recent immigrants to prefer significantly more same-race neighbors than both their longer-term-immigrant counterparts and the native-born, net of other factors. Moreover, native- and foreign-born differences tended to decline with the accumulation of time in the United States, in a manner consistent with the traditional assimilation or adaptation models. Here again the exception was native-born Koreans, who, on average, preferred more same-race neighbors compared to both coethnic immigrants and other native-born Asians. English-language ability had the anticipated impact on Asians' preferences for same-race neighbors—increasing ability decreased preferences for same-race neighbors—particularly among the most recent arrivals (an additional –4.16, $p < .01$; see table 5.5).

Perhaps the most striking differences in preferences among Asian ethnic groups was in their preferences for black and Latino neighbors; these results are presented in the middle two columns of table 5.6. All immigrant groups shared a preference for fewer black and Latino neighbors compared to native-born coethnics and, with one exception (U.S.-born Chinese preferences for black neighbors), U.S.-born Japanese. Native-born Korean respondents stand out again, this time for expressing preferences for substantially fewer minority-group neighbors—nearly 9.5 percent fewer blacks and almost 12 percent fewer Latinos—net of other characteristics. English-language proficiency, moreover, had no significant effect on preferences for either blacks or Latinos as neighbors (see table 5.5).

Among the more obvious differences between Asians and other groups is that Asians' beliefs about out-groups' relative economic status had a much more consistent impact on their preferences for integration. As shown in table 5.5, the impact of perceived social class disadvantage on neighborhood racial composition preferences was most pronounced when potential neighbors were black (beta = –0.12, $p < .001$). Indeed, among the racial attitudes included to predict Asian preferences for black neighbors, the perception of blacks as economically disadvantaged was more important than any of the other racial attitudes. Although class attitudes are among the more salient attitudes for understanding Asians' preferences for same-race neighbors, they were only marginally influential with regard to Asians' preferences for Latino neighbors, and not at all influential when potential neighbors were white.

In-group attachment also appears to be more salient among Asians compared to other groups: it has a significant impact on their preferences for white, black, and same-race neighbors. In keeping with the argument that preferences are primarily a function of strong feelings of in-group solidarity, those Asians with a high degree of common fate identity preferred fewer white neighbors and more same-race neighbors on average. When potential neighbors were black, a moderate level of in-group attachment was modestly associated with declining interest in integration with blacks. A strong sense of common fate identity mattered only for intermediate-term immigrants; indeed, for this subset of Asians, in-group attachment outweighed the perception of blacks as economically disadvantaged. Once again, the results seem to support seemingly race-neutral explanations for preferences: for Asians, avoiding coresidence with poor people and maintaining group cohesion emerged as primary factors influencing their neighborhood racial composition preferences. This was most evident in Asians' preferences for same-race neighbors: here strong feelings of in-group attachment were the most influential of the attitudes considered, and among only two reaching statistical significance.

Out-group-directed racial attitudes—racial stereotyping, social distance, white discrimination, and racial-group threat—tended to be both less consistent and less influential predictors of preferences among Asians. Of these measures, social distance was one of the more robust attitudes: it had a significant impact on preferences for all out-groups, though it was not influential with respect to same-race neighbors. Interestingly, perceived social distance appeared to matter most (compared to both other target groups and other attitudes included in the same model) when Asians contemplated integration with Latinos, another group that includes substantial numbers of immigrants. Note, however, that the impact of social distance on preferences for Latino neighbors depended on nativity status: its impact was significant only among recent arrivals and the native-born; for intermediate- and long-term immigrants, the effect was virtually zero. Racial stereotypes were influential only when potential neighbors were other minority groups; in both instances, however, effects were fairly modest. And as with both blacks and Latinos, Asians' perception of whites as tending to discriminate against members of other groups significantly reduced their preferences for neighborhood integration with whites, but their perception of minority groups as competitive threats had no significant impact on their preferences. None of the out-group-directed attitudes mattered for Asians' preferences for same-race neighbors.[12]

Finally, the social background and neighborhood contact measures used for control purposes showed little in the way of consistent patterns of association with preferences, across respondent categories. In the case of Asians, however, there were a couple of findings worthy of mention. First, age was most consistently associated with preferences among this group. In particular, the oldest group of Asians—those age seventy and older—preferred fewer minority neighbors (about 5.2 percent) and substantially more same-race neighbors (14.2 percent) compared to younger coethnics. Second, and potentially more interesting, is the effect of prior residence in public housing on preferences for both black and Latino neighbors. In both cases, having lived in public housing significantly increased preferences for integration (by a little over 6 percent). Similarly, prior residence in public housing reduced preferences for same-race neighbors by about 10 percent on average.[13] These were the only instances in which experience with public housing exerted any significant impact on preferences, and it appears that, for this group, past contact with other minority groups in public housing had a favorable impact on preferences.

Much as with Latinos, immigration-related characteristics turned out to be of primary importance for understanding Asians' neighborhood racial composition preferences. This was apparent both in the complicated manner in which national-origin groups and nativity-status categories varied across target groups and in an examination of the relative importance of factors (looking at the betas that correspond to each coefficient). Moreover, Asian respondents—both native- and foreign-born—offered the clearest evidence of being concerned with the relative social class position of their neighbors, though only when potential neighbors were other minority groups or coethnics. This pattern of effect suggests that Asians may in fact use race as a proxy for class status and that they actively seek to avoid class disadvantage. Here too the fact that it was the relative class status of blacks and Latinos that mattered is telling and suggests that Asians as a group are more intensely concerned with economic mobility and work to distance themselves from those groups on the lowest rungs of the socioeconomic hierarchy.

Asians differ from Latinos in that their preferences vary in important ways by national origin. Specifically, the comparatively intense desire shown by native-born Koreans to avoid neighborhood contact with blacks and Latinos is curious to the extent that the tense black-Korean relations in Los Angeles are overwhelmingly likely to involve *immigrant* Korean merchants and black and Latino customers. The severity of these tensions became evident in 1992 when Korean merchants saw their stores looted—and in some cases burned to the ground—by blacks and Latinos during the civil unrest following the acquittal of four LAPD officers in the beating of the black motorist Rodney King. As had happened during the 1965 Watts riot, the immediate source of black and Latino discontent was the rampant and seemingly unchecked police brutality directed against minorities in Los Angeles. (Recall that the beating of Rodney King was captured on videotape and that recordings of the audio transmissions revealed that several officers engaged in racially offensive language.) Their feelings of discontent grew, however, to include the Korean merchants who did business in minority neighborhoods and were perceived as having little respect for their largely black and Latino clientele.[14] That immigrant Koreans exhibited preferences for more black and Latino neighbors than their native-born counterparts (though still significantly fewer than U.S.-born Japanese) is consistent with previous research by Jennifer Lee (2002), who finds that relations between Korean merchants and black customers are largely positive. Indeed, in the aftermath of the civil unrest, substantial effort was made to improve relations between these groups; that effort, combined with the passage of time, may explain the absence of aversion to black and Latino neighbors on the part of immigrant Koreans.[15]

Out-group-directed racial attitudes are generally less influential but still matter in important ways for understanding Asians' neighborhood racial composition preferences. Racial stereotyping and perceived social distance were consistently important when potential neighbors were other minority groups; each of these attitudes, in addition to a perception of whites as discriminatory, mattered for Asian attitudes toward residential integration with the dominant group. Overall, and contrary to the view of immigrant adaptation that includes the internalization of a specifically American racial ideology, the impact of these attitudes did not vary much by nativity status (with the exception of social distance and preference for Latino neighbors). Finally, although class-based attitudes emerged as important factors in Asians' thinking about neighborhood racial integration, clearly racial attitudes mattered as well, particularly when potential neighbors were other-race. Moreover, none of the attitudinal measures was as important as the immigration-related characteristics.

In the end, understanding neighborhood racial composition preferences is a complicated matter for groups characterized by massive immigration. Clearly, nuanced, multidimensional approaches are needed and "one-size-fits-all" analyses are to be avoided.

CONCLUSIONS

One of the goals of this chapter (and the previous one) was to assess the relative importance of various racial attitudes as driving forces behind neighborhood racial composition preferences, while situating these preferences within the broader context of historic and contemporary American race relations. The good news—clearly evident in the previous chapter—is that all groups are *willing* to live in neighborhoods that are more integrated than is currently the case. The bad news is that most whites still hold decidedly negative racial attitudes, even many of those whites who express a willingness to share residential space with other groups. At the same time, most racial minorities have a keen sense of their subordinate position relative to whites and of whites' attitudes toward them, and that sense often leaves them suspicious of overwhelmingly white areas (a sort of "better safe than sorry" mentality).

Available evidence indicates that active, present-day racial prejudice and concerns among racial minorities about white hostility play important roles in driving neighborhood racial preferences. In nearly every case, the effect of negative racial attitudes is always stronger and more consistent than the effects of perceived social class disadvantage and in-group attachment. And though the results support both the traditional and group-position variants of racial prejudice, they are particularly persuasive with respect to the latter. This is especially true for whites, the group at the top of the status hierarchy and, arguably, the group with the most to lose. Maintaining their status advantages and privilege requires a certain amount of social distance from nonwhites—particularly blacks and Latinos, the groups at the bottom of the racial queue—since more than token integration would signal an unwelcome change in status relations. Indeed, this racial hierarchy—in which whites occupy the top position and blacks the bottom—is so pervasive that immigrant adaptation includes the internalization and even exaggeration of it among Latinos and Asians, as seen in the patterns of preferences for both groups.

Although whites attempt to preserve their status and to avoid "too much" integration, nonwhites traditionally associate upward social mobility with increased proximity to whites. This helps us understand why blacks, Latinos, and Asians can adhere to negative stereotypes of whites but still express a desire to share residential space with them (Charles 2005; Jankowski 1995; Jaynes and Williams 1989; Massey and Denton 1993). Similarly, however, racial minorities' beliefs about discrimination are associated with decreasing interest in integration with whites and, for Latinos at least, increasing preferences for same-race neighbors. To some extent, then, preferences for same-race neighbors in whites reflect a desire to maintain their status, while in racial minorities they reflect a desire to avoid white hostility.

At the same time, ethnocentrism does appear to play a role in minority-group preferences, though often not in the way that has traditionally been hypothesized. It does turn out to be true that a high level of in-group attachment is associated with an increased preference for same-race neighbors among Latinos and Asians (and marginally for blacks); however, it is also the case that a moderate level of in-group attachment significantly *increases* blacks' preferences for white neighbors and *decreases* both blacks' and Latinos' preferences for same-race neighbors. This pattern is more consistent with an integrationist than a separatist worldview. Conversely, in-group attachment has no significant effect on whites' preferences irrespective of target-group race. This pattern of effect casts doubt on the applicability of explanations for persisting residential segregation that focus primarily on neutral in-group attachment, since in-group solidarity tells us nothing substantial about the preferences of the most residentially isolated group—whites—and often operates counter to expectation for the two most segregated minority groups.

Quite simply, *race matters irrespective of social class position*. This is evident not only through the clear patterns of association between various racial attitudes and preferences, but also through the relative absence of meaningful associations between social background characteristics and preferences. Results from the full models presented in tables 5.2 through 5.6 (located in the appendix) show very few significant associations between preferences and any of the individual characteristics considered (sex, age, education, income, political ideology, homeownership status, and family structure). Of the characteristics controlled for, only the percentage of target-group members in the respondent's actual neighborhood was consistently associated with preferences; consistent with the contact hypothesis (Allport 1954), increased exposure to target groups tended to increase preferences for that group. For Asians, prior residence in public housing also had a positive impact on preferences for both black and Latino neighbors—again consistent with the contact hypothesis.

This is not to say, however, that personal characteristics never matter, since immigration-related characteristics were often the most potent predictors of preferences for both Latinos and Asians; the results from this analysis also highlight the importance of acculturation, particularly for Latinos, but to a lesser extent for Asians as well. How immigrants—whether Latino or Asian—thought about the racial composition of their neighborhoods varied meaningfully by the number of years they had lived in the United States and their level of English proficiency, particularly when potential neighbors were either white or same-race. English proficiency, which was especially important for the most recently arrived immigrants, was positively associated with preferences for white neighbors and negatively associated with preferences for same-race neighbors. The greater import of language among the most recent arrivals is consistent with an adaptation process in which language ability increases over time (Espinosa and Massey 1997), as well as with the heterogeneity of English ability among new arrivals. Overall, these patterns are entirely consistent with the tenets of the spatial assimilation hypothesis and hint at a connection between preferences and actual behavior for these groups (for a detailed discussion on the link between attitudes and residential behavior, see Bobo and Zubrinsky 1996).

The pattern of effects for racial attitudes is also consistent with the claim that these beliefs and the status advantages associated with racial-group membership have specific meanings in the United States that are internalized with the passage of time as part of the acculturation process. Although racial attitudes were often less predictive of recent immigrants' racial neighborhood preferences compared to those of longer-term immigrants and the native-born, this does not mean that newly arrived Latinos and Asians were less likely to express negative attitudes toward other groups. In fact, the reverse tended to be true: a comparison of mean racial stereotype scores across categories of time in the United States reveals that recent and intermediate-term immigrants held the most negative stereotypes of both whites and blacks.[16] This result also supports the prejudice-as-group-position hypothesis: racial attitudes are often most negative among more recent immigrants, but the potential for those attitudes to influence behavior increases over time, arguably as these immigrants internalize and negotiate America's racialized status hierarchy.

All told, these results do not bode well for the dynamics of intergroup relations in multiracial-multiethnic contexts. As racial minorities, Latinos and Asians are located in subordinate positions in the U.S. racial hierarchy: they are better off than blacks (at least perceptually), but they are locked out of the dominant group by their phenotypic distinctiveness or their surname. Thus, the end-game of assimilation is decidedly different than it was (and is) for white immigrants, since "blending into" the dominant group is not an option for Latinos and Asians.[17] As immigrants of color come to understand this, distancing themselves from blacks—and therefore from the bottom of the status hierarchy—takes on special importance. This is seen in Latino and Asian immigrants' greater preference for white neighbors relative to their native-born counterparts as well as to blacks. Despite potential concerns about hostility or discriminatory treatment from whites—which does have a negative impact on preferences—it appears that greater proximity to whites symbolizes upward mobility and, as such, is desirable for immigrants in a way that may be less true among the native-born. Heightened mobility-consciousness is also implicated in immigrants' avoidance of blacks and in the impact of perceived social class disadvantage on Latino and (especially) Asian preferences for blacks as neighbors.

While highlighting important nonracial predictors of preferences associated with immigration—length of time in the United States and English-language proficiency—this analysis clearly details the persistence of a powerful racial ideology in America (Bashi and McDaniel 1997) that is internalized by newcomers, fosters tensions and competition, and makes increased or sustained residential contact between immigrant groups and blacks all the more challenging, if not simply unlikely.[18] Sadly, patterns of racial attitudes and preferences among Latino and Asian immigrants reflect an adaptation process that reinforces and sustains the common belief among early-twentieth-century blacks that one of the first English words an immigrant learns on the path to becoming American is "nigger" and that even for groups that cannot "become white" the ability to distance oneself from blacks is itself social currency, ensuring a social position at least once removed from the bottom (Toni Morrison, in Angelo 1989; Ignatiev 1995; Malcolm X 1964, 339).

Chapter Six | Race and Class Aligned

THE PREVIOUS CHAPTERS offer compelling evidence that racial prejudice is implicated in patterns of neighborhood segregation. Equally compelling is evidence that mere in-group preferences and (except for Asians) efforts to avoid coresidence with groups perceived as relatively disadvantaged economically play a minimal role at best. First, a detailed analysis of the relationship between individual-level social background characteristics and actual neighborhood outcomes (chapter 3) found that whites live in whiter, more affluent neighborhoods irrespective of their individual characteristics, while almost the exact opposite is true for blacks. That is, individual-level socioeconomic status characteristics explain little about blacks' neighborhood exposure to whites or the median household income of their neighborhoods—both in absolute terms and relative to other groups. These results for a large multiracial sample of Los Angeles County residents are consistent with those based on national data from the U.S. census.

Next, a survey of racial attitudes in Los Angeles County showed a high degree of consistency with national trends. Whites continue to adhere to negative racial stereotypes, particularly toward blacks and Latinos, but to a lesser extent toward Asians as well. They perceive systematic prejudice and discrimination as largely a relic of the past and are likely to see minority disadvantage as being the result of "bad culture." And to some extent, whites perceive minority groups as threats to their economic and political opportunities. Blacks, Latinos, and Asians also adhere to negative stereotypes—toward each other as well as toward whites. They tend, however, to be "on the same page" when it comes to their beliefs about inequality. For them, discrimination is pervasive and systematic; it is most problematic for blacks, followed by Latinos and then Asians. All four groups also tend to perceive a good deal of social distance between themselves and other groups and to view one another as threats to their own economic opportunities and political power.

Patterns of neighborhood racial composition preferences, detailed in chapter 4, evince a racial hierarchy of out-groups as desirable neighbors that is consistent with both general patterns of racial-group economic status and trends in racial attitudes. Quite simply, whites are hands-down the most desirable out-group neighbors, and blacks are unambiguously the least desirable; Asians and Latinos, in this order, are in between (except among blacks, who rate Asians as the least desirable out-group). This rank-ordering is evident both in terms of the average percentage of each group included in respondents' ideal multiethnic neighborhoods and with respect to the likelihood of a group's complete exclusion. Especially interesting here is that foreign-born Latinos and Asians are about twice as likely as whites to exclude blacks completely from their ideal multiethnic neighborhoods. This exaggerated tendency toward exclusion of blacks suggests not only a heightened concern with upward mobility and an equally heightened awareness of patterns of American racial stratification but also exposure to negative images of blacks prior to entering the United States and, in the absence of counterbalancing experiences, an exaggerated tendency to internalize these images. The latter possibility is bolstered by average negative stereotypes of blacks among the foreign-born that exceed those of both whites and their native-born counterparts. Ironically, blacks stand out as generally open to a wide variety of out-groups as neighbors, despite showing a clear rank-ordering of preferences (as all groups do).

Moreover, active racial prejudice—both traditional, simple out-group hostility and the group-position variant—is deeply implicated in patterns of preferences for neighborhood racial integration. This is most evident in the roles that perceived racial-group threat and social distance attitudes play in explaining whites' neighborhood racial composition preferences, but negative racial stereotypes are also critically important. In short, all of the out-group-directed racial attitudes are potent predictors of whites' neighborhood racial composition preferences—except for beliefs about out-groups' relative economic status. Whites' degree of in-group attachment is also unimportant.

Concerns about relative group position are also somewhat apparent among blacks, whose preferences for both Asian and same-race neighbors are negatively influenced by the belief that this group poses a competitive threats to economic opportunities and political power; social distance attitudes also play a significant role, irrespective of the race of potential neighbors, as do negative stereotypes. Blacks' perceptions of whites as tending to discriminate against other groups are also influential. At the same time, however, in-group attachment increases blacks' preferences for both white and same-race neighbors. Indeed, the favorable impact of moderate in-group attachment on preferences for white neighbors was quite unexpected. Finally, as with whites, blacks' beliefs about the relative economic status of out-groups have no meaningful impact on their neighborhood racial composition preferences.

The story tends to be more complicated for Latinos and Asians, groups with large immigrant populations. Being foreign-born weighs heavily on Latinos' preferences; recent arrivals must also confront the issues associated with their level of English-language proficiency. The combined effects of recent immigration and English ability are particularly important for understanding the preferences of Latinos and Asians for white and same-race neighbors. In general, foreign-born Latinos and Asians prefer more of both groups; this preference may reflect counterbalancing desires for coethnic camaraderie and parallel social institutions during the transitional period, on the one hand, and the upward socioeconomic mobility that is often symbolized by neighborhood proximity to whites, on the other. Korean-origin respondents (both immigrant and native) stand out among Asians for having substantially less interest in sharing residential space with both blacks and Latinos; their pattern of difference, moreover, is consistent with the particularities of Korean relations with both groups since the 1992 civil unrest.

Still, the impact of racial attitudes is clear. The perception of whites as discriminatory has a negative impact on both groups' preferences for white neighbors; this belief also increases Latinos' preferences for same-race neighbors. Social distance figures prominently in Asian and Latino preferences in the anticipated ways; however, its effect often depends on length of time in the United States. This is also true with respect to negative racial stereotypes, which again have the anticipated—though often less consistent—impact on preferences. That is, for immigrants (and especially recent immigrants), perceived social distance and negative stereotypes often have little effect on preferences. This is most true for Asians, the only group whose concerns about the relative economic position of other minority groups significantly affect preferences for neighborhood racial integration. The relative social class status of blacks is also influential among Latinos. Once again, there appears to be a heightened concern with upward social mobility for these two "middleman" groups. For immigrants, upward mobility was probably central to their decision to migrate; for the native-born, this concern may have more to do with maintaining a relative status position. Both groups learn early that if proximity to whites signals successful mobility, proximity to blacks signals failure.

For both Asians and Latinos, strong in-group attachment is associated with preferences for increased contact with same-race neighbors. Once again, these groups may be looking to avoid hostility rather than expressing in-group preference per se. (Recall that beliefs about discrimination also have the anticipated effects on preferences for white and same-race neighbors.) In-group solidarity has a negative impact on Latino preferences for black neighbors as well, but only for the most recent arrivals. As a shortage of affordable housing has forced recent Latino immigrants to take up residence in historically black communities, and as Asian immigrants continue to pursue entrepreneurial endeavors that often serve a poor, black clientele, interminority-group conflict has become more commonplace; in this environment, the belief that "what happens to my group happens to me" takes on added meaning. Strong in-group attachment also diminishes Asian preferences for white neighbors, which are already diminished by the perception of whites as discriminators. Thus, even for a group with more varied social background characteristics and higher relative social and economic status, the potential for white hostility appears to be salient.[1]

All told, Los Angeles County residents exhibit a powerful association between various racial attitudes and neighborhood racial composition preferences (with the exception of the immigration-related characteristics of Latinos and Asians); none of the social background characteristics come close to exhibiting as strong or consistent an effect. The consistency and strength of these associations across respondent- and target-group racial categories, among both the native- and foreign-born, and in the absence of meaningful associations between preferences and the individual-level characteristics thought to influence attitudes (such as age and education) sends a clear and convincing message. Still, evidence of a direct association between attitudes toward residential integration and actual housing outcomes is elusive, particularly in multiracial contexts.

Several studies have examined the effect of interracial contact on whites' racial attitudes (Jackman and Crane 1986; Sigelman and Welch 1993; Wilson 1996). Consistent with analyses of preferences, both Jackman and Crane (1986) and Sigelman and Welch (1993) find that whites who have black neighbors also express stronger preferences for black neighbors. Christopher Ellison and Daniel Powers (1994) report a similar positive effect of contact on blacks' attitudes toward whites. None of these studies controls, however, for the endogeneity of neighborhood contact. Put more plainly, while it is quite possible that contact influences racial attitudes and preferences, it may also be that preferences have an impact on residential decisionmaking and thus, ultimately, residential segregation. This association is the foundation upon which studies of neighborhood racial composition preferences are based and is central to the arguments made by Massey and Denton (1993), Yinger (1995), and others. To date, however, researchers have had to rely largely upon circumstantial evidence to make their case. Even Alba, Logan, and their colleagues have pursued their prejudice-based explanation for blacks' residential segregation based on what they *do not* find—direct relationships between individual characteristics and neighborhood outcomes.

PREFERENCES AND OUTCOMES: WHICH CAME FIRST?

And so we arrive at that age-old question: which came first, the attitudes or the behavior? Even a preliminary answer to this question, based on rigorous empirical analysis, would add substantially to our understanding of how individual-level attitudes contribute to aggregate-level housing patterns and focus our efforts to address long-standing intergroup divisions and emerging tensions. What we learn from trying to answer this question could also assist policymakers in developing and implementing programs intended to provide better-quality low-income housing or to promote stable, racially integrated neighborhoods. Prior efforts to address this question suggest that our preferences for neighborhood racial integration are associated with the racial composition of our actual neighborhoods (Ilandfeldt and Scafidi 2002b, 2004). These efforts, however, have been limited to considerations of whites and blacks only and to models of preferences that do not pay sufficient attention to the various other racial attitudes shown in the previous chapter to be influential.

The LASUI can address this unresolved issue by offering what amounts to a measure of neighborhood racial composition preferences in the residential attainment models presented in chapter 3. This is accomplished via three stage least squares regression (3SLS), a system of simultaneous equations—one predicting a neighborhood-level outcome (in this case neighborhood racial composition), the other predicting neighborhood racial composition preferences—in which each outcome is also an explanatory variable in the other model (for example, preferences are a predictor of neighborhood outcomes, and vice versa), thereby addressing the issue of endogeneity.[2] Thus, the analyses in this chapter bridge the gap between analyses based on census data, which emphasize the spatial assimilation model, and those that employ survey data, deal mainly in the realm of attitudes, and emphasize the place stratification model. Though both areas of research have been fruitful, each has also suffered from its inability to address the other with rigor.

We begin with a consideration of the influence of preferences on neighborhood proximity to whites, revisiting the residential attainment analyses presented in chapter 3. The measure of preferences for white respondents is preferences for out-group neighbors (black, Latino, and Asian combined); for all nonwhite respondents, the measure is preferences for white neighbors. This model is paired in the simultaneous equations for each racial-respondent group with a second model that is an estimate of preferences, including the neighborhood-level outcome (either neighborhood proximity to whites or neighborhood proximity to out-group minorities). The pairing of these two models is akin to using the models of residential attainment presented in chapter 3 and the preference models estimated in chapter 5 together in the 3SLS process.[3] Full results for both models are presented in tables 6.1 through 6.4; we focus here, however, on models that predict neighborhood-level outcomes, and especially on the impact of neighborhood racial composition preferences on these outcomes.

The reason to consider the impact of preferences on neighborhood proximity to whites is straightforward: this is how segregation is typically studied (that is, in reference to whites), and we know that "whiter" neighborhoods tend to have less poverty, less crime, better-quality schools and other public services, and so on. Thus, aside from any possible benefits of neighborhood racial integration for improving intergroup relations, increasing disadvantaged minority groups' residential integration with whites would also improve the material quality of their lives and is therefore a critical step in the direction of eradicating racial inequality. A consideration of proximity to out-group minorities takes advantage of the rare opportunity to examine potential similarities and differences in processes of residential distribution by race and to assess the impact of interminority-group relations—particularly with blacks—on actual residential patterns, both in the present and for the future. After summarizing and discussing the results for each set of models, I turn to the overall conclusions to be drawn from the research presented in this volume and discuss the implications of these results for the future of integration and intergroup relations in an increasingly diverse society.

PREFERENCES AND NEIGHBORHOOD PROXIMITY TO WHITES

Table 6.1 revisits the residential attainment model predicting proximity to non-Hispanic whites (see table 3.6), adding a measure of preferences. For ease of interpretation, the measure of preferences for all respondent racial categories is preference for white neighbors. The results show a statistically significant association between preferences and neighborhood proximity to whites after accounting for endogeneity and other relevant factors. This is especially true for whites, blacks, and Latinos; the association

Table 6.1 Factors Influencing Neighborhood Proximity to Non-Hispanic Whites: 3SLS Regression Coefficients

	Whites	Blacks	Latinos	Asians
Preference for white neighbors	0.52***	0.82***	0.43***	0.21†
Education				
Less than high school (ref)	—	—	—	—
High school graduate	10.79**	2.09	−0.21	4.39*
Some college	6.86	0.79	1.74	7.30**
BA or BS degree	5.78	2.62	6.53*	10.04***
Graduate or professional degree	15.02***	18.58***	17.00**	5.68
Income				
Less than $20,000 (ref)	—	—	—	—
$20,000 to $39,999	11.39***	1.56	4.34***	4.29*
$40,000 to $59,999	16.34***	4.81***	10.34***	12.23***
$60,000 to $89,999	16.91***	6.38**	14.69***	16.69***
$90,000 and over	18.75***	6.79*	10.83*	18.33**
Missing income	−0.78	1.79	−0.87	2.77
Net financial assets				
Negative or none (ref)	—	—	—	—
$1 to $5,000	−1.58	0.65	0.67	1.14
$5,001 to $10,000	1.59	0.49	1.95	0.25
Over $10,000	3.16	2.01	4.05	2.27
Missing net financial assets	−5.64*	−0.38	−0.72	−4.30**
Homeowner	2.33	−3.30*	−0.73	6.56***
Married with children	4.14	−2.15	−0.46	1.12
Public housing experience				
Never (ref)	—	—	—	—
In the past	−5.59	−1.02	4.23	6.10
Currently	−7.69	−2.66	−6.04	3.89
Years at residence	−0.06	−0.23***	−0.34***	−0.42***
National origin				
Mexican (ref)			—	—
Central American			−3.17*	—
Japanese (ref)			—	—
Chinese				4.10
Korean			—	−3.54
Nativity status				
U.S.-born (ref)			—	—
Foreign-born: five years or less in the U.S.			−11.15***	0.79
Foreign-born: six to ten years in the U.S.			−12.17***	2.19
Foreign-born: over ten years in the U.S.			−10.23***	2.25
English-language ability			0.70	−0.24
Constant	5.48	−7.54*	11.89***	14.10***
X^2	199.17***	149.94***	335.18***	429.21***
Number of cases	704	1,038	908	1,014

Source: Author's compilation.

*** p < .001; ** p < .01; * p < .05; † p < .10

is quite modest for Asians, in terms of both coefficient size and statistical significance. Looking first at whites, this means that preferences for racial integration do in fact play a part in the racial composition of the neighborhoods that whites tend to reside in: as whites' preference for same-race neighbors increased, so too did the percentage white in their actual neighborhoods, net of other individual-level characteristics and accounting for the endogeneity of preferences and actual neighborhood racial composition. Recall from chapter 4 (table 4.5) that the average white respondent created a multiethnic neighborhood that was about 53 percent same-race. In terms of the predicted impact of preferences on actual neighborhood outcomes, this level of preference for coethnic neighbors translates into a 28 percent increase in whites' neighborhood isolation ($.52*53 = 27.56$, $p < .001$).

Among nonwhite groups, the impact of preferences on actual neighborhood outcomes is greatest for blacks. Again, recall that the average black respondent preferred a neighborhood that was about 22 percent white. On average, then, the racial composition preferences of blacks can be expected to increase their neighborhood proximity to whites by about 18 percent, controlling for other factors ($.81*22 = 18.04$, $p < .001$). For Latinos, the impact of preferences is about half as large (.43, $p < .001$), resulting in a predicted increase in proximity to whites of about 11 percent for both the native- and foreign-born in this group. Preferences are least influential for Asians' neighborhood proximity to whites: the coefficient is only one-quarter the size of the black coefficient, half the size of the Latino coefficient, and only marginally significant (.21, $p < .10$). Thus, on average, Asians' neighborhood proximity to whites should increase by only 6 or 7 percent, net of other factors.

Looking only at coefficient size and statistical significance, the influence of preferences on actual neighborhood proximity to whites is largest for blacks, followed by whites, Latinos, and Asians, in this order. Here again, results support the general tendency of blacks to be the group most interested in sharing their neighborhoods with others—in this case whites (see also Bobo and Zubrinsky 1996; Farley et al. 1993; Zubrinsky and Bobo 1996). It is certainly possible that this tendency represents an interest in upward social mobility; however, prior research on the motivations behind blacks' tendency to prefer racially integrated neighborhoods points to the importance of racial harmony and the need for increased interaction to achieve that harmony (Farley et al. 1978; Krysan 2002).

The patterns of association between the individual-level demographic and SES characteristics remain fairly consistent with those reported in chapter 3. In both cases, the association between socioeconomic status characteristics and neighborhood proximity to whites is weakest for blacks—further confirmation of prior tests of the spatial assimilation hypothesis. One noteworthy change between the previous residential attainment model and this updated one is the increase in differences between native-born Latinos and their various foreign-born counterparts once we account for preference for white neighbors. In the previous model, native-born Latinos lived in neighborhoods that were between 6 and 8 percent more white on average than the neighborhoods of their immigrant coethnics (see table 3.6). Reestimating proximity to whites with a simultaneous equations model that also accounts for preferences increases the native-/foreign-born gap to between 10 and 12 percent on average, depending on the length of time immigrants have been in the United States.

Table 6.2 summarizes results from the second model, which predicts neighborhood racial composition preferences accounting for the endogeneity of neighborhood proximity to whites. For whites, the percentage of same-race residents in their neighborhoods is not significantly associated with same-race preferences, net of the other factors in the model and, again, taking into consideration the endogeneity of neighborhood contact. An alternative and more troubling interpretation is that increasing contact with nonwhites does not significantly alter whites' preferences for neighborhood-level contact with other racial groups. It is also evident that, as was true in the previous chapter, whites' attitudes toward minority groups are potent predictors of their preferences for same-race neighbors, but in-group attachment and the perceived relative social class position of out-groups have no significant influence on whites' preferences. Conversely, neighborhood exposure to whites is positively and significantly associated with black, Latino, and Asian preferences for sharing residential space with this group. Unlike its effect on whites, then, this form of contact may help blacks, Latinos, and Asians by neutralizing the strength and influence of stereotypes, reducing perceptions of social distance, and allaying concerns about being the target of white hostility.

The patterns of association between racial attitudes and preferences persist, remaining generally consistent with those detailed in chapter 5. Note, however, that white respondents with missing values on the perceived social class disadvantage item preferred about 9 percent more same-race neighbors relative to those with valid responses, and that whites who were interviewed by nonwhite interviewers preferred nearly 15 percent fewer same-race neighbors compared to those who were interviewed by whites. These patterns are entirely consistent with social desirability bias. It is possible that those whites who were reluctant to respond to the perceived social class disadvantage item were significantly more concerned with the class status of their neighbors than with the race of

Table 6.2 Factors Influencing Preference for White Neighbors: 3SLS Regression Coefficients

	Whites	Blacks	Latinos	Asians
Racial Attitudes				
Social class disadvantage	1.12	0.25†	0.12	0.73
In-group attachment (ref = none or low)				
Medium	1.45	1.13*	−0.29	0.70
High	−0.09	−0.89	−0.58	−2.59*
Racial stereotyping	4.05***	−0.52*	−1.05**	0.20
Social distance	1.71**	−0.52***	−0.63***	−0.77**
Racial-group threat	1.65***	—	—	—
White discrimination	—	−0.31†	−0.47*	−0.79*
Immigration-related characteristics				
Mexican (ref)			—	—
Central American			3.73**	—
Japanese (ref)			—	—
Chinese			—	−2.39
Korean			—	17.25*
Time in the U.S. (ref = U.S.-born)			—	—
Foreign-born: five years or less			9.41**	1.55
Foreign-born: six to ten years			9.00***	7.99**
Foreign-born: over ten years			7.38***	5.98*
English-language ability			0.36	0.85
Interactions				
Korean × five years or less in the U.S.			—	−16.26*
Korean × six to ten years in the U.S.			—	−21.13**
Korean × over ten years in the U.S.			—	−19.48**
Five years or less in the U.S. × English ability			2.49*	3.12**
Five years or less in the U.S. × stereotyping			2.78**	—
Potential intergroup contact				
Percentage white in neighborhood	−0.03	0.26**	0.46***	0.21*
Public housing (ref = never)				
In the past	−0.37	0.91	−0.93	−3.84
Currently	−1.70	3.84***	7.09	1.59
Social background characteristics				
Male	2.98*	0.65	−1.23	−2.06
Age (ref = 20 to 29)				
30 to 39	−4.55*	0.35	−0.06	2.10
40 to 49	−4.08	0.79	0.00	3.11
50 to 59	−0.87	1.75	4.90*	−0.58
60 to 69	3.71	2.46*	6.06*	−2.98
70 and over	6.33*	2.90*	5.16	−2.85

Table 6.2 (Continued)

	Whites	Blacks	Latinos	Asians
Education (ref = less than high school)				
High school graduate	0.08	–1.29	0.26	0.59
Some college	3.32	–0.59	3.35	1.77
BA or BS degree	2.58	–1.30	–1.43	1.56
Graduate or professional degree	–5.07	–6.43	2.46	4.06
Homeowner	2.10	2.13*	0.05	1.09
Married with children	–0.13	0.59	1.06	–1.07
Political conservatism	–0.57	0.10	0.84*	0.39
Other controls				
Missing social class disadvantage	8.64*	–3.59	–4.87	1.16
Missing racial stereotyping	–4.46	1.15	0.39	1.00
Missing social distance	12.98*	–5.84†	1.40	–1.42
Missing white discrimination	—	–0.42	–5.67	–7.82**
Non-race-matched	–14.73***	4.53**	1.98	–6.18
Female ballot	2.04	–0.48	–1.73	–4.61***
Male ballot	0.54	0.35	–2.64*	–5.69***
Constant	40.85***	17.87***	7.67†	26.07***
X^2	231.03***	203.99***	216.43***	264.08***
Number of cases	704	1,038	908	1,014

Source: Author's compilation.
*** p < .001; ** p < .01; * p < .05; † p < .10

their neighbors, compared to those who answered the question. Still, this accounts for only a small fraction of white respondents; therefore, the general conclusion to be made is that other racial attitudes outweigh class-based concerns in whites' calculations regarding the preferred racial composition of their neighborhoods. Similarly, Asians who refused to rate whites as either tending to discriminate against other groups or tending to treat other groups equally preferred about 8 percent fewer white neighbors compared to coethnics who provided valid responses. Finally, note that there was a tendency among Asians and, to a lesser extent, Latinos to respond differently to the stereotype items, depending on whether they were asked to rate group males or females instead of evaluating the group as a whole. In each instance of a significant difference, gendered evaluations tended to be more negative.

PREFERENCES AND NEIGHBORHOOD PROXIMITY TO MINORITIES

Throughout this volume, every effort has been made to capitalize on the richness of this multiracial dataset. Central to this endeavor is a concerted effort to gain insight into minority-minority relations as well as the more typically studied minority-majority scenarios. Given the role that high-volume immigration has played in intensifying tensions between blacks and both Latinos and Asians, this attention seems warranted. Looking at minority-minority relations also illuminates the similarities and differences in the *processes* of intergroup relations—and their potential impact on residential outcomes—when all concerned parties lack dominant-group status and maintain different positions in the status hierarchy. To this end, the final piece of this analysis is a consideration of how preferences influence actual residential contact with minority groups, again taking into account the endogeneity of preferences and actual neighborhood racial composition. Specifically, for whites, minority-group neighbors are black, Latino, and Asian; for blacks, Latinos, and Asians, the target groups are other-race minority groups (for example, for Latinos the target groups are blacks and Asians). The results are summarized for each racial respondent group in tables 6.3 and 6.4. The discussion centers largely on minority-minority relations, but in the interests of full comparison, results for white respondents are also shown. Note, however, that in this instance modeling exposure to out-group neighbors and preference for those neighbors are two sides of the same coin, since preference for minority neighbors and neighborhood exposure to minorities are what remain after considering neighborhood isolation and preference for same-race neighbors.

Once again, after controlling for the endogeneity of preferences and actual neighborhood racial composition, all groups revealed a sizable, statistically significant positive association between preferences for residential integration with minority-group members and their actual neighborhood choices. Differences across respondent racial groups were similar to those in the previous analysis of proximity to whites—strongest for blacks, weakest for Asians—except that the influence of preferences was larger among Latinos than it was among whites. It is interesting that, for both whites and Asians, preferences for contact with minority groups had roughly the same size impact on actual contact as was true in the model predicting contact with whites; furthermore, for Asians, preferences for other minority neighbors were stronger predictors of exposure than was true in the comparable model predicting exposure to whites. Among both blacks and Latinos, on the other hand, the impact of preferences was larger when predicting actual contact with other-race minorities than with whites.

In each case, as anticipated, the association between preferences and actual neighborhood exposure to minority-group members was positive. For the average white respondent, preference for minority-group contact was associated with a 24 percent increase in neighborhood exposure to blacks, Latinos, and Asians, net of other factors (for mean preferences, see table 4.5; 0.52*47% = 24.44%, $p < .001$). The average black respondent saw the biggest increase in neighborhood contact with out-group minorities: on average, blacks expressed a preference for neighborhoods that were about 36 percent Latino and Asian; this translates into residence in a neighborhood that is predicted to be more than half other-race-minority (1.50*36 = 54%, $p < .001$). Among Latinos, there was once again little in the way of native-/foreign-born differences. For the average native-born Latino, preferences were associated with a 29 percent increase in exposure to blacks and Asians; for the typical immigrant Latino, the anticipated increase in minority exposure was about 24 percent, net of other factors. Preferences were least influential for Asians, for whom they were expected to increase neighborhood contact with blacks and Latinos by between 6 and 9 percent (foreign-born and native-born, respectively).

Of the other individual-level characteristics, there were few consistently significant associations with minority-group exposure to other minorities. Income was the most consistent of these, and as we might expect, increasing income decreased exposure to minority groups, net of other factors; again, the impact of income was largest for whites and Asians. Homeownership actually increased Latino exposure to other-race minorities, possibly because, as with blacks, the options available to Latino homeowners are constrained. For both groups, the consequence of these constraints is residence in areas with more blacks. Length of time in the United States was also a significant factor for Latinos, but not for Asians. The most recent Mexican and Central American immigrants experienced the most exposure to blacks and Asians compared to their native-born counterparts, and this exposure declined with the accumulation of time in the United States (though the difference between intermediate- and long-term immigrants was not that great). And interestingly, Korean-origin Asians resided in neighborhoods with significantly more other-race minorities compared to their Japanese- and Chinese-origin counterparts. Recall that, across national-origin categories, Korean respondents were least interested in sharing neighborhood space with blacks and Latinos.

This difference is evident once again in table 6.4, which reestimates preferences taking into consideration the endogeneity of actual neighborhood contact, thus perhaps explaining, for this group at least, why actual

Table 6.3 Factors Influencing Neighborhood Proximity to (Out-Group) Minorities: 3SLS Regression Coefficients

	Whites	Blacks	Latinos	Asians
Preference for (out-group) minority neighbors	0.52***	1.50***	0.92***	0.25**
Education				
Less than high school (ref)	—	—	—	—
High school graduate	−10.51**	−2.48	−2.03	−1.40
Some college	6.68	−2.98	−5.33	−4.33*
BA or BS degree	−5.46	−1.93	−8.90*	−6.99***
Graduate or professional degree	−14.83***	−11.67	3.87	−5.48*
Income				
Less than $20,000 (ref)	—	—	—	—
$20,000 to $39,999	−11.29***	−3.82*	−0.56	−3.97**
$40,000 to $59,999	−16.29***	−6.06*	−8.19**	−10.67***
$60,000 to $89,999	−16.79***	−6.04*	−8.75*	−14.91***
$90,000 and over	−18.50***	−9.16*	−2.46	−14.59***
Missing income	0.93	−0.97	3.42	−1.18
Net financial assets				
Negative or none (ref)	—	—	—	—
$1 to $5,000	1.63	−0.72	−0.03	1.27
$5,001 to $10,000	−1.49	−2.95	−2.50	0.31
Over $10,000	−3.12	−1.05	−2.15	−1.94
Missing net financial assets	5.61*	3.30*	3.11	2.76*
Homeowner	−2.27	−4.44*	8.71***	0.16
Married with children	−4.31	0.45	1.00	−1.04
Public housing experience				
Never (ref)	—	—	—	—
In the past	5.37	0.07	−4.04	−1.59
Currently	7.84	−8.16**	4.33	10.62***
Years at residence	0.06	0.01	−0.12	0.31***
National origin				
Mexican (ref)			—	—
Central American			0.53	—
Japanese (ref)			—	—
Chinese			—	0.33
Korean			—	7.83***
Nativity status			—	—
U.S.-born (ref)			—	—
Foreign-born: five years or less in the U.S.			14.90***	−1.34
Foreign-born: six to ten years in the U.S.			9.44**	−0.40
Foreign-born: over ten years in the U.S.			8.77***	−1.84
English-language ability			0.37	0.37
Constant	41.42***	−10.61	−11.66†	33.31***
X^2	197.27***	99.15***	74.76***	364.76***
Number of cases	704	1,038	908	1,014

Source: Author's compilation.

*** p < .001; ** p < .01; * p < .05; † p < .10

neighborhood contact had no significant effect on Asian preferences for integration with other minority groups. In fact, actual contact with out-group minorities had no significant effect on preferences for any of the respondent racial categories. On the other hand, a brief perusal of the second equation—reconsidering the factors that influence preferences—largely reconfirms analyses from the previous chapter, except for the impact of actual neighborhood contact, which was largely positive and significant.[4] Among whites, each of the three measures of prejudice—racial stereotyping, social distance, and perceived racial-group threat—substantially reduced preferences for neighborhood racial integration. Moreover, these factors stood out as the most consistently significant among those considered. Once again, whites who did not provide valid responses to the perceived social class disadvantage and social distance items and/or were not race-matched with their interviewer responded in ways that were meaningfully different from their counterparts and consistent with a desire to meet social desirability standards.

Social class concerns remained salient among Asians—once again the only group for whom class differences were salient. Racial stereotyping and perceptions of blacks and Latinos as socially distant also had the anticipated effect on preferences. The national-origin and nativity-status differences detailed in the previous chapter also persisted. Overall, immigrants preferred significantly fewer minority-group neighbors than the native-born, both within and across national-origin groups; as indicated previously, Koreans were most resistant to integration with blacks and Latinos. And consistent with the results reported in the previous chapter, Asians who once lived in public housing preferred markedly more contact with other racial minority groups compared to those with no such experience.

Very few factors were significant predictors of minority-group preferences for blacks. As has been the case throughout, racial attitudes were least influential for this group—only racial stereotyping had a significant impact on preferences for integration with Asians and Latinos, net of other factors. Furthermore, blacks were the only group other than Asians to show a positive association between preference for minority-group neighbors and experience with public housing. For this group, however, it was those currently residing in public housing who differed, preferring slightly more minority neighbors relative to other blacks. The only other significant factor in the black-respondent preference model was the race of the interviewer: those black respondents interviewed by nonblacks tended to prefer about 9 percent more out-group minority neighbors relative to black respondents with race-matched interviewers, a finding that, once again, is in keeping with social desirability concerns. (Bear in mind

Table 6.4 Factors Influencing Preference for (Out-Group) Minority Neighbors: 3SLS Regression Coefficients

	Whites	Blacks	Latinos	Asians
Racial attitudes				
Social class disadvantage	–1.13	–0.01	0.26	–1.15**
In-group attachment (ref = none or low)	—	—	—	—
Medium	–1.42	–0.09	1.92†	–0.57
High	0.10	0.39	–1.95†	1.25
Racial stereotyping	–4.03***	–0.87*	0.13	–1.71**
Social distance	–1.70**	–0.13	–0.52*	–0.60†
Racial-group threat	–1.66***	–0.06	–0.24	–0.40
Immigration-related characteristics				
National origin				
Mexican (ref)			—	—
Central American			0.41	—
Japanese (ref)			—	—
Chinese			—	–3.53*
Korean			—	–19.52**
Time in the U.S. (ref = U.S.-born)			—	
Foreign-born: five years or less			–4.94	–6.40*
Foreign-born: six to ten years			–1.10	–6.30†
Foreign-born: over ten years			0.85	–6.62**
English-language ability			0.65	1.00†
Interactions				
Korean × five years or less in the U.S.			—	19.81**
Korean × six to ten years in the U.S.			—	27.40***
Korean × over ten years in the U.S.			—	18.77**
Six to ten years in the U.S. × high in-group attachment			—	–8.46**
Potential intergroup contact				
Percentage (out-group) minority in neighborhood	–0.03	0.18	–0.05	0.02
Public housing (ref = never)	—	—	—	—
In the past	0.37	–0.42	–3.44	12.46**
Currently	1.65	3.00*	1.73	0.85
Social background characteristics				
Male	–3.01*	0.01	0.71	2.62*
Age (ref = 20 to 29)	—	—	—	—
30 to 39	4.53*	0.52	0.43	–1.28
40 to 49	4.06	1.28	–1.27	–2.30
50 to 59	0.91	0.67	0.68	–3.01
60 to 69	–3.66	1.48	–5.00	–5.80**
70 and over	–6.22*	1.56	–8.14*	–9.76***

Table 6.4 (*Continued*)

	Whites	Blacks	Latinos	Asians
Education (ref = less than high school)	—	—	—	—
High school graduate	−0.06	1.57	−0.15	0.74
Some college	−3.29	1.75	0.94	1.05
BA or BS degree	−2.53	2.34	1.68	3.04
Graduate or professional degree	5.12	5.97	−6.81	0.94
Homeowner	−2.14	1.61	−0.61	−0.52
Married with children	0.16	2.05	−0.08	−1.03
Political conservatism	−0.57	0.02	0.38	−0.66†
Other controls				
Missing social class disadvantage	−8.74*	2.26	−6.67*	−0.40
Missing racial stereotyping	4.51	0.34	−2.39	−0.65
Missing social distance	−12.99*	0.28	1.86	−1.89
Non-race-matched	14.88***	9.38*	10.71**	8.67*
Female ballot	−2.05	0.05	1.20	0.63
Male ballot	−0.56	−0.46	−0.08	0.85
Constant	62.48***	23.34***	28.46***	34.54***
X^2	232.09***	492.94***	151.73***	261.58***
Number of cases	704	1,038	908	1,014

Source: Author's compilation.
*** p < .001; ** p < .01; * p < .05; † p < .10

that black respondents who were not race-matched to a black interviewer were extremely likely to be interviewed by a Latino interviewer.)

Racial attitudes were a bit more influential for Latinos than for blacks. In-group attachment was a marginally significant predictor of Latino preferences—a high level of attachment had the anticipated negative effect on preference for integration with blacks and Asians, but a moderate level increased preferences for integration with other-race minorities. One reason a moderate amount of in-group solidarity actually increases preferences for integration with other minority groups may be that those with more centrist views are also more inclined toward coalition-building or are at least better able to see similarities among disadvantaged minority groups, irrespective of their racial-group membership. Or perhaps the association between a high degree of common fate identity and preferences for integration is a simple expression of ethnocentrism. An alternative, more pessimistic view is that this subset of Latinos is expressing the consequences of tense relations with both blacks and Asians. Furthermore, those Latinos who did not provide valid responses to the perceived social class disadvantage item tended to prefer significantly fewer minority-group neighbors, suggesting that there was some small role for class-based attitudes among this group as well. Non-race-matched interviewers, once again, increased preferences for neighborhood integration, thus completing an across-the-board pattern of social desirability pressure across respondent categories. Finally, Latinos differed from Asians in that immigration-related characteristics had no significant impact on their preferences for integration with blacks and Asians. Indeed, there were no meaningful differences along national-origin or nativity-status lines or by level of English proficiency; nor did any of these characteristics interact with one another or with racial attitudes in any meaningful way.

Looking Ahead

These results provide striking empirical evidence that there is a direct association between individuals' neighborhood racial composition preferences and their actual residential outcomes and that active racial prejudice is a driving force in that relationship. This is not to say that individual social background characteristics and various life-course and lifestyle factors are insignificant; such factors can and do influence many of the important decisions we make in life, including where we "set up house." But this is to say that all of us—scholars, policymakers, politicians, the public—must take seriously the evidence that we remain a society organized along racial lines and that we must begin now to deal with the serious consequences of such stratification, both for our own life chances and for public efforts to improve intergroup relations and move toward greater racial harmony.

CONCLUSIONS

The goal of this volume has been to elucidate the individual-level processes of racial residential segregation in multiracial contexts. Fine-grained analyses of the ways in which both class and race figure into the residential decisionmaking process have been central to this exercise. After spending a good deal of time detailing patterns of socioeconomic inequality across racial groups and their impact on monthly housing expenditures, rates of homeownership, and processes of residential attainment, I turned to a detailed consideration of patterns of neighborhood racial composition preferences and the forces that drive them. What becomes abundantly clear is that racial preferences are situated within the broader context of historic and contemporary American race relations. Preferences both for and against integration with various out-groups are part and parcel of more generalized racial stereotypes, beliefs about social distance, perceptions of minority groups as competitive threats to the economic opportunities and political power of one's own group, and beliefs about discrimination. The patterns of racial attitudes and their impact on preferences reveal the persistence of both traditional racial prejudice and the group-position variant.

Whites, not surprisingly, provide the most powerful evidence of prejudice as a sense of group position. Whites are at once the dominant group socially and economically and a numerical minority in Los Angeles. Feelings of competitive threat are quite common across groups, but they are influential for preferences only among whites. Negative racial stereotypes and feelings of social distance are also potent predictors of preferences; these measures also capture both simple out-group antipathy and perceptions of out-groups as inferior relative to one's own group. To the extent that whites perceive racial-ethnic minorities as socially distant and tending to be less intelligent, lazier (preferring welfare to self-sufficiency), more criminally oriented, and so on, contact with out-groups may suggest a loss of status advantages and privileges. The primary importance of whites' racial prejudice is further supported by the evidence that their perceptions of racial-ethnic minority groups as economically disadvantaged—and they perceive both blacks and Latinos as substantially disadvantaged—never influence their preferences for neighborhood integration (or isolation) in any meaningful way; nor do their feelings of in-group attachment.

Whites are not unique, however, in this regard. To varying, albeit lesser, degrees, prejudice has a meaningful impact on the neighborhood racial composition preferences of blacks, Latinos, and Asians as well. Nevertheless, group positioning in the nation's status hierarchy is critically important to understanding differences in the factors that influence the neighborhood racial composition preferences of whites and nonwhites. As the dominant group, whites seem to be primarily concerned about maintaining their elevated position and all of the privileges that come with dominant-group status; this motive is probably why concerns about racial-group competition are salient for whites' preferences but not for those of other groups. Alternatively, the preference for white neighbors of each of the nonwhite groups is significantly affected by the extent to which they believe that whites tend to discriminate against members of other racial-ethnic groups. Also influential are nonwhite groups' perceptions of whites as socially distant or hard to get along with socially. The finding that racial-ethnic minorities tend to perceive whites as both difficult to get along with and likely to discriminate against other groups suggests that they are consciously concerned that white neighbors would treat them in a hostile way. Negative stereotypes are also important, but the primacy of two of the three most influential racial attitudes (the perception of whites as socially distant—difficult to get along with—and tending to discriminate against others) suggests that nonwhite groups are trying to balance integration with self-preservation by avoiding those they perceive as unfriendly or downright hostile.

Racial-ethnic minorities also differ from whites in terms of the salience of in-group attachment and its effect on neighborhood racial composition preferences. In a couple of instances, strong in-group solidarity does have the hypothesized negative effect on preferences for neighborhood racial integration. It is also the case, however, that a moderate degree of in-group attachment increases preferences for integration with whites, contrary to expectations. Recall too that the importance of in-group attachment varies with nativity status and is associated with immigrant adaptation. Indeed, immigration-related characteristics weigh heavily on the neighborhood racial composition preferences of both Latinos and Asians. For the former, recent arrival and English-language ability interact to influence preferences for both white and same-race neighbors; for the latter, national-origin and nativity-status differences are key. Perceived differences in social class status also matter a great deal for Asians; indeed, this racial attitude has the greatest influence on Asians' preferences for minority-group neighbors.

There is good news in all this. Despite persisting negative racial attitudes and a strikingly clear association between racial attitudes and preferences and between preferences and actual neighborhood outcomes, whites are increasingly *willing* to live in close proximity to racial minorities, and a sizable number of blacks, Latinos, and Asians are still *willing* to live in predominantly white areas. To capitalize on this willingness, however, requires being ever mindful of how race shapes both our day-to-day interactions and our overall worldviews. As the primary driving forces in preferences, these attitudes ultimately shape our residential choices. Preferences for integration lead to residence in more integrated neighborhoods. And contrary to the assertions of conservatives (both white and black), it is out-group hostility and concern about becoming a target of hostility that best explain preferences for self-segregation, not mutually expressed ethnocentrism (Patterson 1997; McWhorter 2000; Thernstrom and Thernstrom 1997).

However, the finding that a sizable minority of whites still prefer predominantly or overwhelmingly white neighborhoods, combined with the tendency for nonwhites to prefer more same-race neighbors than whites are willing to tolerate, provides less encouraging news. A majority of whites still adhere to negative stereotypes, even many of those who are willing to share residential space with racial minorities. Conversely, with their keen sense of both their subordinate position relative to whites and whites' negative views of them, most blacks, Latinos, and Asians remain suspicious of overwhelmingly white areas. In short, given group-level differences in preferences, when people cannot achieve their preferred level of integration in their residential decisionmaking, they more often err on the conservative side.

Across racial groups, patterns of neighborhood racial composition preferences reveal a clear and consistent racial rank-ordering of out-groups as potential neighbors. Whites are always the most preferred out-group neighbors, and they are also the most likely to prefer entirely same-race neighborhoods or only limited contact with nonwhites—especially blacks. By contrast, blacks are always the least preferred out-group neighbors but are the group most open to substantial integration with all other groups and the least likely to prefer entirely same-race neighborhoods. Asians and Latinos are in between these extremes. To varying degrees, all groups express preferences for both meaningful integration and a strong coethnic presence, yet preferences for the latter appear to depend on the race of potential neighbors and are strongest when potential neighbors are black.

Thus, one way or another, the available evidence indicates that racial prejudice plays a particularly important role in driving neighborhood racial composition preferences. For nearly all groups, the effects of racial stereotyping, social distance, perceived racial-group competition, and perceived white discrimination are almost always stronger and more consistent than the effects of perceived social class disadvantage or in-group attachment. In fact, in both absolute and relative terms, neither the perception of social class disadvantage nor ethnocentrism emerges as a driving force in neighborhood racial preferences (with the exception of class attitudes among Asians). And again, although the evidence supports both variants of racial prejudice, it is particularly persuasive with respect to the group-position variant given the importance of social distance attitudes and the perception of minority groups as competitive threats. This is especially true for whites, the group at the top of the status hierarchy: maintaining their status advantages and privilege necessitates a certain amount of social distance from nonwhites—particularly blacks and Hispanics, who occupy the lowest positions on the racial hierarchies. For many whites, more than token integration with these groups signals an unwelcome change in status relationships. Indeed, the racial pecking order is so widely known that Hispanics and Asians—many of them unassimilated immigrants—mirror (and arguably exaggerate) it in their preferences for integration.

Conversely, with whites clearly in the most privileged positions of the economic, political, and prestige hierarchies in American society, nonwhites have traditionally associated upward social mobility with proximity to whites. That many nonwhites hold negative stereotypes of whites but still want to share residential space with them is indicative of this orientation (Jankowski 1995; Jaynes and Williams 1989; Massey and Denton 1993). At the same time, minority-group members tend to rate as less desirable those communities they perceive as hostile toward them, and overwhelmingly white communities are often perceived in this way (Zubrinsky and Bobo 1996). Nonwhites' beliefs about discrimination and hostility and their awareness that whites are not "on the same page" appear to cause some minority home-seekers to limit their housing searches to areas where they feel welcome, and sometimes they decide not to search at all (Yinger 1995; Charles 2001b). Thus, rather than reflecting ethnocentrism, a neighborhood's racial composition acts as a signal for minority home-seekers: those areas with substantial coethnic representation are viewed as welcoming, while those with very few or no coethnic residents evoke concerns about hostility, isolation, and discomfort, both psychological and, sometimes, physical (Meyer 2000). For all groups, preferences for same-race neighbors have more to do with aversion to—or fear of—others far more than with group solidarity. *These are clearly racial concerns, and they cut across class lines.*

Indeed, studies of the attitudes and experiences of middle-class blacks suggest that, paradoxically, this subset of blacks may be most pessimistic about the future of race relations, most likely to believe that whites have negative attitudes toward them, and increasingly less interested in predominantly white neighborhoods (Feagin and Sikes 1994; Hochschild 1995; Sigelman and Tuch 1997). Thus, the most upwardly mobile blacks may be more suspicious of whites than other blacks and less interested in sharing residential space with them. For this group, whites' racial prejudice, both real and perceived, poses a serious obstacle because most whites—irrespective of their own social class status—adhere to negative racial stereotypes, deny the persistence of pervasive racial prejudice and discrimination, and are quite likely to oppose race-targeted social policies. A sizable number of whites also perceive racial-ethnic minority groups as competitors for valued societal resources and therefore as threats to their own privileged status.

This is not to say that class-based explanations must take a backseat to explanations based in racial prejudice and minority responses to it—far from it. Objective group differences in social class characteristics are as much a reality in America as they have ever been, and these differences have monumental consequences for actual neighborhood outcomes, which, in turn, are implicated in racial disparities in income, education, health, safety, and the like. This is especially evident with respect to the analysis of racial and nativity-status group differences in the likelihood of homeownership presented in chapter 3. When differences in objective social class characteristics are accounted for, racial-ethnic minorities—both native- and foreign-born—either do not differ significantly from whites or are significantly more likely to own homes. And when non-owners were asked if they would like to buy a house in the Los Angeles area if they could, 64 and 65 percent of blacks and Latinos, respectively, said yes, compared to roughly half of whites and only 41 percent of Asians.[5] Racial-ethnic group differences in sociodemographic and financial characteristics are also implicated in what each group is able to spend on housing each month. Again, these things being equal, there are few racial-ethnic or nativity-status group differences in monthly housing expenditures; the remaining disadvantages are limited to more recently arrived Latino immigrants. (Recall that, other things being equal, Asian immigrants either do not differ significantly from whites or spend more on housing each month.)

In critically important ways, then, social class disadvantage patterned along racial lines must factor into understanding aggregate housing patterns. Indeed, many believe that it is the correlation between racial-ethnic group membership and social class status that explains the persistence of racial residential segregation: some groups simply lack the financial means to share neighborhoods with other groups. This argument is closely linked to the belief that whites and other groups avoid proximity to groups that are disproportionately poor irrespective of race; this is the essence of racial proxy hypotheses (Ellen 2000; Harris 1997). In most cases, there is no evidence to support proxy interpretations—particularly among whites, the group that is most segregated from everyone else and in control of most of society's "goodies."

We might expect, however, that given equal social class status, *individuals* of various racial-ethnic backgrounds would have similar "neighborhood purchasing power." If this is true, we might expect that over time, as disadvantaged minority groups gain in educational attainment and income in the aggregate, racial residential segregation would decline. Unfortunately, this is not the case: racial-ethnic groups often differ in meaningful ways in the returns to their human capital characteristics, and these differences again disadvantage the groups that already occupy the most disadvantaged positions. Thus, only blacks and Latinos with an advanced degree see significant improvements in their residential contact with whites, and interestingly, their returns are a bit larger than for comparable whites and Asians. This accounts for a very small percentage, however, of the black and Latino population; the rest do not differ significantly from their counterparts with less than a high school diploma. Alternatively, whites and Asians attain significant neighborhood improvements at every increment of educational attainment. Potentially more disconcerting, however, is that accumulated wealth—long thought to be a crucial omitted variable in tests of spatial assimilation—may modestly improve white outcomes but provides no meaningful advantage to minority-group members in Los Angeles County. (Whites in the highest category of net financial assets benefit in both neighborhood racial composition and neighborhood median income, and Asians benefit only with respect to the latter; see tables 3.6 and 3.7).[6]

There are two reasons why any consideration of the role played by racial differences in social class characteristics in understanding persisting racial residential segregation invariably leads back to a discussion of persisting racial prejudice—both individual and structural. First, quite simply, human capital characteristics should be of equal value across racial-ethnic group boundaries. That this is generally not the case seems borne out by the differential outcomes of racial-ethnic groups: some get less neighborhood for their human capital, whether by having to achieve more to see any payoff or by getting less at all levels. Such outcomes may be a consequence of differential treatment: those groups perceived as "less desirable" may get fewer returns, and those groups perceived as "more desirable" may get more than they deserve. Either way, the outcome severely disadvantages blacks and Latinos, setting the stage to disadvantage these groups in other material outcomes as well, such as education, safety, and health.

The second reason why class disadvantage leads back to racial prejudice is fairly straightforward but often more difficult to "sell" to white America. The disadvantaged status of blacks and Latinos began with the systematic exclusion of these groups as full members of American society. Legalized segregation, particularly of blacks but also of native-born, multigenerational Latinos in the Southwest, along with laws that made it extremely difficult for these groups to earn a living, get an education, or accumulate wealth through homeownership, confined these groups to overcrowded, subpar neighborhoods and concentrated poverty (Meyer 2000; Mindiola et al. 2002; Massey and Denton 1993; Oliver and Shapiro 1995).

Moreover, this history of oppression and the racial ideology that emerged to justify the systematic oppression of racial minority groups are the not-so-distant relatives of the widely documented racial attitudes and patterns of systematic discrimination that prevail today in public places (Cose 1993; Feagin and Sikes 1994) and in the labor and housing markets

(Bertrand and Mullainathan 2004; Pager and Quillian 2005; Turner et al. 2002; Yinger 1995). Admittedly, the whites walking the streets of America today are not responsible for the behavior of their forebears; unfortunately, this is often the knee-jerk rationale for discounting any solutions that are perceived as penalizing dominant-group members for the mistakes of the past. Thus, Americans are widely supportive of policies that target "the poor" but increasingly reluctant to back policies aimed at "redressing past racial wrongs."

As we move headlong into the twenty-first century and continue to struggle with racial inequality in all areas of American life, we must be ever mindful that race still matters, and that it matters over and above social class characteristics. At the same time, we must remember how and why race matters. White objections to race-targeted social policy point to the necessity for well-crafted, universal housing policies that can gain widespread public support but also address issues more directly tied to race. Studies documenting the characteristics of stably integrated neighborhoods provide us with potentially useful strategies for encouraging whites and nonwhites to share residential space. Residents of these communities often work together on community betterment projects (building playground equipment for a park, working to have street lights installed) or engage in other community-building efforts that bring people of varied racial backgrounds together to work toward a common goal. Such activities, particularly when they become part of the larger neighborhood culture, can fundamentally alter attitudes on both sides of the racial divide by highlighting what residents share in common, helping to build trust, and reducing stereotypes (Allport 1954).

Another common strategy is to launch aggressive public relations campaigns that sing the praises of particular communities. Some of these may stress the value added by diversity; others highlight desirable neighborhood amenities, services, and community events that make the area generally attractive; those that do both may ultimately be the most successful (Ellen 2000). Aggressive marketing strategies seem particularly beneficial when neighborhoods can be advertised as among "the best" in a particular metropolitan area. Positive marketing may also help to attract blacks, Hispanics, and Asians to overwhelmingly white areas by informing these groups that they are open to creating stable, friendly, and racially diverse communities.

Active, diligent enforcement of antidiscrimination laws is both appropriate and necessary but is likely to be a far more difficult and potentially less rewarding task. As it stands, the burden of proving discrimination is placed on the victim, yet empirical evidence suggests that present-day discrimination is often so subtle that few victims are likely to suspect that their housing choices are being constrained (Briggs 2003; Galster and Godfrey 2003; Turner et al. 2002; Yinger 1995). Add to this issue the gulf of racial misunderstanding separating whites and racial minorities: where blacks and, to a lesser extent, Latinos and Asians see "a racist moment," whites see "an isolated incident" or a "misinterpretation of events," or even worse, they argue that minorities are "overreacting." In response, blacks and other minorities become increasingly distrustful of a system that is supposed to protect them, pessimistic about the future of race relations, and less inclined to incur the psychic costs associated with filing a complaint. Add to this the growing mistrust and tension between racial minority groups resulting from high-volume immigration and constrained housing opportunities and it becomes even more difficult to imagine a future in which, to quote Rodney King, we all "just get along."

To give teeth to antidiscrimination enforcement, we need "a new enforcement strategy that builds the capacity of local, state, and federal civil rights agencies to conduct widespread, ongoing" audit studies as a credible deterrent (Galster and Godfrey 2003, 24). Randomly selected real estate agencies and those suspected of discrimination could be tested; those agencies found to treat clients and others with consistent fairness could be publicly rewarded, while those shown to discriminate could be sanctioned, both publicly and financially. Audit studies in the lending market are more difficult, but regular analysis of Home Mortgage Disclosure Act (HMDA) data presents a method for charting the practices of lenders. Such strategies could create meaningful deterrents. Furthermore, regular monitoring could lead to documentation of systematic discrimination that not only could help to alter whites' beliefs about inequality and discrimination but also could be used by victims as evidence in complaints. Such efforts could move us toward better racial understanding as whites obtain the "proof" they need to believe what blacks and other racial minorities "just know" (Briggs 2005).

A more obvious and equally difficult challenge for reducing residential segregation and improving housing options for the poor (including those who participate in public housing programs) is posed by whites' racial prejudice, and minority responses to it. For many, the obvious material benefits of such programs will clearly outweigh concerns about experiences of prejudice and discrimination (Briggs 2005). For a nontrivial few, however, fears of isolation and hostility will prevail, and those participants will return to the ghetto; others will opt out entirely when confronted with the reality of moving to a potentially hostile environment (Rubinowitz and Rosenbaum 2000). Asians and Latinos are not at the bottom of the status hierarchy, but they are also subordinate groups that grapple with similar racial issues. Patterns of racial attitudes and preferences among these groups suggest that a similar paradox is emerging for them as well.

We once thought that increasing racial diversity might create a "buffer" for blacks, opening up opportunities for residential mobility, contact with whites, and minority-group coalition-building and making it easier for all of us to embrace that diversity. Yet Latinos and Asians are at least as likely to hold negative stereotypes of blacks as whites are, and even more likely to object to sharing residential space with them. Furthermore, while whites hold negative stereotypes of both Latinos and Asians, those stereotypes tend to be less severe than their stereotypes of blacks. Thus, whites are likely to view blacks as culturally deficient, while perceiving largely immigrant Latino and Asian populations as culturally distinct. Similarly, stereotypes of immigrants working hard at menial jobs and complaining less may fuel anti-black sentiment, fostering the belief that blacks "push too hard" or "are always looking for a handout." Hence, rather than operating as a buffer or a source of greater options and acceptance for blacks, increasing racial diversity may simply add to the climate of resistance to blacks as neighbors.

Perhaps Mister Rogers' suggestion that "since we're together we might as well say: Would you be mine? Could you be mine? Won't you be my neighbor?" is not likely to become the theme of a national campaign promoting racial residential integration anytime soon. Nevertheless, given the disheartening state of race relations in the United States, any and all efforts to achieve greater racial understanding, including efforts to achieve more equitable housing outcomes, are critical.

Appendix

Table A.1 Racial Attitudes and Neighborhood Racial Composition Preferences, by Respondent Race and Nativity Status: Correlations

Target-Group Race	Whites	Blacks	Native-Born Latinos	Foreign-Born Latinos	Native-Born Asians	Foreign-Born Asians
White Neighbors						
Social class disadvantage	—	0.140***	0.123	–0.006	0.058	0.053
In-group attachment	—	–0.145***	–0.166*	–0.059	–0.031	0.096**
Racial stereotyping	—	–0.079*	–0.172*	–0.048	0.094	0.035
Social distance	—	–0.276***	–0.36***	–0.179***	–0.112	–0.192***
White discrimination	—	–0.216***	–0.173*	–0.091	0.148	0.019
Black neighbors						
Social class disadvantage	–0.051	—	–0.130	0.017	0.174	–0.305***
In-group attachment	0.004	—	0.017	–0.040	–0.001	0.016
Racial stereotyping	–0.360***	—	–0.055	–0.056	–0.134	–0.128***
Social distance	–0.270***	—	–0.216**	–0.147***	–0.264**	–0.054
Racial-group threat (blacks)[a]	–0.213***	—	–0.116	0.035	–0.102	–0.295***
Latino neighbors						
Social class disadvantage	–0.035	0.014	—	—	0.051	–0.223***
In-group attachment	–0.062	0.021	—	—	0.025	–0.092**
Racial stereotyping	–0.248***	–0.057	—	—	–0.118	–0.197***
Social distance	–0.186	–0.043	—	—	–0.192*	–0.024
Racial-group threat (Latinos)[a]	–0.280***	–0.022	—	—	–0.428***	–0.002
Asian neighbors						
Social class disadvantage	–0.103**	0.109***	–0.051	–0.001	—	—

(*Table continues on p. 191.*)

In-group attachment	–0.053	–0.066*	–0.120	–0.015	—	—
Racial stereotyping	–0.261***	–0.078*	0.025	–0.029	—	—
Social distance	–0.202***	–0.263***	–0.154*	–0.124***	—	—
Racial-group threat (Asians)[a]	–0.303***	–0.192***	–0.283*	–0.084	—	—
Same-race neighbors[b]						
Social class disadvantage	0.080*	–0.045	–0.014	–0.050	–0.166	0.120***
In-group attachment	0.049	0.124***	0.192*	0.073*	0.009	–0.034
Racial stereotyping	0.343***	0.090**	0.113	–0.022	0.022	–0.032
Social distance	0.245***	0.236***	0.410***	0.188***	0.198*	0.018
Racial-group threat	0.317***	0.146***	0.161*	0.074*	0.179*	0.126***
White discrimination	—	–0.093**	0.070	0.113**	–0.010	–0.043

Source: Author's compilation.

a. Owing to a split ballot, roughly one-third of whites considered blacks (N = 234), Latinos (N = 241), and Asians (N =228); about half of each nonwhite group considered group competition with each remaining group (512 blacks got the Latino ballot, and 523 got Asians; 96 native-born and 345 foreign-born Latinos got the black ballot, 78 native-born and 389 foreign-born Latinos got Asians; 58 native-born and 447 foreign-born Asians considered blacks, 65 native-born and 443 foreign-born Asians considered Latinos).

b. For same-race neighbors, racial attitudes combine responses for all out-groups (for example, for white respondents, attitudes toward blacks, Latinos, and Asians are combined for perceived SES and stereotype difference measures, social distance, and competitive threat; for nonwhites, these and the second instance of housing discrimination are pooled).

*** $p < .001$; ** $p < .01$; * $p < .05$

Table A.2 Factors Influencing Whites' Preferences: OLS Regression Coefficients

	Blacks	Latinos	Asians	Race
Constant	25.12***	18.53***	18.67***	28.63***
Social background				
Sex (1 = male)	–1.33	–0.93	–1.38	3.81
Age (ref = 20 to 29)				
30 to 39	1.11	0.30	1.06	–2.81
40 to 49	–1.48	1.40	1.51	–1.91
50 to 59	–1.13	–0.11	–1.12	2.41
60 to 69	–3.10	–1.05	–0.71	5.11
70 and over	–5.24***	–3.63*	–0.55	9.68**
Education (ref = less than high school)				
High school graduate	–2.34	–0.06	2.74	0.33
Some college	–4.54*	–0.33	1.91	3.54
BA or BS degree	–4.48*	–1.92	2.69	4.09
Graduate or professional degree	–2.19	1.57	4.51*	–3.32
Income (ref = less than $20,000)				
$20,000 to $39,999	0.46	2.49*	1.55	–3.48
$40,000 to $59,999	–1.66	0.26	–1.18	3.58
$60,000 to $89,999	0.24	–0.18	0.30	0.43
$90,000 and over	1.41	1.63	2.23	–3.89
Homeowner (1 = yes)	–1.38	1.61	–0.05	0.13
Married with children (1 = yes)	0.35	0.61	–1.00	0.07
Political ideology	–0.22	–0.20	–0.29	0.76
Potential intergroup contact				
Past public housing resident	–0.65	0.66	–0.45	0.22
Current public housing resident	1.46	1.89	–0.07	–3.97
Percentage target group in neighborhood	0.14***	0.10***	0.08*	0.04
Racial attitudes				
Social class disadvantage	0.44	–0.14	–0.42	0.35
In-group attachment (ref = none or low)				
Medium	0.17	0.68	–0.89	0.66
High	0.30	–1.19	–0.89	1.66
Racial stereotyping	–1.92***	–1.36***	–2.23**	5.00***
Social distance	–0.75**	–0.69*	–1.15**	1.95**
Racial-group threat	–0.56*	–0.62***	–0.61**	1.83***
Other controls				
Missing income	–2.33*	–0.35	2.90	0.15
Missing social class disadvantage	1.60	–2.46	–2.27	8.51
Missing racial stereotyping	–3.00	1.76	–1.59	–1.03
Missing social distance	–0.50	–3.65	–3.09	8.06
Non-race-matched	0.59	1.27	3.36***	–6.34***
Female ballot	0.76	–0.31	–0.97	0.87
Male ballot	–0.16	0.58	–1.20	0.75
R-squared	0.28***	0.16***	0.16***	0.23***

Source: Author's compilation.

Notes: N = 705.

*** $p < .001$; ** $p < .01$; * $p < .05$

Table A.3 Factors Influencing Blacks' Preferences: OLS Regression Coefficients

	Whites	Latinos	Asians	Race
Constant	20.37***	19.00***	13.97***	43.91***
Social background				
Sex (1 = male)	−0.19	0.28	−0.34	0.30
Age (ref = 20 to 29)				
30 to 39	0.81	0.32	0.87	−2.40
40 to 49	1.99	−0.25	1.94	−4.14*
50 to 59	2.86	0.17	1.88	−5.29*
60 to 69	2.58	−0.74	2.01	−4.10
70 and over	2.65	1.04	2.20	−7.06*
Education (ref = less than high school)				
High school graduate	−1.67	1.36	0.81	−0.65
Some college	−1.13	0.58	1.79	−1.31
BA or BS degree	−1.68	1.24	2.43*	−2.07
Graduate or professional degree	−3.04	0.56	6.97**	−4.66
Income (ref = less than $20,000)				
$20,000 to $39,999	2.82**	−1.76*	−0.20	−1.03
$40,000 to $59,999	1.83	−2.72*	0.99	−0.69
$60,000 to $89,999	3.55*	−0.91	0.44	−3.43
$90,000 and over	3.08	−1.20	0.44	−3.09
Homeowner (1 = yes)	−0.04	−0.05	−0.24	0.54
Married with children (1 = yes)	0.39	1.60	1.45	−3.46*
Political conservatism	0.25	−0.01	0.32	−0.57
Potential intergroup contact				
Past public housing resident	1.11	−0.56	0.07	−0.37
Current public housing resident	3.71**	0.85	0.04	−4.69**
Percentage target group in neighborhood	0.09***	0.05	0.06	0.05
Racial attitudes				
Social class disadvantage	0.33†	−0.09	0.51**	−1.11**
In-group attachment (ref = none or low)				
Medium	1.82**	0.14	−0.00	−1.97*
High	−1.20	−0.60	−0.50	2.47†
Racial stereotyping	−0.72*	−1.06*	−0.53*	2.68***
Social distance	−0.73***	−0.32	−0.54***	1.11**
White discrimination	−0.50*	—	—	0.26
Racial-group threat	—	−0.16	−0.28†	0.45†
Other controls				
Missing income	1.96	0.39	0.10	−1.94
Missing social class disadvantage	−2.08	1.80	−0.95	−2.11
Missing stereotyping	1.41	3.26	−0.58	−1.02
Missing social distance	−5.82	−1.75	0.99	2.66
Missing white discrimination	−4.11	—	—	3.44
Non-race-matched	1.38	1.57	0.96	−4.64
Female ballot	−1.34	−0.86	1.40	0.90
Male ballot	−0.54	0.12	0.21	0.36
R-squared	0.12***	0.05***	0.09***	0.13***

Source: Author's compilation.

Notes: N = 1,038.

*** $p < .001$; ** $p < .01$; * $p < .05$; † $p < .10$

Table A.4 Factors Influencing Latinos' Preferences: OLS Regression Coefficients

	Whites	Blacks	Asians	Same-Race
Constant	13.27***	13.15***	10.43***	41.62***
Social background				
Sex (1 = male)	–1.26	1.65	0.13	–0.43
Age (ref = 20 to 29)				
30 to 39	–0.76	0.22	1.42	–1.27
40 to 49	–2.05	1.69	–0.08	–0.59
50 to 59	4.05	2.39	3.43**	–11.03***
60 to 69	4.61	–2.17	–1.21	–2.01
70 and over	2.38	–0.81	–6.15*	3.88
Education (ref = less than high school)				
High school graduate	0.25	0.14	0.99	–0.92
Some college	4.07	–0.59	1.89	–5.59
BA or BS degree	1.59	1.01	1.66	–4.48
Graduate or professional degree	9.08	–5.39	1.29	–7.52
Income (ref = less than $20,000)				
$20,000 to $39,999	1.82	0.61	–0.15	–3.08
$40,000 to $59,999	3.61	0.03	–0.11	–5.03*
$60,000 to $89,999	–2.93	3.30	1.34	–3.97
$90,000 and over	4.65	–5.91	–3.44	3.02
Political conservatism	1.11*	–0.05	0.40	–1.52**
Homeowner (1 = yes)	0.13	–1.83*	–0.12	2.71
Married with children (1 = yes)	0.78	–0.71	0.46	–0.54
Potential intergroup contact				
Past public housing resident	–0.09	–0.86	–1.05	2.02
Current public housing resident	6.43	–2.89	2.18	–5.68
Percentage target group in neighborhood	0.21***	0.12***	0.21***	0.10**
Immigration-related characteristics				
Central American	3.53*	0.89	–0.34	–3.74*
Time in the U.S. (ref = U.S.-born)				
Five years or less	6.27*	–0.78	–3.68*	13.97***
Six to ten years	5.33*	–2.65	–0.02	2.46
Over ten years	4.59**	–2.92*	0.44	6.65
English-language ability	0.89†	0.94**	0.10	–0.26
Racial attitudes				
Social class disadvantage	0.18	–0.65*	–0.21	–0.18
In-group attachment (ref = none or low)				
Medium	0.00	0.19	2.35*	–2.79†
High	–0.63	0.36	–0.96	2.63†

Table A.4 *(Continued)*

	Whites	Blacks	Asians	Same-Race
Racial stereotyping	–1.40**	–0.50	–0.81*	0.65
Social distance	–0.72***	–0.90***	–0.44**	1.17***
White discrimination	–0.66*	—	—	–0.74*
Racial-group threat	—	0.06	–0.32	0.31
Interactions				
Five years or less in the U.S. × English ability	2.82*	—	—	–5.61***
Over ten years in the U.S. × English ability	—	—	—	–2.80**
Five years or less in the U.S. × racial stereotyping	3.21***	—	—	—
Five years or less in the U.S. × social class disadvantage	—	1.55*	—	—
Five years or less in the U.S. × high in-group attachment	—	–5.60**	—	—
Five years or less in the U.S. × social distance	—	0.98*	—	—
Other controls				
Missing income	–3.57*	–0.73	–1.27	6.63*
Missing social class disadvantage	–6.59	–0.04	–2.26	5.80
Missing stereotyping	1.29	–3.82**	–1.46	1.17
Missing social distance	2.83	0.05	–1.01	–4.09
Missing white discrimination	–7.98*	—	—	15.11**
Non-race-matched	1.16	0.49	1.67	–3.78
Female ballot	–1.29	–1.45	2.07*	0.94
Male ballot	–2.48*	–0.54	0.49	2.60
R-squared	0.19***	0.15***	0.14***	0.23***

Source: Author's compilation.
Notes: N = 908.
*** p < .001; ** p < .01; * p < .05; † p < .10

Table A.5 Factors Influencing Asians' Preferences: OLS Regression Coefficients

	Whites	Blacks	Latinos	Same-Race
Constant	27.51***	18.41***	17.58***	34.26***
Social background				
Sex (1 = male)	−1.19	1.08†	1.04	−0.37
Age (ref = 20 to 29)				
30 to 39	2.37	−0.89	−0.54	−0.43
40 to 49	3.04	−1.38	−0.77	−0.40
50 to 59	−1.06	−2.13	−0.89	4.20
60 to 69	−2.63	−3.83**	−2.68	9.60***
70 and over	−3.76	−5.14***	−5.15**	14.20***
Education (ref = less than high school)				
High school graduate	1.01	0.44	0.85	−3.00
Some college	2.29	0.58	0.61	−4.37
BA or BS degree	2.19	1.79†	1.34	−6.56**
Graduate or professional degree	3.89	1.41	−0.90	−6.84*
Income (ref = less than $20,000)				
$20,000 to $39,999	0.24	−1.10	−0.79	1.20
$40,000 to $59,999	0.73	−0.25	0.01	−2.04
$60,000 to $89,999	2.21	−1.04	0.50	−3.99
$90,000 and over	4.26	0.54	1.30	−7.76*
Political conservatism	0.33	−0.45*	−0.04	0.22
Homeowner (1 = yes)	1.36	−0.51	−0.01	−0.79
Married with children (1 = yes)	−1.41	−0.73	−0.41	2.92*
Potential intergroup contact				
Past public housing resident	−3.29	6.13**	6.46**	−9.62*
Current public housing resident	1.71	−0.62	0.44	0.43
Percentage target group in neighborhood	0.13***	0.01	0.03	0.13**
Immigration-related characteristics				
Chinese	−2.92	−1.42	−2.31*	2.70
Korean	16.67*	−9.44***	−11.86**	6.97*
Time in the U.S. (ref = U.S.-born)				
Five years or less	0.79	−3.42*	−2.58†	7.91†
Six to ten years	8.35**	−3.34†	−6.08***	5.42
Over ten years	6.62**	−4.05***	−3.62**	−4.25
English-language ability	0.82	0.38	0.73	−1.94*
Racial attitudes				
Social class disadvantage	0.47	−0.82***	−0.44†	1.21*
In-group attachment (ref = none or low)				
Medium	1.40	−1.02	0.05	−0.13
High	−2.78†	1.09	−0.81	3.40*

Table A.5 (*Continued*)

	Whites	Blacks	Latinos	Same-Race
Racial stereotyping	–0.15	–0.79*	–0.89*	0.53
Social distance	–0.70†	–0.41**	–0.96**	0.36
White discrimination	–0.83†	—	—	0.70
Racial-group threat	—	–0.25	–0.08	0.05
Interactions				
Korean × five years or less in the U.S.	–15.56*	10.41**	11.31*	–8.98*
Korean × six to ten years in the U.S.	–20.66**	12.87***	15.64***	–11.10**
Korean × more than ten years in the U.S.	–19.72**	9.92***	12.02**	—
Chinese × more than ten years in the U.S.	—	—	—	8.03*
Five years or less in the U.S. × English ability	3.61*	—	—	–4.16**
Six to ten years in the U.S. × high in-group attachment	—	–4.25**	—	—
Six to ten years in the U.S. × social distance	—	—	1.00*	—
Over ten years in the U.S. × social distance	—	—	0.91*	—
Other controls				
Missing income	–0.99	–0.44	–0.99	2.97
Missing social class disadvantage	0.86	–0.35	–0.24	–2.72
Missing stereotyping	0.93	0.44	–0.28	–0.95
Missing social distance	–0.99	–0.98	–1.43	3.80
Missing white discrimination	–7.89*	—	—	9.10*
Non-race-matched	–9.42***	3.65	3.82	2.17
Female ballot	–4.55**	–0.04	0.71	3.86**
Male ballot	–5.90***	0.59	0.30	5.13***
R-squared	0.22***	0.20***	0.15***	0.31***

Source: Author's compilation.
Notes: N = 1,014.
*** p < .001; ** p < .01; * p < .05; † p < .10

Notes

INTRODUCTION

1. © 1967 / McFeely-Rogers Foundation. Used with permission of Family Communications, Inc.

CHAPTER 1

1. William Frey and Reynolds Farley (1996) define a multiethnic metropolis as one in which at least two of three minority groups exceed their percentage in the U.S. population as a whole.
2. Regions that are currently majority-minority are Los Angeles, Riverside–San Bernardino, Oakland, and San Jose, California; Houston and San Antonio, Texas; Miami, Florida; and New York, New York. Two other regions—Orange County and San Francisco, California—are currently just over 51 percent white.
3. The indices were developed and calculated by Global Insight, a highly regarded international consulting firm. Weights are based on a poll of invited participants in a leadership summit held to prepare for the report. For the economics index, 50 percent of the weighted score is based on median income, 30 percent on employment issues, and 15 percent on poverty; 5 percent of the weighted index reflects the ownership of business firms (for additional details, see United Way of Greater Los Angeles and Los Angeles Urban League 2005, appendix).
4. The two most notable instances of black-Korean conflict in Los Angeles prior to 1992 were the 1991 murders of two black shoppers—thirteen-year-old Latasha Harlans and Lee Aurther Mitchell—by two different Korean merchants.
5. Approximately half of the LACSS interviews were completed prior to the 1992 unrest, and the remaining half afterward. This allowed a comparison of responses pre- and postrebellion.

6. Studies of residential segregation generally rely on one or more of six measures, each of which captures a different dimension of the spatial distribution of groups. *Evenness*, measured as the index of dissimilarity (D), describes the degree to which a group is evenly distributed across neighborhoods or tracts. A score over 60 is interpreted as extreme segregation between two groups, indicating the percentage of either group that would have to move to another tract to achieve within-tract population distributions that mirror those of the metro area. *Isolation*, measured as (P^*_{xx}), is interpreted as the percentage of the same race in the average group member's neighborhood or tract; scores of 70 and over, indicating that the average person lives in an area that is 70 percent same-race, are considered extreme. The inverse of isolation is *exposure* (P^*_{xy}), interpreted as the average probability of contact with a person of an other-race comparison group (usually whites). These are the most commonly reported measures. On three other measures—*concentration* (a group's degree of density), *clustering* (proximity to the central business district), and *centralization* (the contiguity of their neighborhoods)—a group is hypersegregated if it scores over 60 on at least four of these measures (Denton 1994; Massey and Denton 1989, 1993).
7. According to official estimates, nearly 85 percent of the 15.5 million immigrants to the United States between 1971 and 1993 were of Latin American or Asian origin (roughly 50 percent and 35 percent, respectively). Including estimates of undocumented or illegal immigrants—the majority of whom are Mexican—pushes the total up by at least another 3 million (Massey 1995).
8. The table uses tract-level data, the most commonly used level of census geography. Census tracts typically have between 2,500 and 8,000 residents and are closest in size to what most consider a neighborhood. Some researchers (such as Farley and Frey 1994) report segregation measures based on smaller, block-group data. This unit of geography usually contains only a few hundred residents who are, on average, more homogeneous. As a result, calculating segregation indices at the block-group level yields higher results (Ellen 2000, 14).
9. These compositional shifts influence residential segregation in meaningful ways. Isolation is generally low for a small group but is expected to rise with increasing group size even if its level of segregation remains constant. Moreover, the larger the relative size of an out-group's population, the greater the exposure to that group is likely to be. Both exposure and isolation are also influenced by group settlement patterns. Specifically, the chain migration patterns common among both Latino and Asian immigrants concentrate rapidly growing groups in a small number of metro areas and within a small number of neighborhoods in these areas—increasing their isolation and decreasing their exposure to out-groups (Logan 2001a; Massey and Denton 1987).
10. Data for minority-minority group exposure are not shown here but are

available from the Lewis Mumford Center at www.albany.edu/mumford/census.

11. The LASUI is part of the larger multidisciplinary project known as the Multi-City Study of Urban Inequality, which includes similar surveys in Atlanta, Boston, and Detroit.
12. This design includes a basic stratifying criterion of majority versus nonmajority status in a census tract for white, black, Latino, and Asian respondents. Because economic inequality was also a core aspect of the project, the sample design stratified income levels as well. Census tracts were classified by poverty level (less than 20 percent, 20 to 39 percent, and 40 percent or more of the residents below the poverty level). We had to use a multistratified sampling frame with variable sampling fractions to achieve the desired sample. Sampling proceeded in three stages: (1) selection of census tracts; (2) selection of blocks within tracts; and (3) selection of households within blocks. Probability proportional to size selection was utilized in the first two stages; the third stage utilized equal probability sampling (Bobo et al. 2000, 267–68). To identify participants, we employed block listers during the third stage to identify and list all housing units in selected blocks. We selected single housing units using systematic random sampling from the lists of housing units. To identify respondents, screeners visited each selected housing unit and asked a household member (whoever answered the door) to complete a household roster; the respondent was randomly selected from that list.
13. In addition, to ensure that foreign-language translations maintained the original purpose and intent, we employed highly skilled and experienced translators. To maintain the integrity of the questionnaire, after translation the foreign-language instruments were back-translated into English by translators who did not participate in the original translation.
14. Ninety-two percent of Asian interviews were race-matched, 82 percent of African American interviews, 74 percent of Latino interviews, and 53 percent of white interviews. Whites who were not race-matched were usually interviewed by an Asian interviewer. Latinos who were not race-matched were usually interviewed by a white interviewer.
15. The latter presumes that nonrespondents would have responded the same as respondents on average.
16. All foreign-born whites and blacks—124 and 43, respectively—were excluded from the analyses, largely because they were too few in number to include national-origin categories that would have been consistent with the treatment of foreign-born Latinos and Asians. Furthermore, studies of racial inequality tend to focus on native-born white and black populations, comparing them to Latinos and Asians, the largest immigrant groups. Seventy-four Latinos with ancestries other than Mexican or Central American were also excluded because there were too few of them from any single location to

say anything substantive about them. Eleven Asians were excluded for similar reasons.

17. Note that, for these purposes, "neighborhood" is defined as the census tract. Although this is not necessarily the level of geography that individual respondents had in mind, it is commonly used in social science research.

CHAPTER 2

1. For an overview of other popular theories of the underclass, see Wilson (1987) and Massey and Denton (1993); for detailed discussions of the characteristics of concentrated-poverty neighborhoods, see, besides these two works, Jargowsky (1996).
2. Massey and Denton (1993) and others (for example, Logan, Alba, and Leung 1996) argue that groups of an obvious African phenotype are similarly disadvantaged, explaining the divergence between black and white Latinos.
3. Because of space limitations, I limit my discussion of the spatial assimilation model to group differences in socioeconomic status and acculturation. The majority of multivariate analyses of spatial assimilation include one or more measures of metropolitan context (generally group size, rate of population growth, region, and/or new housing supply) and find associations between contextual effects and segregation consistent with those outlined in the previous section (see, for example, Alba and Logan 1993; Logan et al. 1996; Massey and Denton 1987; Massey, Gross, and Shibuya 1994; South and Crowder 1997a, 1997b, 1998; South and Deane 1993). Older, larger cities, located primarily in the Northeast and Midwest, are more segregated than the newer cities of the West and Southwest. Older cities have ecological structures more conducive to segregation: densely settled cores, densely populated working-class neighborhoods, and older housing stock built prior to the passage of the 1968 Fair Housing Act (for a detailed discussion, see Farley and Frey 1994).
4. Two types of aggregate-level analysis are common. In the first, a population is separated into socioeconomic indicator categories (such as education, occupation, and income), and segregation indices are recalculated within categories of the selected indicator. If segregation within categories of the indicator is similar to the overall level, we conclude that socioeconomic status is not influential in residential outcomes for that group (see, for example, Darden 1995; Denton and Massey 1988; Massey and Fischer 1999). In the second type of aggregate-level analysis, multivariate models predict residential outcomes (for example, probability of contact with whites) using the average characteristics of blacks, Latinos, and Asians for a set of metropolitan areas (Massey and Denton 1987, 1988).
5. In fairness, it should be emphasized that, until recently, obtaining census

data with both individual- and aggregate-level data was extremely difficult. Gross and Massey (1991), Massey and Denton (1985), and Villemez (1980) are exceptions to the type of analysis noted here; all are individual-level analyses (using special editions of the 1970 and 1980 public use files, to which the Census Bureau appended neighborhood racial composition data) that do not suffer from problems of ecological inference. Results are consistent with those of aggregate-level studies; Massey and Denton (1985, 94) conclude that any errors of substantive interpretation (of aggregate-level analyses) are conservative in nature. Still, these exceptions, like their aggregate-level counterparts, rely on a limited number of indicators (see Alba and Logan 1993).

6. The residential mobility model is similar, in that it considers the influence of individual-level characteristics on the likelihood of moving as well as the locational returns to individual characteristics; it differs in that it limits analysis to movers and data are taken from national panel studies (such as the Panel Survey of Income Dynamics [PSID] or the Annual Housing Survey; see Massey, Gross, and Shibuya 1994; South and Crowder 1997a, 1997b, 1998; South and Deane 1993). I focus here on individual-level analyses of census data because their results are more broadly generalized; however, the pattern of results is consistent for the two types of studies.
7. These analyses focus on suburban residents for two reasons. First, segregation is lower in the suburbs compared to the central city for all groups (see Massey and Denton 1988), suggesting that the influence of individual-level characteristics is different for the two locations. And second, focusing on suburban residents reveals the process that determines location within suburbia and elaborates differences in the characteristics of suburban neighborhoods across racial-ethnic groups (Alba and Logan 1993, 1400).
8. It has also been suggested that important differences in socioeconomic status among West Indian immigrants may influence residential outcomes. Black immigrants from the British West Indies (mainly Jamaica) have significantly higher incomes, educational levels, and employment and homeownership rates and are more concentrated in high-status occupations than French West Indians (mainly Haitians); Dutch West Indians fall in between (Crowder 1999, 103).
9. Alba and his colleagues (1999) suggest that the countertrend among the Vietnamese is attributable to their refugee status during the 1970s, when housing location was determined largely by resettlement agencies. In the 1980s, by contrast, housing decisions were more often made on the basis of household needs. These authors conclude that the Vietnamese may be entering a settlement phase comparable to the earlier phases of nonrefugee groups (Alba et al. 1999, 457).
10. Negative racial stereotypes are in play here as well, because stereotypes are

probabilistic judgments—there can be a kernel of truth to them. So, for example, as a group, blacks and Latinos do "tend to be poor." As such, what some call prejudice or discrimination might also be thought of in terms of "statistical discrimination," as described by the racial proxy and race-based neighborhood proxy hypotheses. Reliance on these probabilistic judgments is problematic when we use them to characterize individual group members who may deviate considerably from these group-level stereotypes. For the best recent treatment of stereotyping by quantitative sociologists, see Bobo and Massagli (2001).

11. The 1976 Detroit Area Study introduced an innovative and highly regarded method for measuring views on residential segregation. In the experiment, white respondents were asked about their comfort with and willingness to enter neighborhoods with varying degrees of integration with blacks; black respondents participated in a similar experiment: they were asked to rate neighborhoods of various racial compositions from most to least attractive and to indicate their willingness to enter each area. In both cases, the scenarios represented realistic assumptions regarding the residential experiences and options of both groups. The results from this study have influenced important general assessments of the status of African Americans (see, for example, Jaynes and Williams 1989, 141–44; Bok 1996, 182), as have two important treatises on racial residential segregation: Massey and Denton (1993) and Yinger (1995).
12. Using a split-ballot technique, we randomly assigned one-third of each racial category in Los Angeles (whites, blacks, Latinos, and Asians) and Boston (whites, blacks, and Latinos) to one of three out-groups. (For example, one-third of Latinos completed the Latino-white experiment, one-third completed the Latino-black experiment, and the remaining one-third considered integration with Asians.) Except for differences in target groups, black, Latino, and Asian respondents all completed the same variation of the experiment. For details, see Charles (2001b) and Zubrinsky and Bobo (1996).
13. Research suggests important differences by immigrant status and acculturation. The foreign-born—particularly those with five years or less in the United States and/or those with limited English proficiency—preferred substantially more same-race neighbors compared to their native-born and long-term-immigrant counterparts and those who communicated effectively in English (Charles 2000b, 2001b, 2002).
14. The measure of preferences used in the 2000 GSS is identical to the measure I used in Charles (2000a). Respondents were shown a single neighborhood card similar to those shown in figure 2.1 except that the houses were blank. They were then instructed: "Now I'd like you to imagine a neighborhood that has an ethnic and racial mix *you personally* would *feel most comfortable in*. Here is a blank neighborhood card, which depicts some houses that sur-

round your own. Using the letters A for Asian, B for Black, H for Latino/a or Latin American, and W for White, please put a letter in each of these houses to represent your preferred neighborhood where *you would most like to live.* Please be sure to fill in all of the houses."

15. Ingrid Gould Ellen (2000) argues that the heightened sensitivity of white homeowners and/or families with children to racial composition (whether it is actual or measured as change over time) is evidence that pure prejudice is less important than race-based neighborhood stereotyping; pure prejudice does not vary, she argues, and should not be affected by a white household's homeowning status or inclusion of children. The presence and strength of these differences among whites, she argues, indicates that whites are expressing concerns about property values and school quality. It is also possible, however, that these differences simply reflect the increased salience of particular aspects of black stereotypes—welfare dependence and intellect, for example—for white homeowners and/or parents. To test this, I compared whites' racial stereotypes of blacks by housing tenure and parenting status using the LASUI data (results not shown, but available upon request). Owners expressed significantly more negative stereotypes of blacks relative to whites ($p < .001$); a similar pattern emerges when comparing white parents to nonparents, though the difference is not statistically significant. Differences in perceptions of blacks' social class status by tenure and parenting status were nonsignificant. These results are consistent with a pure prejudice interpretation: for whites, these statuses increase the salience of widely held negative stereotypes of blacks and may increase their motivation to act on these attitudes or the likelihood that they will do so.
16. Negative racial stereotypes capture two variants of prejudice: simple out-group hostility and "a sense of group position" that members of one group have about another group; and a collective process whereby groups define their social positions vis-à-vis each other and make socially learned commitments to maintaining group status or relative status position. What matters is the magnitude of difference that in-group members perceive between their own group and particular out-groups (Blumer 1958, 3–4; Bobo 1999).
17. In other work (Charles 2000a) I distinguish between native- and foreign-born within categories of race for Asians and Latinos; the clearest result is that the effect of racial stereotyping on preferences for same-race neighbors is smaller among the foreign-born of both groups than for their native-born counterparts. This finding is consistent with my acculturation argument here. Alternatively, no nativity-status differences emerge with respect to in-group attachment or perceived social class difference.
18. Despite its advantages, the audit methodology is not without critics, most notably James Heckman and Peter Siegelman (1993; see also Heckman 1998). For instance, by sampling housing units only from major newspapers, audit

studies are likely to underestimate the incidence of discrimination. Other aspects of the method run the risk of overstating the frequency of discrimination. Because auditors are fully informed in their training of the purpose of the study, they may be unintentionally motivated to find discrimination; similarly, it has been suggested that other characteristics of the auditors besides race may influence agent behavior, such as the presence or absence of facial hair or an accent. Concern has also been expressed about the use of gross measures of discrimination that count "all errors made" by agents and landlords as unfavorable or as discriminatory treatment; such measures inaccurately assume, it is argued, that firms never make race-neutral errors and confound random and systematic effects. These critics suggest beginning with a net measure of the discrimination experienced by minority testers relative to their white teammates; a net measure takes race-neutral errors into account, and if it reveals evidence of discrimination, the gross measure does as well (Heckman and Siegelman 1993, 272). In response, John Yinger (1993, 1995, 1998) agrees that audit studies measure discrimination in a major segment of the housing market (units advertised in major newspapers) that is accessible to all home-seekers irrespective of race or ethnicity; though results cannot be generalized to all housing transactions, they do account for a large share of the action. Conceding the potential benefits of "blind" audits for avoiding experimenter effects, proponents of full disclosure nevertheless argue for deliberately informing auditors of the nature and purpose of the study and, at the same time, emphasizing the importance of accurate, complete reporting of other kinds of "experimenter effects." Specifically, some minority auditors may be upset by blatant mistreatment and find themselves unable to make accurate and complete evaluations, thus invalidating the audit. Moreover, both members of an audit team must receive identical training to minimize behavioral differences. Bringing teammates together without full disclosure opens the door for their (usually inaccurate) speculation about the purpose of the study and about appropriate behavior. With respect to aspects of auditors' appearance or behavior—aside from race—that could influence agents' behavior, more recent audit studies are more careful in selecting testers, particularly when assessing the advantages or disadvantages of an accent (Yinger 1995). Finally, though simple gross measures of discrimination almost certainly overestimate the frequency of systematic discrimination and should be interpreted as upper-bound estimates of discrimination, net measures subtract both random and systematic differences in treatment and probably underestimate the frequency of discrimination. As a consequence, net measures underestimate the gross incidence of discrimination (Yinger 1995, 45–46). Analyses of audit studies generally present net measures followed by gross measures. Yinger (1995, 46) points out that the "story told by the simple net measure is bleak enough . . .

[but] in some ways the story may be even worse." As a result of such intense scrutiny, research on housing market discrimination based on audit studies has become highly regarded in both the research and legal communities and is now widely accepted both as an enforcement tool and, in U.S. courts, as evidence of discrimination (Metcalf 1988; Yinger 1998).

19. A growing body of evidence documents racial discrimination in lending as well (Dedman 1988, 1989; Jackson 1994). The Boston Fed Study compares conventional loan denial rates for whites, blacks, and Latinos in Boston using 1990 data from the Home Mortgage Disclosure Act (HMDA), supplemented by other variables known to influence credit decisions. Together, these data offer "the most comprehensive set of credit characteristics ever assembled" (Yinger 1995, 71; for details, see Munnell et al. 1996). Results from the Boston Fed Study indicate that, controlling for "the risk and cost of default and for loan and personal characteristics," blacks and Latinos are 56 percent more likely than whites to be denied a conventional mortgage loan, which amounts to a minority denial rate of 17 percent, compared to a white rate of 11 percent. An analysis of the Boston Fed data by James Carr and Isaac Megbolugbe (1993) finds that minorities receive systematically lower credit ratings, so that, for example, a "slow-paying" white applicant would be considered creditworthy but a similar black applicant would not. There is evidence of racial bias in nearly every other aspect of the lending process, including the selling of private mortgage insurance, redlining by home insurance companies, and methods of advertising and outreach (Yinger 1995, 83–85); bank branch locations and closing patterns (Caskey 1992); and the relationship between blacks' loan approval rates and the racial composition of the financial institution workforce (Squires and Kim 1995). Studies of the last issue have confirmed that prejudice and economic interests motivate biased behavior (Yinger 1995; Ondrich et al. 1998).
20. Los Angeles is one of the metro areas included in all phases of HDS 2000; the full report provides summaries at the metropolitan-area level (see Turner et al. 2002, annex 8).
21. This approach—using the telephone rather than face-to-face interaction—addresses the possibility that differences in treatment between pairs of testers result from unmeasured differences in their personal characteristics. Similarly, a recent study of racial discrimination in the Chicago and Boston labor markets employed the audit methodology to respond to advertised positions by mail. Matched pairs of résumés manipulated the perception of race by using either an obviously African American name (such as Tamika or Jamal) or a very white-sounding name (such as Kristen or Brad), eliminating possible bias in treatment resulting from other experimenter characteristics. Marianne Bertrand and Sendhil Mullainathan (2004) report that this manipulation produced a significant gap in the rate of callbacks for interviews.

Specifically, white names received roughly 50 percent more callbacks than African American names. Moreover, a manipulation of qualifications resulted in a 30 percent higher callback rate for whites with higher-quality résumés; for blacks, résumé quality had no effect on the likelihood of callback. Results from this study and from Massey and Lundy (2001) support the reliability of face-to-face audit studies as evidence of discrimination, since both find ample evidence of such without face-to-face contact.

CHAPTER 3

1. To measure monthly housing expenditures, renters were asked to report their monthly rent and utility expenditures; homeowners were asked to report the amount of principal and interest paid each month on all mortgages (including seconds, home improvement loans, and so on). In a follow-up question, respondents indicated whether this amount included taxes and insurance. The mean housing expenditures reported in table 3.1 are not adjusted for these differences; however, the multivariate analyses in table 3.2, in which monthly housing expenditures are the outcome, do control for what was included in this figure.
2. According to data from the 1990 census (file STF3A), 69.1 percent of whites in the United States owned their homes, as did 52.2 percent of Asians, 43.4 percent of blacks, and 42.4 percent of Latinos, for an overall rate of 65 percent. The lower rates found among LASUI respondents relative to the national figures are probably tied to the high cost of housing in Los Angeles compared to other U.S. cities.
3. An examination of tract-level owner occupancy rates confirms this hypothesis. The average LASUI homeowner lives in a neighborhood that is 58 percent owner-occupied; the neighborhoods of non-owners, on average, are only 35 percent owner-occupied ($p < .001$). Among non-owners, foreign-born Latinos and Asians have the lowest rates of owner-occupied housing in their neighborhoods (28 and 30 percent, respectively). Among owners, the two groups with the highest rates of owner occupancy in their neighborhoods were whites (62 percent) and native-born Asians (just over 63 percent).
4. We asked LASUI respondents who did not own their home: "If you could, would you like to buy a house in the Los Angeles area?" Across groups, 58 percent said yes. Affirmative responses were lowest for native- and foreign-born Asians (43 and 41 percent, respectively) and highest for foreign-born Latinos (66 percent); half of white non-owners and 64 percent of black non-owners expressed a desire to purchase a home in the L.A. area ($p < .001$).
5. As stated previously, the measure of monthly housing expenditures does not account for the fact that some homeowners included taxes and/or insurance in their responses, despite being asked for only the amount of the principal

and interest on all mortgages. To account for these differences, models 3 through 6 include a set of dummy variables to distinguish between those who included (1) taxes, (2) insurance, or (3) both. (The reference category is to report only principal and interest.) In all cases, only those who included both taxes and insurance differed significantly from those reporting only principal and interest. In the full model, those reporting both taxes and insurance in addition to principal and interest spent about $114 more each month on housing ($p < .01$).

6. Admittedly, this analytic strategy may mask the substantial heterogeneity within the broad categories "Latino" and "Asian" with respect to both nativity status and national origin. The strategy confronts the nativity-status issue but leaves the issue of national origin untouched, largely so as to present the most information while at the same time allowing for ease of interpretation. Additional analyses (not shown here, but available from the author upon request) break down Latino and Asian respondents into national-origin and nativity-status categories (such as native-born Mexican or foreign-born Mexican with over ten years in the United States). The results are consistent with those presented here for the racial-group and nativity-status categories.
7. As might be expected, LASUI respondents exhibited considerable differences in length of time at their current address. Whites and native-born Asians had the most time at their current addresses (on average, twelve years and ten years, respectively), and consistent with their foreign-born status, foreign-born Latinos and Asians reported the fewest years at their current residence (on average, just over four years for both groups). Black respondents reported an average of nine years at their current address. Only the foreign-born respondents differed significantly from whites ($p < .001$).
8. For example, the total effect of age for a twenty-five-year-old is $(18.38*25) + (-.20*25^2)$, or $334.50; for a sixty-five-year-old, it is $(18.38*65) + (-.20*65^2)$, or $319.70. The effect of age for these two ends of the age distribution is substantially less than the $422.10 for a forty-five-year-old respondent: $(18.38(45) + (-.20*45^2)$.
9. In a second set of analyses (not shown here), I use national-origin categories instead of the racial categories "Latino" and "Asian" along with nativity status. The results indicate that the greater propensity for homeownership (net of other factors) found among Latinos and Asians is specific to Mexican and Chinese respondents.
10. Net of nativity status, English ability, and other factors, only the most recently arrived immigrants differ from the native-born in their likelihood of homeownership. As expected, this group is significantly disadvantaged relative to the native-born (odds ratio = .47, $p < .01$). The remaining results do not differ substantially from those presented in model 4 of table 3.3.
11. Models comparable to the full model in table 3.3 (for Latinos, $p < .05$).

12. Results are not shown here but are available upon request. The pattern of results is roughly the same when Asians and Latinos are separated by nativity status: for both native- and foreign-born, $p < .001$.
13. In *A Raisin in the Sun*, Mama Younger's dream of homeownership is a central theme, evidenced in part by her ritual tending of a houseplant meant to represent her hope of one day having her own garden. The play ends with the Younger family moving out of their tenement building to a new home purchased with the proceeds from the insurance check Mama Younger receives after her husband's death (Hansberry 1959/1994; Magill 1992). Similarly, the television sitcom *Good Times* ended its multi-year run with the Evans family leaving their inner-city public housing project for a home of their own. Most recently, MTV's *Cribs* highlighted the importance of this dream at the extremes of the black community. This show takes viewers into the homes of the "rich and famous," who quite often are black, rags-to-riches hip-hop artists (rap and/or R&B) or professional athletes who show off their new, expensive, well-furnished homes in exclusive neighborhoods. This example highlights another tendency among this crowd, which is to take good care of immediate and extended family members—particularly mothers—by providing them with a home of their own.
14. Although native-born Latinos are substantially more likely than their foreign-born counterparts to own their home, ongoing high-volume immigration into the United States suggests that the foreign-born and, more specifically, recent arrivals will at some point outnumber their native-born coethnics. If so, then the overall rate of Latino homeownership will be closer to the 20 percent rate found among the foreign-born than the 45 percent rate of homeownership reported among native-born Latinos.
15. Consistent with Alba and Logan (1991, 1992b), we measured proximity to non-Hispanic whites as the percentage white in respondents' actual neighborhoods. When respondents are non-Hispanic white themselves, this measure is interpreted as isolation; when respondents are nonwhite, it is interpreted as exposure to non-Hispanic whites (Alba and Logan 1993).
16. These categories are similar to those presented in Logan and Alba (1995).
17. For Chinese and Korean renters, the incidence of discrimination is generally low; however, there are differences in treatment. For instance, both groups are told about and shown more units compared to non-Asian minorities, but black and Hispanic testers receive better service from agents than either Asian group (Turner et al. 2002).

CHAPTER 4

1. Those results are not shown here but are available upon request.
2. Because social scientists have only recently attempted to study the racial atti-

tudes of Latinos and Asians, we know very little about trends in their racial attitudes. Thus, most of this discussion is centered on the racial attitudes of whites and blacks. When possible, however, I include what is known about Asian and Latino attitudes.

3. Changes in attitudes toward interracial marriage depend heavily on the wording of the question. Specifically, when no specific racial group is mentioned (for example, the question is simply about a close relative marrying someone "of another race"), support is substantially higher than when a specific out-group (particularly blacks) is mentioned.
4. This set of items follows the models of the 1990 General Social Survey (Smith 1990; Bobo and Kluegel 1993, 1996). The selection of these items was heavily influenced by earlier multiracial-multiethnic focus group discussions (Bobo et al. 1994, 1995). To assess stereotypes, the LASUI employed a split-ballot format in which one-third of each respondent-racial-group category was asked to rate the four racial groups as a whole (whites, blacks, Latinos, and Asians), one-third rated racial-group males, and the remaining one-third rated racial-group females. Respondents were randomly assigned to one of the three subcategories, making it possible to generalize to the entire sample category. The scores presented here are based on pooled responses and do not take experimental ballots into account, although it is noted that some ballot-specific differences exist for specific items (see Bobo and Johnson 2000). There are fewer ballot-specific differences for the index measures (the overall rating, as well as the two difference scores). To address these potentially important gender differences, multivariate models include dummy variables to control for experimental ballot (see also Charles 2000a, 2000b).
5. The negative-leaning ratings of both native- and foreign-born Latinos on the English ability trait are probably tied to immigration. For both, the knowledge that such a large percentage of the total Latino population is foreign-born no doubt figures into this evaluation.
6. This was not the case when discussing means in table 4.2. Recall that, to be clear about the expression of clearly negative views of out-groups relative to in-groups, figures 4.1 and 4.2 are restricted to values greater than 1.00.
7. Only 1.5 percent of whites had stereotype differences scores indicating positive stereotypes of blacks relative to their own group (values of –.50 or less); even fewer whites (.68 percent) had positive stereotypes of Latinos.
8. All groups believe that Asians face very little racial discrimination, including Asians themselves. Blacks and Latinos also tend to downplay the structural barriers facing each other.
9. This index is extremely reliable, with Cronbach's alpha values of .79 for the black and Latino target groups and .91 for the Asian target group.
10. The analyses are not shown here but are available upon request.
11. Again, however, support varies according to the type of integration involved:

whites' support for such policies is highest when more public and impersonal domains are involved and lowest for efforts to integrate more personal domains, such as neighborhoods and public schools. By the early 1970s, for example, nearly all whites believed that public transportation should be integrated and employment opportunities made equal; by the mid-1990s, 96 percent of whites favored school integration. As recently as 1988, however, only about half of whites expressed support for a law barring racial discrimination in the sale or rental of housing, and in 1990 20 percent of whites opposed interracial marriage (Bobo 2001; Schuman et al. 1997). It should be noted that antiminority animus is not the only source of opposition to government involvement in effecting positive racial change. Schuman and Bobo (1988) conclude that whites' policy-related attitudes are motivated by objections to government coercion as well as by negative racial attitudes.

12. The original items were five-category items ranging from "strongly disagree" to "strongly agree," with a neutral category ("neither agree nor disagree") in the middle. These were recoded such that high scores represented high perceived out-group competition. Cronbach's alphas are .78, .76, and .80 for black, Latino, and Asian target groups, respectively. This measure is similar to those used by Bobo and Hutchings (1996) and Bobo and Johnson (2000).
13. None of the respondents preferred being the only member of their group in the neighborhood.
14. Results based on the Farley-Schuman methodology suggest somewhat less aversion; see Zubrinsky and Bobo (1996) or Charles (2000b).
15. To minimize the likelihood of inauthentic, socially desirable responses (particularly to questions about racial attitudes and preferences for racially integrated neighborhoods), we knew it was important to match the race of the respondent and the interviewer as often as possible. The results presented in table 4.5 do not include a control for interviewer race. A comparison of race-matched to non-race-matched respondents reveals little or no deviation from the results in table 4.5 among respondents whose interviewer was the same race and the following deviations for non-race-matched respondents: (1) on average, non-race-matched Latinos and Asians preferred neighborhoods with more white and same-race neighbors than their race-matched counterparts; (2) for all groups, blacks were still the least preferred out-group, with rates of total exclusion that were slightly higher for whites and slightly lower for Latinos and Asians when the respondent and interviewer were not race-matched; (3) non-race-matched Latinos and Asians—but not blacks—preferred the fewest same-race neighbors (because they preferred more white neighbors).
16. To some extent, this may reflect socially desirable response bias for many respondents (especially whites) who were reluctant to object to interracial

neighborhood contact. It is difficult to conclude, however, that the patterns reflect serious bias of this kind, nor do they represent a sharp disjuncture with actual aggregate-level residential patterns.

CHAPTER 5

1. Because of the split-ballot format used for the racial-group threat measure, correlations are restricted to the subset of respondents who answered these items for their own group; however, bear in mind that because respondents were randomly assigned to a target group, results for this subset of respondents can be generalized to the full sample.
2. Additional analyses of these correlations by nativity status suggest important differences between native- and foreign-born Latinos. Most notably, correlations tended to be stronger and more powerful among the native-born compared to the foreign-born. For example, the correlation between social distance and preference for white neighbors was –.360 ($p < .001$) for native-born Latinos, roughly twice that for their foreign-born counterparts (–.179, $p < .001$). This difference is even more striking with respect to preferences for same-race neighbors, where the correlation between perceived out-group social distance and preferences for same-race neighbors was .410 ($p < .001$) for native-born Latinos, but only .188 ($p < .001$) for the foreign-born. Correlations by race and nativity status and preferences are reported in the appendix (table A1).
3. Once again, consideration of nativity status proves fruitful and suggests that these class concerns are specific to foreign-born Asians. Class concerns are consistent with a potentially heightened interest in improving one's economic status—a common concern among immigrants. Similarly, the correlation between in-group attachment and preference for white neighbors was statistically significant only for the foreign-born (.096, $p < .01$) but otherwise nearly identical to that shown in table 5.1. Indeed, the overall pattern is the exact opposite of that found among Latinos: most of the meaningful correlations among Latinos were found among the native-born, but for Asians it was often the foreign-born who exhibited the stronger correlations. There were two important exceptions: correlations were stronger among native-born Asians between social distance and preference for black neighbors (native-born Asians: –.264, $p < .01$; foreign-born Asians: –.054, p = not significant) and between racial-group competition and preference for Latino neighbors (native-born Asians: –.428, $p < .001$; foreign-born Asians: –.002, p = not significant). These differences provide further evidence to support the notion that, at least among Asians, immigrants are more concerned with social class position and that these concerns may outweigh any anti-out-group attitudes (see appendix, table A1).

4. Recall that this item was part of a split-ballot format in which respondents were randomly assigned a target group to respond to. As a consequence, initial analyses of preferences for black, Latino, or Asian neighbors included a dummy variable for the target-group-specific ballot to ascertain whether perceptions of out-group competition were target-group-specific or whether those who felt threatened by any out-group were simply less interested in residential contact with all other groups. If concerns about racial-group threat were target-group-specific, then those who considered the target group threatening should have been more reluctant to share residential space with that group than their coethnics who considered another target group threatening. This turns out not to be the case. To the extent that perceived racial-group competition had an impact on preferences for integration, its effect was universal (target-group-specific differences were nonsignificant). This effect seems to be "provincialism" working in reverse: just as a positive attitude toward or experience with a certain group can improve attitudes about all other groups, a negative belief about one target group has an impact on preferences toward all minority groups (see Pettigrew 1982).
5. All models also control, where appropriate, for missing values on income, social class disadvantage, racial stereotyping, social distance, and white discrimination (all of which were imputed using best-subset imputation); respondent-interviewer race-matching; and gender-specific ballots on the stereotyping items. Owing to intercorrelations among several of the racial attitude measures, the tables show statistical significance to the .10 level on these items only.
6. The dependent variables in all cases are percentages, and the distribution of outcomes is therefore limited to values between 0 and 100 percent. In many instances, distributions are also truncated. For these reasons, I considered estimating models using alternative methods—specifically either logit transformations of all dependent variables or a series of Tobit regressions. Neither alternative improves upon the OLS results.
7. Increasing education was associated with declining preference for integration with blacks; the most-educated whites preferred increased contact with Asians. The oldest group of whites preferred to avoid contact with both blacks and Latinos and to increase residential isolation. Alternatively, it appears that increasing neighborhood contact with out-groups (the percentage of target-group members in the respondent's own neighborhood) had a positive impact on preferences for integration with those groups. This was especially true for integration with both blacks and Latinos. For full results, see the appendix (table A.2).
8. If this is the case, it is not borne out by the data. A test of interactive effects for in-group attachment and perceptions of whites as discriminators found no statistically significant relationships. I also considered the possibility that

in-group attachment is similarly associated with perceived racial-group competition, but found no such association.

9. David Harris (2001) suggests that both whites and blacks as groups use race as a proxy to avoid black neighbors.
10. Recall that Japanese have been the reference group for Asian respondents throughout, owing to the greater tendency among this subset of Asians to be U.S.-born.
11. Specifically, they did not differ significantly from U.S.-born Japanese; similarly, U.S.-born Chinese did not differ significantly from the reference group.
12. In models that considered the effect of each attitude individually on preferences for white neighbors, medium in-group attachment, social distance, and the perception of whites as discriminatory were all statistically significant at the .05 level. In a similar set of models run for Asian preferences for same-race neighbors, the perception of whites as discriminatory was statistically significant at the .05 level. In a model of Asian preferences for black neighbors that included only the competitive threat item, this perception of blacks had a negative impact on preferences at the .10 level.
13. It should also be mentioned that Asians who opted not to answer the white discrimination item preferred significantly fewer white neighbors (–9.42, $p < .01$) and significantly more same-race neighbors (9.10, $p < .05$) compared to those providing valid responses on these items. This pattern of nonresponse was consistent with respondent concerns about social desirability. A similar pattern of difference was evident for gender-specific ballots on the stereotyping item. Specifically, Asians who were asked about their stereotypes of white men or white women showed a larger negative effect of stereotyping on preferences for white neighbors (for women, –4.55, $p < .01$; for men, –5.90, $p < .001$) and a larger positive effect of stereotyping on preferences for same-race neighbors (for women, 3.86, $p < .01$; for men, 5.13, $p < .001$) (for full results, see table A5).
14. Although it is certainly true that Koreans' relations with blacks have garnered most of the media and research attention, Latinos tend to share neighborhood space with blacks and thus are just as likely to be alienated from the police and to have less than friendly relationships with local merchants. Both blacks and Latinos felt disenfranchised by the 1992 verdict, and both groups probably harbored resentment against local nonresident merchants, who were often believed to both benefit from and look down on the local residents.
15. Indeed, it is possible that the aversion among native-born Koreans to residential contact with blacks and Latinos is a consequence of the lingering effects of the civil unrest for this group, combined with a general lack of contact between native-born Koreans and blacks and/or Latinos. Efforts at improving relations may have bypassed this subset of the Korean community.
16. Results are not shown but are available from the author upon request.

17. Admittedly, however, both Asians and Latinos experience much higher rates of intermarriage with whites and thus, one can conclude, greater social acceptance by whites.
18. The increasing residential contact of Asians and Latinos with blacks has been attributed to an artifact of immigration. With the passage of time, new arrivals distance themselves from blacks, so that it is the continuous flow of immigrants that accounts for the increase (Massey 1995).

CHAPTER 6

1. It could be argued that the associations between in-group attachment and Latino and Asian preferences simply reflect a desire for group contact, maintenance of culture, and the like. However, if this were the case, we should expect in-group attachment to affect preferences for various out-groups in a similar fashion, and this is not the case.
2. Three-stage least squares regression produces the most efficient estimates when endogeneity is an issue. If, when used as explanatory variables, preferences or neighborhood outcomes are correlated with the error term, relying on single-equation estimates from OLS regression results in biased and inconsistent estimates. By allowing the error terms in both equations to be correlated, 3SLS also yields more efficient estimates than would be the case with a single-equation OLS model, since the disturbance is correlated with the endogenous variable and this violates assumptions (Stata Press 2003 47–48; see also Greene 2000, 692–93). This analysis is similar to one by Keith Ilandfeldt and Benjamin Scafidi (2004), who also point out that measurement error in the variables measuring preferences requires treating them as endogenous. This measurement error is tied to perceptions of social desirability that can lead respondents to give dishonest responses (probably erring on the side of greater preference for integration) and also to the framing of the question itself. Measurement error could also be a concern if the respondent's preferences have changed since he or she last moved (Greene 2000, 344).
3. It is necessary to identify the simultaneous relationships between preferences and the neighborhood-level outcomes by including certain variables in one equation that are excluded from the other (Greene 2000). The preferences model is identified by the measures of perceived social class disadvantage, in-group attachment, racial stereotyping, social distance, white discrimination, and perceived racial-group competition, based on hypothesized relationships between these attitudes and preferences, in addition to the results presented in the previous two chapters. Models estimating neighborhood racial composition preferences are also identified by respondents' sex and political ideology, as both have been shown to affect racial attitudes more generally (Schuman et al. 1997); dummy variables for non-race-matched interviewers (which

could bias responses) and missing values on racial attitude measures also identify preferences models. The neighborhood proximity to whites model is identified by household income and net financial assets and by number of years at current residence, since each characteristic is hypothesized to have a direct influence on actual neighborhood-level outcomes. Income is excluded from the preferences models, since this was shown in the previous chapter (and in other research; see Farley et al. 1994) not to be especially correlated with preferences. Age, education, experience in public housing, and the immigration-related characteristics are included in both sets of models for substantive reasons. Age and education, though not consistently influential in the preferences models presented here, are known to be important factors for understanding a variety of racial attitudes and public opinions (Schuman et al. 1997), and they are also directly implicated in locational attainment. Experience in public housing was significantly associated with neighborhood-level outcomes in chapter 3. Furthermore, the opportunity for neighborhood-level interracial contact (or, for blacks, racial isolation) stemming from experience in public housing had an impact on preferences for integration in some cases. Finally, the immigration-related characteristics remain in both models because of their importance to understanding both preferences and actual neighborhood outcomes.

4. Bear in mind, however, that the analyses in chapter 5 include actual contact but cannot account for the endogeneity of preferences and actual neighborhood racial composition. This is a common problem with cross-sectional data and OLS regression.
5. These results are not shown here but are available upon request. This question was followed by an inquiry about the barriers to homeownership. Not surprisingly, given the cost of housing in Los Angeles, the inability to make a down payment and affordability were top concerns for most, regardless of race.
6. Admittedly, the LASUI does not contain the best measure of accumulated wealth. Future research would be wise to address this issue.

References

ACORN. 2003. *The Great Divide: Home Purchase Mortgage Lending Nationally and in 115 Metropolitan Areas*. Available at: www.acorn.org.

Alba, Richard D., Nancy A. Denton, Shu-yin J. Leung, and John R. Logan. 1995. "Neighborhood Change Under the Conditions of Mass Immigration: The New York City Region, 1970–1990." *International Migration Review* 31(3): 625–56.

Alba, Richard D., and John R. Logan. 1991. "Variations on Two Themes: Racial and Ethnic Patterns in the Attainment of Suburban Residence." *Demography* 28: 431–53.

———. 1992a. "Assimilation and Stratification in the Homeownership Patterns of Racial and Ethnic Groups." *International Migration Review* 26: 1314–41.

———. 1992b. "Analyzing Locational Attainments: Constructing Individual-Level Regression Models Using Aggregate Data." *Sociological Methods and Research* 20: 367–97.

———. 1993. "Minority Proximity to Whites in Suburbs: An Individual-Level Analysis of Segregation." *American Journal of Sociology* 98(6): 1388–1427.

Alba, Richard D., John R. Logan, and Paul E. Bellair. 1994. "Living with Crime: The Implications of Racial-Ethnic Differences in Suburban Location." *Social Forces* 73(2): 395–434.

Alba, Richard D., John R. Logan, and Brian J. Stults. 2000a. "The Changing Neighborhood Contexts of the Immigrant Metropolis." *Social Forces* 79(2): 587–621.

———. 2000b. "How Segregated Are Middle-Class African Americans?" *Social Problems* 47(4): 543–58.

Alba, Richard D., John R. Logan, Brian J. Stults, Gilbert Marzan, and Wenquan Zhang. 1999. "Immigrant Groups in the Suburbs: A Reexamination of Suburbanization and Assimilation." *American Sociological Review* 64: 446–60.

Alexander, Karl L., Scott Holupka, and Aaron M. Pallas. 1987. "Social Background and Academic Determinants of Two-Year Versus Four-Year College Attendance: Evidence from Two Cohorts a Decade Apart." *American Journal of Education* 96: 56–80.

Allport, Gordon W. 1954. *The Nature of Prejudice*. New York: Doubleday Anchor.

Anderson, Elijah. 1990. *Streetwise: Race, Class, and Change in an Urban Community*. Chicago: University of Chicago Press.

———. 1999. *Code of the Street: Decency, Violence, and the Moral Life of the Inner City*. New York: Norton.

Angelo, Bonnie. 1989. "The Pain of Being Black." *Time*, May 22. Retrieved June 13, 2003 from: http://www.time.com/time/community/pulitzerinterview.html.

Ashmore, Richard D., and Frances K. Del Boca. 1981. "Conceptual Approaches to Stereotypes and Stereotyping," In *Cognitive Processes in Stereotyping and Intergroup Behavior*, edited by David L. Hamilton. Hillsdale, N.J.: Lawrence Erlbaum.

Baldasarre, Mark, ed. 1994. *The Los Angeles Riots: Lessons for the Urban Future*. Boulder, Colo.: Westview.

Bashi, Vilna, and Antonio McDaniel. 1997. "A Theory of Immigration and Racial Stratification." *Journal of Black Studies* 27(5): 668–82.

Bauman, Kurt J. 1998. "Schools, Markets, and Family in the History of African-American Education." *American Journal of Education* 106: 500–31.

Bennett, Pamela R., and Yu Xie. 2003. "Revisiting Racial Differences in College Attendance: The Role of Historically Black Colleges and Universities." *American Sociological Review* 68: 567–80.

Bertrand, Marianne, and Sendhil Mullainathan. 2004. "Are Emily and Brendan More Employable Than Lakisha and Jamal? A Field Experiment on Labor Market Discrimination." *American Economic Review* 94(4): 991–1013.

Bickford, A., and Douglas S. Massey. 1991. "Segregation in the Second Ghetto: Racial and Ethnic Segregation in American Public Housing, 1977." *Social Forces* 69: 1011–36.

Blumer, Herbert. 1958. "Race Prejudice as a Sense of Group Position." *Pacific Sociological Review* 1: 3–7.

Bobo, Lawrence. 1988. "Group Conflict, Prejudice, and the Paradox of Contemporary Racial Attitudes." In *Eliminating Racism: Profiles in Controversy*, edited by Phyllis A. Katz and Dalmas A. Taylor. New York: Plenum Press.

———. 1989. "Keeping the Linchpin in Place: Testing the Multiple Sources of Opposition to Residential Integration." *International Review of Social Psychology* 2(3): 305–23.

———. 1999. "Prejudice as Group Position: Micro-Foundations of a Sociological Approach to Racism and Race Relations." *Journal of Social Issues* 55(3): 445–72.

———. 2001. "Racial Attitudes and Relations at the Close of the Twentieth Century." In *America Becoming: Racial Trends and Their Consequences*, edited by Neil J. Smelser, William Julius Wilson, and Faith Mitchell. Washington, D.C.: National Academy Press.

Bobo, Lawrence, and Vincent Hutchings. 1996. "Perceptions of Racial Competition in a Multiracial Setting." *American Sociological Review* 61(6, December): 951–72.

Bobo, Lawrence D., and Devon Johnson. 2000. "Racial Attitudes in a Prismatic

Metropolis: Mapping Identity, Stereotypes, Competition, and Views on Affirmative Action." In *Prismatic Metropolis: Inequality in Los Angeles*, edited by Lawrence D. Bobo, Melvin L. Oliver, James H. Johnson Jr., and Abel Valenzuela Jr. New York: Russell Sage Foundation.

Bobo, Lawrence, James Johnson, Melvin Oliver, Reynolds Farley, Barry Bluestone, Irene Browne, Sheldon Danziger, Gary Green, Harry Holzer, Maria Krysan, Michael Massagli, and Camille Zubrinsky Charles. 1998. *Multi-City [Atlanta, Boston, Detroit, and Los Angeles] Study of Urban Inequality, 1992–1994: Household Survey Data*. Computer file. 3rd ICPSR version. Atlanta: Mathematica; Boston: University of Massachusetts, Survey Research Laboratory; Ann Arbor: University of Michigan, Detroit Area Study and Institute for Social Research, Survey Research Center; Los Angeles: University of California, Survey Research Program. Distributed by Interuniversity Consortium for Political and Social Research (ICPSR), 2000.

Bobo, Lawrence, and James R. Kluegel. 1993. "Opposition to Race-Targeting: Self-Interest, Stratification Ideology, or Racial Attitudes?" *American Sociological Review* 58: 443–64.

———. 1996. "The Difference Between Black and Brown: Explanations of Racial Economic Inequality." Paper presented to the fifty-first annual meeting of the American Association for Public Opinion Research. Salt Lake City, Utah (May 16–19).

Bobo, Lawrence D., and Michael P. Massagli. 2001. "Stereotypes and Urban Inequality." In *Urban Inequality: Evidence from Four Cities*, edited by Alice O'Connor, Chris Tilly, and Lawrence D. Bobo. New York: Russell Sage Foundation.

Bobo, Lawrence D., Melvin L. Oliver, James H. Johnson Jr., and Abel Valenzuela Jr. 2000. "Analyzing Inequality in Los Angeles." In *Prismatic Metropolis: Inequality in Los Angeles*, edited by Lawrence D. Bobo, Melvin L. Oliver, James H. Johnson Jr., and Abel Valenzuela Jr. New York: Russell Sage Foundation.

Bobo, Lawrence D., and Ryan A. Smith. 1994. "Antipoverty Policy, Affirmative Action, and Racial Attitudes." In *Confronting Poverty: Prescriptions for Change*, edited by Sheldon H. Danziger, Gary D. Sandfur, and Daniel H. Weinberg. Cambridge, Mass.: Harvard University Press.

Bobo, Lawrence D., and Susan Suh. 2000. "Surveying Racial Discrimination: Analyses from a Multiethnic Labor Market." In *Prismatic Metropolis: Inequality in Los Angeles*, edited by Lawrence D. Bobo, Melvin L. Oliver, James H. Johnson Jr., and Abel Valenzuela Jr. New York: Russell Sage Foundation.

Bobo, Lawrence D., and Camille L. Zubrinsky. 1996. "Attitudes Toward Residential Integration: Perceived Status Differences, Mere In-Group Preference, or Racial Prejudice?" *Social Forces* 74(3): 883–909.

Bobo, Lawrence, Camille L. Zubrinsky, James H. Johnson Jr., and Melvin L. Oliver. 1994. "Public Opinion Before and After a Spring of Discontent." In *The Los Angeles Riots: Lessons for the Urban Future*, edited by Mark Baldassare. Boulder, Colo.: Westview.

———. 1995. "Work Orientation, Job Discrimination, and Ethnicity: A Focus Group Perspective." In *Research in the Sociology of Work*, vol. 5, edited by Richard L. Simpson and Ida Harper Simpson. Greenwich, Conn.: JAI Press.

Bok, Derek. 1996. *The State of the Nation: Government and the Quest for a Better Society*. Cambridge, Mass.: Harvard University Press.

Briggs, Xavier de Souza. 2003. "Desegregating the City: Space and Inequality in Global Perspective." In *Desegregating the City: Enclaves Yes, Ghettos No*, edited by David Varady. New York: SUNY Press.

———, ed. 2005. *The Geography of Opportunity: Race and Housing Choice in Metropolitan America*. Washington: Brookings Institution Press.

Carr, James H., and Isaac F. Megbolugbe. 1993. "The Federal Reserve Bank of Boston Study on Mortgage Lending Revisited." *Journal of Housing Research* 4(2): 277–313.

Caskey, John. 1992. "Bank Representation in Low-Income and Minority Urban Communities." Working paper (December RWP 1992–10). Kansas City, Mo.: Research Division of the Federal Reserve Bank of Kansas City.

Charles, Camille Zubrinsky. 2000a. "Neighborhood Racial-Composition Preferences: Evidence from a Multiethnic Metropolis." *Social Problems* 47(3): 379–407.

———. 2000b. "Residential Segregation in Los Angeles." In *Prismatic Metropolis: Inequality in Los Angeles*, edited by Lawrence D. Bobo, Melvin L. Oliver, James H. Johnson Jr., and Abel Valenzuela Jr. New York: Russell Sage Foundation.

———. 2001a. "Socioeconomic Status and Segregation: African Americans, Hispanics, and Asians in Los Angeles." In *Problem of the Century: Racial Stratification in the United States*, edited by Elijah Andersen and Douglas S. Massey. New York: Russell Sage Foundation.

———. 2001b. "Processes of Residential Segregation." In *Urban Inequality: Evidence from Four Cities*, edited by Alice O'Connor, Chris Tilly, and Lawrence Bobo. New York: Russell Sage Foundation.

———. 2002. "Comfort Zones: Immigration, Assimilation, and the Neighborhood Racial Composition Preferences of Latinos and Asians." Paper presented to the annual meeting of the American Sociological Association, Chicago.

———. 2003. "Comfort Zones: Immigration, Acculturation, and the Neighborhood Racial Composition Preferences of Latinos and Asians." Unpublished paper.

———. 2005. "Can We Live Together? Racial Preferences and Neighborhood Outcomes." In *The Geography of Opportunity: Race and Housing Choice in Metropolitan America*, edited by Xavier de Souza Briggs. Washington: Brookings Institution Press.

Charles, Camille Zubrinsky, Vincent J. Roscigno, and Kimberly C. Torres. Forthcoming. "Racial Inequality and College Attendance: The Mediating Role of Parental Investments." Social Science Research.

Chen, Hsiang-Shui. 1992. *Chinatown No More: Taiwan Immigrants in Contemporary New York*. Ithaca, N.Y.: Cornell University Press.

Cheng, Lucie, and Yen Espiritu. 1989. "Korean Businesses in Black and Hispanic Neighborhoods: A Study of Intergroup Relations." *Sociological Perspectives* 32(4): 521–34.

Clark, W. A. V. 1986. "Residential Segregation in American Cities: A Review and Interpretation." *Population Research and Policy Review* 5: 95–127.

———. 1988. "Understanding Residential Segregation in American Cities: Interpreting the Evidence: A Reply to Galster." *Population Research and Policy Review* 8: 193–97.

———. 1989. "Revealed Preferences and Neighborhood Transitions in a Multiethnic Setting." *Urban Geography* 10(5): 434–48.

———. 1992. "Residential Preferences and Residential Choices in a Multiethnic Context." *Demography* 29(3): 451–66.

———. 2002. "Ethnic Preferences and Ethnic Perceptions in Multiethnic Settings." *Urban Geography* 23(3): 237–56.

Conley, Dalton. 1999. *Being Black, Living in the Red: Race, Wealth, and Social Policy in America*. Los Angeles: University of California Press.

Cose, Ellis. 1993. *The Rage of a Privileged Class*. New York: HarperCollins.

Coulson, Edward. 1999. "Why Are Hispanic and Asian-American Homeownership Rates So Low? Immigration and Other Factors." *Journal of Urban Economics* 45(2): 209–27.

Crowder, Kyle D. 1999. "Residential Segregation of West Indians in the New York–New Jersey Metropolitan Areas: The Roles of Race and Ethnicity." *International Migration Review* 33: 79–113.

Cutler, David M., and Edward L. Glaeser. 1997. "Are Ghettos Good or Bad?" *Quarterly Journal of Economics* 112(3): 827–72.

Cutler, David M., Edward L. Glaeser, and Jacob L. Vigdor. 1999. "The Rise and Decline of the American Ghetto." *Journal of Political Economy* 107(3): 455–506.

Darden, Joe T. 1995. "Black Residential Segregation Since the 1948 *Shelley v. Kraemer* Decision." *Journal of Black Studies* 25(6): 680–91.

Davis, Mike. 1992. *City of Quartz: Excavating the Future of Los Angeles*. New York: First Vintage Books.

Dawson, Michael C. 1994. *Behind the Mule: Race and Class in African American Politics*. Princeton, N.J.: Princeton University Press.

Dedman, Bill. 1988. "The Color of Money." *Atlanta Journal and Constitution*, May 1–4.

———. 1989. "Blacks Turned Down for Home Loans from S&Ls Twice as Often as Whites." *Atlanta Journal and Constitution*, January 22.

De la Garza, Rodolfo O., Angelo Falcon, and Chris F. Garcia. 1996. "Will the Real Americans Please Stand Up?: Anglo and Mexican-American Support of Core American Political Values." *American Journal of Political Science* 40(2): 335–51.

Denton, Nancy A. 1994. "Are African Americans Still Hypersegregated?" In *Residential Apartheid: The American Legacy*, edited by Robert Bullard, Charles Lee, and J. Eugene Grigsby. Los Angeles: UCLA Center for African American Studies.

Denton, Nancy A., and Douglas S. Massey. 1988. "Residential Segregation of Blacks, Hispanics, and Asians by Socioeconomic Status and Generation." *Social Science Quarterly* 69: 797–817.

———. 1989. "Racial Identity Among Caribbean Hispanics: The Effect of Double Minority Status on Residential Segregation." *American Sociological Review* 54: 790–808.

———. 1991. "Patterns of Neighborhood Transition in a Multiethnic World: U.S. Metropolitan Areas, 1970–1980." *Demography* 28(1): 41–63.

Dikoetter, Frank. 1994. "Racial Identities in China: Context and Meaning." *China Quarterly* 138(June): 404–12.

Du Bois, W. E. B. 1990. *The Souls of Black Folk: Essays and Sketches*. New York: Vintage Books. (Orig. pub. in 1903.)

Eagly, A. H., and V. J. Steffen. 1984. "Gender Stereotypes Stem from the Distribution of Women and Men into Social Roles." *Journal of Personality and Social Psychology* 46: 735–54.

Edin, Kathryn, and Maria Kafalas. 2004. *Promises I Can Keep*. Berkeley: University of California Press.

Edmonston, B., and J. S. Passel. 1992. "Immigration and Immigrant Generations in Population Projections." *International Journal of Forecasting* 8(3): 459–76.

Ellen, Ingrid Gould. 2000. *Sharing America's Neighborhoods: The Prospects for Stable Racial Integration*. Cambridge, Mass.: Harvard University Press.

Ellison, Christopher G., and Daniel A. Powers. 1994. "The Contact Hypothesis and Racial Attitudes Among Black Americans." *Social Science Quarterly* 75(2): 385–400.

Emerson, Michael O., Karen J. Chai, and George Yancey. 2001. "Does Race Matter in Explaining Residential Segregation? Exploring the Preferences of White Americans." *American Sociological Review* 66(6): 922–35.

Espinosa, Kristin E., and Douglas S. Massey. 1997. "Determinants of English Proficiency Among Mexican Migrants to the United States." *International Migration Review* 31(1): 28–50.

Espiritu, Yen Le. 1992. *Asian American Pan-Ethnicity: Bridging Institutions and Identities*. Philadelphia: Temple University Press.

Fannie Mae. 2004. *Becoming a Homeowner: How Much House Can You Afford?* Retrieved July 27, 2004, from www.fanniemae.com.

Farley, John E. 1995. "Race Still Matters: The Minimal Role of Income and Housing Cost as Causes of Housing Segregation in St. Louis, 1990. " *Urban Affairs Review* 31(2): 244–54.

———. 1996a. *The New American Reality: How We Are, How We Got There, Where We Are Going*. New York: Russell Sage Foundation.

———. 1996b. "Racial Differences in the Search for Housing: Do Whites and

Blacks Use the Same Techniques to Find Housing?" *Housing Policy Debate* 7: 367–86.

Farley, Reynolds, Elaine Fielding, and Maria Krysan. 1997. "The Residential Preferences of Whites and Blacks: A Four-Metropolis Analysis." *Housing Policy Debate* 8(4): 763–800.

Farley, Reynolds, and William H. Frey. 1994. "Changes in the Segregation of Whites from Blacks During the 1980s: Small Steps Toward a More Integrated Society." *American Sociological Review* 59: 23–45.

Farley, Reynolds, Howard Schuman, Suzanne Bianchi, Diane Colasanto, and Shirley Hatchett. 1978. "Chocolate City, Vanilla Suburbs: Will the Trend Toward Racially Separate Communities Continue?" *Social Science Research* 7: 319–44.

Farley, Reynolds, Charlotte Steeh, Tara Jackson, Maria Krysan, and Keith Reeves. 1993. "Continued Racial Segregation in Detroit: Chocolate City, Vanilla Suburbs." *Journal of Housing Research* 4(1): 1–38.

Farley, Reynolds, Charlotte Steeh, Maria Krysan, Tara Jackson, and Keith Reeves. 1994. "Stereotypes and Segregation: Neighborhoods in the Detroit Area." *American Journal of Sociology* 100(3): 750–80.

Feagin, Joe R., and Melvin P. Sikes. 1994. *Living with Racism: The Black Middle-Class Experience*. Boston: Beacon.

Feagin, Joe R., and Hernán Vera. 1995. *White Racism: The Basics*. New York: Routledge.

Fischer, Mary J., and Douglas S. Massey. 2004. "The Ecology of Racial Discrimination." *City and Community* 3(3): 221–41.

Fix, Michael, and Raymond J. Struyk. 1993. *Clear and Convincing Evidence: Measurement of Discrimination in America*. Washington: Urban Institute Press.

Flippen, Chenoa A. 2001. "Residential Segregation and Minority Homeownership." *Social Science Research* 30(3): 337–62.

Forman, Tyrone, and Nadia Kim. 1999. "Beyond Black and White: Asian Americans' Attitudes Toward Blacks and Latinos." Paper presented to the annual meeting of the Society for the Study of Social Problems. Chicago (August 5–7).

———. 2003. "Beyond Black and White: Asian Americans' Attitudes Toward Blacks and Latinos." Paper presented to the annual meeting of the Society for the Study of Social Problems. Chicago (August 5–7).

Forman, Tyrone, Gloria Martinez, and Eduardo Bonilla-Silva. 2003. "Latinos' Perceptions of Blacks and Asians: Testing the Immigrant Hypothesis." In *Brown and Black Communication: Latino and African American Conflict and Convergence in Mass Media*, edited by Diana I. Rios, and Ali Mohamed. Westport, Conn.: Greenwood Press.

Fossett, Mark A., and Jill K. Kiecolt. 1989. "The Relative Size of Minority Populations and White Racial Attitudes." *Social Science Quarterly* 70(4): 820–35.

Freer, Regina. 1994. "Black-Korean Conflict." In *The Los Angeles Riots: Lessons for the Urban Future*, edited by Mark Baldassare. Boulder, Colo.: Westview.

Frey, William H., and Reynolds Farley. 1993. "Latino, Asian, and Black Segregation in Multiethnic Metro Areas: Findings from the 1990 Census." Research report. Ann Arbor: University of Michigan, Population Studies Center.

Gabriel, Stuart A., and Gary Painter. 2003a. "Paths to Homeownership: An Analysis of the Residential Location and Homeownership Choices of Black Households in Los Angeles." *Journal of Real Estate Finance and Economics* 27(1): 87–109.

———. 2003b. "Mobility, Residential Location, and the American Dream: The Intermetropolitan Geography of Minority Homeownership." Working paper. Los Angeles: University of Southern California, Lusk Center for Real Estate.

Galster, George C. 1988. "Residential Segregation in American Cities: A Contrary Review." *Population Research Policy Review* 7: 93–112.

———. 1990. "Racial Steering in Housing Markets During the 1980s: A Review of the Audit Evidence." *Journal of Planning and Education Research* 9: 165–75.

———. 1991. "Black Suburbanization: Has It Changed the Relative Location of Races?" *Urban Affairs Quarterly* 26: 621–28.

———. 1992. "Research on Discrimination in Housing and Mortgage Markets: Assessment and Future Directions." *Housing Policy Debate* 3(2): 639–83.

Galster, George C., and Erin Godfrey. 2003. "By Words and Deeds: Racial Steering by Real Estate Agents in the U.S. in 2000." Paper presented to the annual meeting of the Urban Affairs Association. Cleveland (March).

Gans, Herbert J. 1999. "The Possibility of a New Racial Hierarchy in the Twenty-first-Century United States." In *The Cultural Territories of Race: Black and White Boundaries*, edited by Michele Lamont. Chicago and New York: University of Chicago Press and Russell Sage Foundation.

GeoLytics, Inc. 2003. CensusCD Neighborhood Change Database (NCDB), 1970–2000 Tract Data.

Gilens, Martin. 1995. "Racial Attitudes and Opposition to Welfare." *Journal of Politics* 57: 994–1014.

———. 1996. "Race Coding and White Opposition to Welfare." *American Political Science Review* 90: 593–604.

Glazer, Nathan. 1980. "Race and the Suburbs." In *The Work of Charles Abrams*, edited by O. H. Koenigsberger, S. Groak, and B. Bernstein. Oxford: Pergamon Press.

Greene, William H. 2000. *Econometric Analysis*. 3rd ed. New York: Macmillan.

Gross, Andrew B., and Douglas S. Massey. 1991. "Spatial Assimilation Models: A Micro-Macro Comparison." *Social Science Quarterly* 72(2): 347–61.

Gurin, Patrician, Shirley Hatchett, and James S. Jackson. 1989. *Hope and Independence: Blacks' Response to Electoral and Party Politics*. New York: Russell Sage Foundation.

Hansberry, Lorraine. 1994. *A Raisin in the Sun*. New York: Vintage. (Orig. pub. in 1959.)

Harris, David R. 1997. "Racial and Nonracial Determinants of Neighborhood Satisfaction Among Whites, 1975–1993." Research report 97–388. Ann Arbor: University of Michigan, Population Studies Center.

———. 1999. "Property Values Drop When Blacks Move In, Because . . .": Racial and Socioeconomic Determinants of Neighborhood Desirability." *American Sociological Review* 64(June): 461–79.

———. 2001. "Why Are Whites and Blacks Averse to Black Neighbors?" *Social Science Research* 30(1): 100–16.

Harrison, Roderick, and Claudette E. Bennett. 1995. "Racial and Ethnic Diversity." In *State of the Union: America in the 1990s*, vol. 2, *Social Trends*, edited by Reynolds Farley. New York: Russell Sage Foundation.

Hauser, Robert M. 1993. "The Decline in College Entry Among African Americans: Findings in Search of Explanations." In *Prejudice, Politics, and the American Dilemma*, edited by P. M. Sniderman, P. E. Tetlock, and E. G. Carmines. Palo Alto, Calif.: Stanford University Press.

Heckman, James J. 1998. "Detecting Discrimination." *Journal of Economic Perspectives* 12(2): 101–16.

Heckman, James J., and Peter Siegelman. 1993. "The Urban Institute Audit Studies: Their Methods and Findings." In *Clear and Convincing Evidence: Measurement of Discrimination in America*, edited by Michael Fix and Raymond J. Struyk. Washington: Urban Institute Press.

Henry, Charles. 1980. "Black-Chicano Coalitions: Possibilities and Problems." *Western Journal of Black Studies* 4: 222–32.

Henry, Charles, and Carlos Munoz. 1991. "Ideological and Interest Linkages in California Rainbow Politics." In *Racial and Ethnic Politics in California*, edited by Byron O. Jackson, and Michael B. Preston. Berkeley, Calif.: IGS Press.

Hochschild, Jennifer. 1995. *Facing Up to the American Dream: Race, Class, and the Soul of the Nation*. Princeton, N.J.: Princeton University Press.

Holzer, Harry. 1987. "Informal Job Search and Black Youth Unemployment." *American Economic Review* 77: 446–52.

———. 1988. "Search Method Used by Unemployed Youth." *Journal of Labor Economics* 6: 1–20.

Hurwitz, Jon, and Mark Peffley. 1997. "Public Perceptions of Race and Crime: The Role of Racial Stereotypes." *American Journal of Political Science* 41: 375–401.

Ignatiev, Noel. 1995. *How the Irish Became White*. New York: Routledge.

Ilandfeldt, Keith R., and Benjamin Scafidi. 2002a. "Black Self-Segregation as a Cause of Neighborhood Racial Segregation: Evidence from the Multi-City Study of Urban Inequality." *Journal of Urban Economics* 31: 366–90.

———. 2002b. "The Neighborhood Contact Hypothesis: Evidence from the Multi-City Study of Urban Inequality." *Urban Studies* 39: 619–41.

———. 2004. "Whites' Neighborhood Racial Preferences and Neighborhood Racial Composition in the United States: Evidence from the Multi-City Study of Urban Inequality." *Housing Studies* 19(3, May): 325–59.

Jackman, Mary R. 1994. *The Velvet Glove: Paternalism and Conflict in Gender, Class, and Race Relations*. Berkeley: University of California Press.

Jackman, Mary R., and Marie Crane. 1986. "'Some of My Best Friends Are Black . . .': Interracial Friendship and Whites' Racial Attitudes." *Public Opinion Quarterly* 50: 459–86.

Jackman, Mary R., and Robert W. Jackman. 1983. *Class Awareness in the United States*. Berkeley: University of California Press.

Jackman, Mary R., and Michael J. Muha. 1984. "Education and Intergroup Attitudes: Moral Enlightenment, Superficial Democratic Commitment, or Ideological Refinement?" *American Sociological Review* 49(6, December): 751–69.

Jackman, Mary R., and Mary Scheuer Senter. 1983. "Different Therefore Unequal: Beliefs About Groups of Unequal Status." *Research in Social Stratification and Mobility* 2: 309–35.

Jackson, William E., III. 1994. "Discrimination in Mortgage Lending Markets as Rational Economic Behavior: Theory, Evidence, and Public Policy." In *African Americans and the New Policy Consensus: Retreat of the Liberal State,* edited by Marilyn E. Lashley, and Melanie Njeri Jackson. Westport, Conn.: Greenwood Press.

Jankowski, Martin Sanchez. 1995. "The Rising Significance of Status in U.S. Race Relations." In *The Bubbling Cauldron: Race, Ethnicity, and the Urban Crisis,* edited by Michael Peter Smith, and Joe R. Feagin. Minneapolis: University of Minnesota Press.

Jargowsky, Paul A. 1996. *Poverty and Place: Ghettos, Barrios, and the American City*. New York: Russell Sage Foundation.

Jargowsky, Paul A., and Mary Jo Bane. 1991. "Ghetto Poverty in the United States, 1970–1980." In *The Urban Underclass,* edited by Christopher Jencks, and Paul E. Peterson. Washington: Brookings Institution Press.

Jasso, Guillermina, and Mark Rosenzweig. 1990. *The New Chosen People: Immigrants in the United States*. New York: Russell Sage Foundation.

Jaynes, Gerald David, and Robin M. Williams Jr. 1989. *A Common Destiny: Blacks in American Society*. Washington, D.C.: National Academy Press.

Johnson, James H., Jr., and Walter C. Farrell Jr. 1993. "The Fire This Time: The Genesis of the Los Angeles Rebellion of 1992." *North Carolina Law Review* 71(5): 1403–20.

Johnson, James H., Jr., Cloyzelle K. Jones, Walter C. Farrell Jr., and Melvin L. Oliver. 1992. "The Los Angeles Rebellion: A Retrospective View." *Economic Development Quarterly* 6(4): 356–72.

Johnson, James H., Jr., and Melvin L. Oliver. 1985. "Black-Brown Conflict in the City of Los Angeles." *Urban Resources* (local interest insert on Los Angeles) 2(3): LA1–5.

———. 1989. "Interethnic Minority Conflict in Urban America: The Effects of Economic and Social Dislocations." *Urban Geography* 10: 449–63.

Kain, John F. 1968. "Housing Segregation, Negro Employment, and Metropolitan Decentralization." *Quarterly Journal of Economics* 82: 175–97.

———. 1986. "The Influence of Race and Income on Racial Segregation and Housing Policy." In *Housing Desegregation and Federal Policy*, edited by John M. Goering. Chapel Hill: University of North Carolina Press.

———. 1992. "The Spatial Mismatch Hypothesis: Three Decades Later." *Housing Policy Debate* 3(2): 371–460.

Kane, John, and Lawrence M. Spizman. 1994. "Race, Financial Aid Awards, and College Attendance: Parents and Geography Matter." *American Journal of Economics and Sociology* 53(January): 85–97.

Kasarda, John. 1989. "Urban Industrial Transition and the Underclass." *Annals of the American Academy of Political and Social Science* 501: 26–47.

———. 1993. "Cities as Places Where People Live and Work: Urban Change and Neighborhood Distress." In *Interwoven Destinies: Cities and the Nation*, edited by Henry Cisneros. New York: Norton.

Katz, Irwin. 1991. "Gordon Allport's *The Nature of Prejudice*." *Political Psychology* 12: 125–57.

Kerner Commission. 1968. *Report of the National Advisory Commission on Civil Disorders*. Washington: U.S. Government Printing Office.

Kirschenman, Joleen, and Kathryn M. Neckerman. 1991. "'We'd Love to Hire Them, But . . .': The Meaning of Race for Employers." In *The Urban Underclass*, edited by Christopher Jencks and Paul E. Peterson. Washington: Brookings Institution Press.

Kluegel, James, and Elliot Smith. 1982. "Whites' Beliefs About Blacks' Opportunity." *American Sociological Review* 47: 518–32.

———. 1986. *Beliefs About Inequality: Americans' Views of What Is and What Ought to Be*. New York: Aldine de Gruyter.

Krivo, Lauren J. 1995. "Immigrant Characteristics and Hispanic-Anglo Housing Inequality." *Demography* 32(November): 599–615.

Krivo, Lauren J., and Ruth D. Peterson. 1996. "Extremely Disadvantaged Neighborhoods and Urban Crime." *Social Forces* 75: 619–48.

Krysan, Maria. 1998. "Privacy and the Expression of White Racial Attitudes: A Comparison Across Three Contexts." *Public Opinion Quarterly* 62: 506–44.

———. 2002. "Whites Who Say They'd Flee: Who Are They, and Why Would They Leave?" *Demography* 39(4): 675–96.

Krysan, Maria, and Reynolds Farley. 2002. "The Residential Preferences of Blacks: Do They Explain Persistent Segregation?" *Social Forces* 80: 937–80.

Lambert, Wallace, and Donald Taylor. 1990. *Coping with Cultural and Racial Diversity in Urban America*. Westport, Conn.: Praeger.

Lee, Jennifer. 2002. *Civility in the City: Blacks, Jews, and Koreans in Urban America*. Cambridge, Mass.: Harvard University Press.

Leven, Charles L., James T. Little, Hugh O. Nourse, and R. Read. 1976. *Neighbor-*

hood Change: Lessons in the Dynamics of Urban Decay. Cambridge, Mass.: Ballinger.

Lieberson, Stanley. 1963. *Ethnic Patterns in American Cities*. New York: Free Press of Glencoe.

Lipset, Seymour, and William Schneider. 1978. "The Bakke Case: How Would It Be Decided at the Bar of Public Opinion?" *Public Opinion* 1: 38–44.

Liska, Allen E., John R. Logan, and Paul E. Bellair. 1998. "Race and Violent Crime in the Suburbs." *American Sociological Review* 63: 27–38.

Logan, John R. 2001a. "Ethnic Diversity Grows, Neighborhood Integration Lags Behind." Report. Albany, N.Y.: Lewis Mumford Center for Comparative Urban and Regional Research (April 3). Available at: www.albany.edu/mumford/census.

———. 2001b. "The New Ethnic Enclaves in America's Suburbs." Report. Albany, N.Y.: Lewis Mumford Center for Comparative Urban and Regional Research.

———. 2001c. "Living Separately: Segregation Rises for Children." Report. Albany, N.Y.: Lewis Mumford Center for Comparative Urban and Regional Research (May 6).

Logan, John R., and Richard Alba. 1993. "Locational Returns to Human Capital: Minority Access to Suburban Community Resources." *Demography* 30(2): 243–68.

———. 1995. "Who Lives in Affluent Suburbs? Racial Differences in Eleven Metropolitan Regions." *Sociological Focus* 28(4).

Logan, John R., Richard D. Alba, and Shu-Yin Leung. 1996. "Minority Access to White Suburbs: A Multiregional Comparison." *Social Forces* 74(3): 851–81.

Logan, John R., Richard D. Alba, and Wenquan Zhang. 2002. "Immigrant Enclaves and Ethnic Communities in New York and Los Angeles." *American Sociological Review* 67: 299–322.

Loury, Glenn C. 2002. *The Anatomy of Racial Inequality*. Cambridge, Mass.: Harvard University Press.

Magill, Frank N., ed. 1992. *Masterpieces of African-American Literature*. New York: HarperCollins.

Malcolm X. 1964. *The Autobiography of Malcolm X*. New York: Ballantine Books.

Massey, Douglas S. 1985. "Ethnic Residential Segregation: A Theoretical Synthesis and Empirical Review." *Sociology and Social Research* 69: 315–50.

———. 1995. "The New Immigration and Ethnicity in the United States." *Population Development Review* 21(3): 631–52.

Massey, Douglas S., and Brooks Bitterman. 1985. "Explaining the Paradox of Puerto Rican Segregation." *Social Forces* 64(2): 306–31.

Massey, Douglas S., Camille Zubrinsky Charles, Garvey F. Lundy, and Mary J. Fischer. 2003. *The Source of the River: The Social Origins of Freshmen at America's Selective Colleges and Universities*. Princeton, N.J.: Princeton University Press.

Massey, Douglas S., Gretchen A. Condran, and Nancy A. Denton. 1987. "The Effect of Residential Segregation on Black Social and Economic Well-being." *Social Forces* 66: 29–57.

Massey, Douglas S., and Nancy A. Denton. 1985. "Spatial Assimilation as a Socioeconomic Outcome." *American Sociological Review* 50: 94–106.

———. 1987. "Trends in the Residential Segregation of Blacks, Hispanics, and Asians: 1970–1980." *American Sociological Review* 52(6): 802–25.

———. 1989. "Hypersegregation in U.S. Metropolitan Areas: Black and Hispanic Segregation Along Five Dimensions." *Demography* 26(3): 373–91.

———. 1993. *American Apartheid: Segregation and the Making of the Underclass.* Cambridge, Mass.: Harvard University Press.

Massey, Douglas S., and Mary J. Fischer. 1999. "Does Rising Income Bring Integration? New Results for Blacks, Hispanics, and Asians in 1990." *Social Science Research* 28: 316–26.

———. 2000. "How Segregation Concentrates Poverty." *Ethnic and Racial Studies* 23(4): 670–91.

———. 2002. "The Long-Term Consequences of Segregation." Paper presented to the annual meeting of the Population Association of America. Atlanta (May 9–11).

Massey, Douglas S., and Eric Fong. 1990. "Segregation and Neighborhood Quality: Blacks, Hispanics, and Asians in the San Francisco Metropolitan Area." *Social Forces* 69: 15–32.

Massey, Douglas S., Andrew B. Gross, and Mitchell Eggers. 1991. "Segregation, the Concentration of Poverty, and the Life Chances of Individuals." *Social Science Research* 20: 397–420.

Massey, Douglas S., Andrew B. Gross, and Kumiko Shibuya. 1994. "Migration, Segregation, and the Geographic Concentration of Poverty." *American Sociological Review* 59(4): 425–45.

Massey, Douglas S., and Garvey Lundy. 2001. "Use of Black English and Racial Discrimination in Urban Housing Markets: New Methods and Findings." *Urban Affairs Review* 36(4): 452–69.

Massey, Douglas S., and Brendan Mullan. 1984. "Process of Hispanic and Black Spatial Assimilation." *American Journal of Sociology* 89(4): 837–73.

McDonald, Katrina Bell, and Thomas A. LaVeist. 2001. "Black Educational Advantage in the Inner City." *Review of Black Political Economy* 29(1): 25–47.

McWhorter, John H. 2000. *Losing the Race: Self-Sabotage in Black America.* New York: Free Press.

Metcalf, George R. 1988. *Fair Housing Comes of Age.* New York: Greenwood Press.

Meyer, Stephan Grant. 2000. *As Long as They Don't Live Next Door: Segregation and Racial Conflict in American Neighborhoods.* New York: Rowman and Littlefield.

Miles, Jack. 1992. "Blacks Versus Browns: The Struggle for the Bottom Rung." *Atlantic* 270(4): 41–68.

Min, Pyong Gap. 1996. *Caught in the Middle: Korean Communities in New York and Los Angeles*. Berkeley: University of California Press.

Mindiola, Tatcho, Jr., Yolanda Flores Niemann, and Nestor Rodriguez. 2002. *Black-Brown Relations and Stereotypes*. Austin: University of Texas Press.

Monk-Turner, Elizabeth. 1995. "Factors Shaping the Probability of Community Versus Four-Year College Entrance and Acquisition of the BA Degree." *Social Science Journal* 32: 255–64.

Moore, Thomas S., and Aaron Laramore. 1990. "Industrial Change and Urban Joblessness: An Assessment of the Mismatch Hypothesis." *Urban Affairs Quarterly* 25: 640–58.

Morenoff, Jeffrey D., and Robert J. Sampson. 1997. "Violent Crime and the Spatial Dynamics of Neighborhood Transition: Chicago, 1970–1990." *Social Forces* 76: 31–64.

Munnell, Alicia H., Geoffrey M. B. Tootell, Lynn E. Browne, and James McEneaney. 1996. "Mortgage Lending in Boston: Interpreting HMDA Data." *American Economic Review* 86(1): 25–53.

Myrdal, Gunnar. 1972. *An American Dilemma: The Negro Problem and Modern Democracy*. New York: Random House. (Orig. pub. in 1944.)

Niemann, Yolanda. 1999. "Social Ecological Contexts of Prejudice Between Hispanics and Blacks." In *Race, Ethnicity, and Nationality in the United States*, edited by Paul Wong. Boulder, Colo.: Westview.

Nyden, Philip, John Lukehart, Michael T. Maly, and William Peterman, eds. 1998. "Racially and Ethnically Diverse Urban Neighborhoods." *Cityscape* 4(2). Washington: U.S. Department of Housing and Urban Development.

Okazawa-Rey, Margo, and Marshall Wong. 1997. "Organizing in Communities of Color: Addressing Interethnic Conflict." *Social Justice* 24(1): 24–39.

Oliver, Melvin L., and James H. Johnson Jr. 1984. "Interethnic Conflict in an Urban Ghetto: The Case of Blacks and Latinos in Los Angeles." *Research in Social Movements, Conflict, and Change* 6: 57–94.

Oliver, Melvin L., and Thomas M. Shapiro. 1995. *Black Wealth/White Wealth: A New Perspective on Racial Inequality*. New York: Routledge.

Ondrich, Jan, Alex Stricker, and John Yinger. 1998. "Do Real Estate Brokers Choose to Discriminate? Evidence from the 1989 Housing Discrimination Study." *Southern Economic Journal* 64(4): 880-902.

Orfield, Gary, with Nora Gordon. 2001. "Schools More Separate: Consequences of a Decade of Resegregation." Cambridge, Mass.: Harvard University, Civil Rights Project (July). Available at: www.law.harvard.edu/civilrights.

Pager, Devah, and Lincoln Quillian. 2005. "What Employers Say Versus What They Do." *American Sociological Review* 70(3): 355–80.

Painter, Gary, Stuart A. Gabriel, and Dowell Myers. 2001. "Race, Immigrant Status, and Housing Tenure Choice." *Journal of Urban Economics* 49(1): 150–67.

Painter, Gary, Lihong Yang, and Zhou Yu. 2003. "Heterogeneity in Asian American Homeownership: The Impact of Household Endowments and Immigrant Status." *Urban Studies* 40(3): 505–30.

Park, Kyeyoung. 1991. "Conception of Ethnicities by Koreans: Workplace Encounters." In *Asian Americans: Comparative and Global Perspectives*, edited by Shirley Hune, Hyung-Chan Kim, Stephen Fugita, and Amy Ling. Pullman: Washington State University Press.

———. 1995. "The Reinvention of Affirmative Action: Korean Immigrants' Changing Conceptions of African Americans and Latin Americans." *Urban Anthropology* 24: 59–92.

Park, Robert E., and Ernest W. Burgess. 1969. *Introduction to the Science of Sociology*. 3rd ed. Chicago: University of Chicago Press.

Patterson, Orlando. 1997. *The Ordeal of Integration: Progress and Resentment in America's Racial Crisis*. Washington, D.C.: Civitas.

Pattillo-McCoy, Mary. 1999. *Black Picket Fences: Privilege and Peril Among the Black Middle Class*. Chicago: University of Chicago Press.

Peffley, Mark, Jon Hurwitz, and Paul M. Sniderman. 1997. "Racial Stereotypes and Whites' Political Views of Blacks in the Context of Welfare and Crime." *American Journal of Political Science* 41: 30–60.

Pettigrew, Thomas F. 1982. "Prejudice." In *Dimensions of Ethnicity: Prejudice*, edited by Stephan Thernstrom, Ann Orlov, and Oscar Handlin. Cambridge, Mass.: Belknap Press of Harvard University Press.

Portes, Alejandro, and Rubén Rumbaut. 1996. *Immigrant America: A Portrait*. Berkeley: University of California Press.

Quillian, Lincoln. 1996. "Group Threat and Regional Change in Attitudes Toward African Americans." *American Journal of Sociology* 102: 816–60.

Rivkin, Steven G. 1995. "Black/White Differences in Schooling and Employment." *Journal of Human Resources* 30: 826–52.

Rosenbaum, Emily. 1994. "The Constraints on Minority Housing Choices, New York City, 1978–1987." *Social Forces* 72(3): 725–47.

———. 1996. "The Influence of Race on Hispanic Housing Choices, New York City, 1978–1987." *Urban Affairs Review* 32(2): 217–43.

Rubinowitz, Leonard S., and James E. Rosenbaum. 2000. *Crossing the Class and Color Lines: From Public Housing to White Suburbia*. Chicago: University of Chicago Press.

Sampson, Robert J., and William Julius Wilson. 1995. "Toward a Theory of Race, Crime, and Urban Inequality." In *Crime and Inequality*, edited by John Hagen and Ruth D. Peterson. Palo Alto, Calif.: Stanford University Press.

Sassen, Saskia. 1990. "Economic Restructuring and the American City." *Annual Review of Sociology* 16: 465–90.

Schelling, Thomas C. 1971. "Dynamic Models of Segregation." *Journal of Mathematical Sociology* 1: 143–86.

Schuman, Howard, and Lawrence Bobo. 1988. "Survey-Based Experiments on

White Racial Attitudes Toward Residential Integration." *American Journal of Sociology* 94: 273–99.

Schuman, Howard, Charlotte Steeh, Lawrence Bobo, and Maria Krysan. 1997. *Racial Attitudes in America: Trends and Interpretations*. 2nd ed. Cambridge, Mass.: Harvard University Press.

Sears, David O. 1994. "Urban Rioting in Los Angeles: A Comparison of 1965 with 1992." In *The Los Angeles Riots: Lessons for the Urban Future*, edited by Mark Baldassare. Boulder, Colo.: Westview.

Sigelman, Lee, and Steven A. Tuch. 1997. "Metastereotypes: Blacks' Perceptions of Whites' Stereotypes of Blacks." *Public Opinion Quarterly* 61: 87–101.

Sigelman, Lee, and Susan Welch. 1993. "The Contact Hypothesis Revisited: Black-White Interaction and Positive Racial Attitudes." *Social Forces* 71(3): 781–95.

Skaburskis, Andrejs. 1996. "Race and Tenure in Toronto." *Urban Studies* 33(2): 223–52.

Skerry, Peter. 1993. *Mexican Americans: The Ambivalent Minority*. Cambridge, Mass.: Harvard University Press.

Smith, Tom W. 1990. "Ethnic Images." General Social Survey topical report 19. Chicago: University of Chicago, National Opinion Research Center (December).

———. 1998. "Intergroup Relations in Contemporary America: An Overview of Survey Research." In *Intergroup Relations in the United States: Research Perspectives*, edited by W. Windborne and R. Cohen.

Sniderman, Paul M., and Edward G. Carmines. 1997. *Reaching Beyond Race*. Cambridge, Mass.: Harvard University Press.

South, Scott J., and Kyle D. Crowder. 1997a. "Residential Mobility Between Cities and Suburbs: Race, Suburbanization, and Back-to-the-City Moves." *Demography* 34(4): 525–38.

———. 1997b. "Escaping Distressed Neighborhoods: Individual, Community, and Metropolitan Areas." *American Journal of Sociology* 103(4): 1040–84.

———. 1998. "Leaving the 'Hood: Residential Mobility Between Black, White, and Integrated Neighborhoods." *American Sociological Review* 63: 17–26.

South, Scoot J., and Glenn D. Deane. 1993. "Race and Residential Mobility: Individual Determinants and Structural Constraints." *Social Forces* 72(1): 147–67.

Squires, Gregory D., and Sunwoong Kim. 1995. "Does Anybody Who Works Here Look Like Me? Mortgage Lending, Race, and Lender Employment." *Social Science Quarterly* 76(4): 823–38.

Stata Press. 2003. *Stata Base Reference Manual*, vol. 3 (N-R), release 8. College Station, Tex.: Stata Press.

Stephan, W. 1985. "Intergroup Relations." In *Handbook of Social Psychology*, vol. 2, 3rd ed., edited by Gardner Lindzey and Elliot Aronson. New York: Random House.

Taeuber, Karl E., and Alma F. Taeuber. 1965. *Negroes in Cities: Residential Segregation and Neighborhood Change*. West Hanover, Mass.: Atheneum.

Tajfel, Henri. 1982. "Social Psychology of Intergroup Relations." *Annual Review of Psychology* 33: 1–39.

Tate, Katherine. 1993. *From Protest to Politics: The New Black Voters in American Elections*. Cambridge, Mass.: Harvard University Press.

Thernstrom, Stephan, and Abigail Thernstrom. 1997. *America in Black and White: One Nation, Indivisible*. New York: Simon & Schuster.

Thornton, Michael C. 1985. "Collective Representations and Japanese Views of African-Descent Populations." *International Journal of Sociology and Social Policy* 6(1): 90–101.

Timberlake, Jeffrey M. 2000. "Still Life in Black and White: Effects of Racial and Class Attitudes on Prospects for Residential Integration in Atlanta." *Sociological Inquiry* 70(4): 420–45.

———. 2002. "Separate, but How Unequal? Ethnic Residential Stratification, 1980 to 1990." *City and Community* 1(3): 251–66.

Tuan, Mia. 1999. *Forever Foreigners or Honorary Whites? The Asian Ethnic Experience Today*. New Brunswick, N.J.: Rutgers University Press.

Turner, J. C., R. J. Brown, and Henri Tajfel. 1979. "Social Comparison and Group Interest in In-group Favoritism." *European Journal of Social Psychology* 9(2): 187–204.

Turner, Margery Austin. 1992. "Discrimination in Urban Housing Markets: Lessons from Fair Housing Audits." *Housing Policy Debate* 3(2): 185–215.

Turner, Margery Austin, and Stephen L. Ross. 2003. *Discrimination in Metropolitan Housing Markets: National Results from Phase II HDS 2000*. Washington: U.S. Department of Housing and Urban Development.

Turner, Margery Austin, Stephen L. Ross, George C. Galster, and John Yinger. 2002. *Discrimination in Metropolitan Housing Markets: National Results from Phase I HDS 2000*. Washington: U.S. Department of Housing and Urban Development.

U.S. Bureau of the Census. 1990. *Census of Population and Housing*. Washington: U.S. Government Printing Office.

———. 2000. *Census of Population and Housing*. Washington: U.S. Government Printing Office.

United Way and Los Angeles Urban League. 2005. *The State of Black Los Angeles*.

Venkatesh, Sudhir Alladi. 2000. *American Project: The Rise and Fall of a Modern Ghetto*. Cambridge, Mass.: Harvard University Press.

Villemez, Wayne J. 1980. "Race, Class, and Neighborhood: Differences in the Residential Return on Individual Resources." *Social Forces* 59(2): 414–30.

Waldinger, Roger. 1996. "Ethnicity and Opportunity in the Plural City." In *Ethnic Los Angeles*, edited by Roger Waldinger and Mehdi Bozorgmehr. New York: Russell Sage Foundation.

Waldinger, Roger, and Tom Bailey. 1991. "The Continuing Significance of Race: Racial Conflict and Racial Discrimination in Construction." *Politics and Society* 19: 291–323.

Waldinger, Roger, and Mehdi Bozorgmehr. 1996. *Ethnic Los Angeles*. New York: Russell Sage Foundation.

Waters, Mary C. 1990. *Ethnic Options: Choosing Identities in America*. Berkeley: University of California Press.

———. 1999. *Black Identities: West Indian Immigrant Dreams and American Realities*. New York: Russell Sage Foundation.

Weitzer, Ronald. 1997. "Racial Prejudice Among Korean Merchants in African American Neighborhoods." *Sociological Quarterly* 38(4): 587–606.

Wilkes, Rima, and John Iceland. 2004. "Hypersegregation in the Twenty-first Century: An Update and Analysis." *Demography* 41(1): 23–36.

Wilson, William Julius. 1987. *The Truly Disadvantaged: The Inner City, the Underclass, and Public Policy*. Chicago: University of Chicago Press.

———. 1996. *When Work Disappears: The World of the New Urban Poor*. New York: Alfred A. Knopf.

Yinger, John. 1993. "Audit Methodology: Comments." In *Clear and Convincing Evidence: Measurement of Discrimination in America*, edited by Michael Fix and Raymond J. Struyk. Washington: Urban Institute Press.

———. 1995. *Closed Doors, Opportunities Lost: The Continuing Costs of Housing Discrimination*. New York: Russell Sage Foundation.

———. 1998. "Evidence on Discrimination in Consumer Markets." *Journal of Economic Perspectives* 12(2): 23–40.

Yoon, In-jin 1997. *On My Own: Korean Businesses and Race Relations in America*. Chicago: University of Chicago Press.

Yuan, Goa. 1989. "In China, Black Isn't Beautiful." *New York Times*, January 25.

Zhou, Min. 1992. *Chinatown: The Socioeconomic Potential of an Urban Empire*. Philadelphia: Temple University Press.

Zuberi, Tukufu. 2001. "The Population Dynamics of the Changing Color Line." In *Problem of the Century: Racial Stratification in the United States*, edited by Elijah Anderson and Douglas S. Massey. New York: Russell Sage Foundation.

Zubrinsky, Camille L., and Lawrence Bobo. 1996. "Prismatic Metropolis: Race and Residential Segregation in the City of the Angels." *Social Science Research* 25: 335–74.

Index

Boldface numbers refer to figures and tables.